"The belief that humans survive bodily death in some form is universal. Long considered superstition, several lines of evidence now suggest that this belief is valid. Dianne Arcangel's *Afterlife Encounters* adds to this body of knowledge, and will provide hope and comfort for anyone who reads it."

—Larry Dossey, M.D., author, *The Extraordinary Healing Power Of Ordinary Things, Reinventing Medicine,* and *Healing Words*

"Many books exist on the afterlife and communications from loved ones who have passed on, but no one is a better guide to the very human interest of accounts of afterlife experiences and their life-changing aftereffects than former director of the Kübler-Ross Center and hospice chaplain Dianne Arcangel, who in this book presents the results of a survey with interviews she conducted."

—Rhea A. White, Exceptional Human Experience Network

"Based on rich narratives and scientific investigation, *Afterlife Encounters* dares to explore the life-enhancing aftereffects of experiencing the worlds beyond physical life. For anyone who has considered the question, 'What's next?', this book offers comfort, surprise, awe, and wonder."

—Suzanne V. Brown, Ph.D., Editor, *The Journal of the American Society for Psychical Research*; Director of Research & Development, The Exceptional Human Experience Network

"*Afterlife Encounters* is a courageous book that combines inspirational personal accounts with impressive empirical data. Drawing upon her extensive experience as hospice chaplain, psychotherapist, and thanatology researcher, Dianne Arcang-' ts the profound power of afterlif uide-lines for helping the bere

Ps

r of

ginia

"Read *Afterlife Encounters* and you will be enlightened and comforted by the powerful experiences of ordinary people when they discover that life continues after physical death. This book will become a classic!

"The afterlife experiences in this book are valuable gifts from the experiencers. Their accounts of the ultimate reality that awaits us after physical death are inspiring and comforting."

—Dale E. Graff, M.S., physics; Former Director, U.S. Army Special Project StarGate; author of *Tracks in the Psychic Wilderness and River*

"Dianne Arcangel is fearlessly exploring one of the most important topics facing modern science: does the human personality survive bodily death? Her findings provide weighty evidence to support this possibility. She writes with balance and a sensitivity to many of the skeptical issues that any intelligent reader will wish to see addressed. Most importantly, she addresses the human, emotional dimensions of the survival question. This is undoubtedly an important book."

—Jeffrey Mishlove, Ph.D., President, Intuition Network; Dean of Consciousness Studies, University of Philosophical Research

"Dianne Arcangel manages to integrate her abundant research and life experiences in order to bring humanity to the science of the soul. It is a careful balance between the heart's need to believe and the mind's need to understand."

—George Anderson

"*Afterlife Encounters* is a must read for anyone with any curiosity or concern about the afterlife, from the committed skeptic to committed believer. This gripping account of real-life experiences challenges and extends the current view of the nature of human consciousness, and provides solid hope and comfort to all who have lost someone they loved."

—Sally Rhine Feather, Ph.D.; coauthor of *The Gift*;
Director of Development, Rhine Research Center

"Dianne Arcangel has written the definitive work for all those who have experienced encounters perceived by means other than the five senses. By carefully analyzing scientific data and relating scores of anecdotal evidence, she has helped us to understand that science and spirituality may be leading us on the same path. This is a must read for both the bereaved and the simply curious. Dianne's research has proven what many psychologists are finally beginning to realize; acknowledgment of afterlife encounters is, in fact, the most effective form of grief therapy. Most importantly, those experiencing such phenomena no longer have to ask 'Am I crazy?'"

—Bob Ginsberg, Co-Founder, Forever Family Foundation Inc

Also by Dianne Arcangel

Life After Loss (coauthored with Raymond Moody, Jr.)

AFTERLIFE

ENCOUNTERS

ORDINARY PEOPLE, EXTRAORDINARY EXPERIENCES

DIANNE ARCANGEL

HAMPTON ROADS
for the evolving human spirit   PUBLISHING COMPANY, INC.

Cover design by Marjoram Productions
Cover digital imagery © PictureQuest/BrandXPictures. All rights reserved.

Hampton Roads Publishing Company, Inc.
1125 Stoney Ridge Road
Charlottesville, VA 22902

434-296-2772
fax: 434-296-5096
e-mail: hrpc@hrpub.com
www.hrpub.com

If you are unable to order this book from your local
bookseller, you may order directly from the publisher.
Call 1-800-766-8009, toll-free.

Library of Congress Cataloging-in-Publication Data

Arcangel, Dianne.
Afterlife encounters : ordinary people, extraordinary experiences /Dianne
Arcangel.
p. cm.
Summary: "Defines characteristics of afterlife encounters; their purpose, meaning,
and aftereffects; and provides six criteria by which encounters are considered
evidence for life's continuance beyond bodily death. Demonstrates that afterlife
encounters are normal, healthy, functional, and comforting; and concludes with
supportive resources"--Provided by publisher.
Includes index.
ISBN 1-57174-436-3 (5-1/2x8-1/2 tp : alk. paper)
1. Death--Miscellanea. 2. Spiritualism. 3. Future life. I. Title.
BF1275.D2A73 2005
133.9--dc22
                              2005015511

ISBN 1-57174-436-3
10 9 8 7 6 5 4 3 2 1
Printed on acid-free paper in the United States

16

To librarians around the globe, especially

Rhea A. White.

Your dedication and enthusiasm

make a difference.

T

Contents

Foreword by Gary E. Schwartz, Ph.D. .ix

Preface xi

Acknowledgments xv

One: The Door Opens 1

Two: The Survey Reveals 16

Three: Addressing the Survival Issue 65

Four: Profiles of Typical Perceivers .105

Five: Heart Strings 115

Six: Considering the Controversial 165

Seven: The World of Mediumship 171

Eight: The Afterlife Watching Experiments 202

Nine: Conclusion 271

Appendix: Afterlife Encounter Survey—Phase 1 277

Endnotes 301

Glossary 305

Supportive Resources 307

Works Consulted 321

Index 327

Foreword

By Gary E. Schwartz, Ph.D.

"Afterlife Encounters" is a phrase introduced to the scientific world by Dianne Arcangel, the courageous author of this remarkable book. The subtitle to her book could not be more appropriate—"ordinary people, extraordinary experiences." As you read her beautifully woven collection of extraordinary afterlife encounters that have been witnessed—and celebrated—by everyday people, you will experience a renewed sense of inspiration and opportunity concerning the future of humanity that can stimulate your intellect as it soothes your spirit.

Few scientists, clinicians, or clergy have had as extensive experience with afterlife encounters as Dianne. And even among this select group, Dianne is unique. Her book is filled with impressive and impeccable evidence. The evidence is presented gracefully and vibrantly for the enthusiastic heart, yet carefully and cautiously for the critical mind. Dianne understands the distinction between empirical truth and pseudo-skepticism. Only the most biased and hardened of cynics can read her book and not come away enlightened and invigorated.

Dianne writes: "Afterlife encounters are beacons of light. They are catalysts, offering a more peaceful, loving, and compassionate world." How does Dianne reach such an encouraging and beautiful conclusion? She does so partly through direct personal experience, and partly through systematic and comprehensive research.

Dianne knows, as a skilled psychotherapist and chaplain, that it can sometimes be dangerous—personally and professionally—to be forthcoming about afterlife encounters. She appreciates that most of us are fearful of receiving intense ridicule, if not scorn, from certain family members, friends, or colleagues, if we confess some of the extraordinary afterlife encounters we have experienced. We worry that if we see a ghost or an apparition and tell someone, will we be labeled crazy? If a medium gives us information, supposedly from a deceased loved one, that can be independently confirmed in our personal lives, does it mean that we have succumbed to superstition and lost our ability to distinguish reality from fantasy? Or, is it possible that such experiences are real, that they have deep purpose, and that we can use them to help heal humankind as well as advance our material and spiritual growth?

One of the reasons that Dianne has written *Afterlife Encounters* is to help remove the taboo and stigma surrounding the phenomenon. Only by documenting them in a safe and nurturing context can their profound significance be acknowledged; their nature be explored by ordinary people, as well as scientists; and their potential applications be developed.

In the end, remaining true to science, Dianne wrote: "Regardless of whether they are, or are not, from the hereafter, we invite you to recognize and appreciate them for what they have been proven to be—growth promoting."

Can you imagine a better invitation for reading this precious book?

Preface

Primitive cave paintings depict humankind's earliest beliefs about life beyond bodily death. Prehistoric remains give us insight into how nomads prepared for the Hereafter. Symbols evolved into hieroglyphics, the first form of written word—explicit documentation inscribed on the interior walls of tombs and scrolled across coffins. Life continued in the Great Beyond, the ancients were certain—so certain that they spent their lives in preparation for their spiritual continuance.

Organized religion came along, wherein many sects demanded, "Spirit is eternal, and to question that fact is a sin." Those who could not accept the doctrine on blind faith often turned from religious organizations.

Philosophers then stepped in, deeming the concept of survival archaic. "What's the big deal?" asked Plato. "So what if I die and that's it? I won't be here to find out. And if I survive after my body dies, then I'll just continue to do my work unencumbered by a body. So what difference does it make?"

Well, Plato, it makes a tremendous difference.

The contemporary world is very different from our early ancestors' world, and yet we are returning to their spiritual convictions. Why? Nothing else has provided what we need. We need answers to life's core questions: How did I get here? Why am I here? What will happen to me after I die? A specialized branch of science—survival—probes, *What, if anything, exists after physical demise? Where does it go and for how long?*

I have been a survivalist for some five decades. Although I systematically investigated afterlife encounters, I kept a low profile—

avoiding controversy was necessary for my work as a psychotherapist and chaplain. Meanwhile, the questions I posed to my parapsychology colleagues haunted me: *What good does our research do if it sits in our files? Who will it help if we take the information to our graves?* My conscience forces me to step out of the survival closet.

This book is based on questions raised by hospice patients, families in mourning, audience members, colleagues, and friends. "Do spirits really exist or are they simply figments of our imaginations?" "Is there scientific proof either way?" "Why do some people experience apparitions, but others do not?" "When do afterlife encounters occur?" "What is their purpose?" "Do mediums help or harm?" "What information have you gathered?"

While I was choosing various stories from my repository, Louise Rhine's words echoed in my mind: "It's possible that an inauthentic report will creep into a mass collection, but the total outweighs that one." I wanted to avoid even one false claim—therefore, I verified the accounts by interviewing the perceivers, corroborating with witnesses, and obtaining written documentation. I further substantiated particular cases by turning to outside resources. All of the anecdotes were given in good faith by heartfelt, emotionally stable, and mentally competent individuals who were not seeking fame, fortune, power, or ego. They offered the lessons they learned and are grateful that their experiences will reach people who are free to make their own decisions about them.

A student decided, during one of my death education classes, "Well, it doesn't make sense to me. Why would apparitions come here for such things as guiding their relatives to money hidden in the rafters and not more important things like saving lives? If there really are spirits, then why didn't they warn us that terrorists were going to attack the World Trade Center so those people wouldn't die?"

"Oh, but they did," I said. "Several weeks after September 11, I was waiting to meet a bereaved family at the gates of Ground Zero. I noticed an elderly gentleman leaning against a barricade. He kept glancing toward the ruins and then staring into my eyes. I sensed he had a story to tell, so I walked closer to him, and asked, 'This is beyond sad, isn't it?'"

"'Would be intolerable if I hadn't been here before . . . before it happened,' he said. 'I saw the whole thing.'

"I asked him, 'How? In a dream?'

"'Not exactly,' he said, but then his voice dropped so low that I had to cup my hand by my ear to hear him above the workmen. 'My wife came to me last month and showed it to me on a big screen. I saw it. I heard it. I felt it. All of it. At first, I thought I was just reliving my days on the battlefield, World War II, ya know? But then I took a closer look and knew it was something else.'

"I asked him, 'Did you tell anyone about your encounter?'

"'Lord no! They'd think I was loony. If I could've . . . along with other people like me . . . maybe we wouldn't be here today.'"

Some afterlife encounters have saved lives. Others could. You see, the problem is, few people talk about them.

Therein lies the heart of my work. Most of the perceivers who described their afterlife encounters began with, "I've never told anybody this." Now, finally, after 50 years, I have the courage to reveal what I have learned. We, the many authors of this book, are tired of living in such a cynical society—therefore, we are joining ranks. Our intention is to educate the public, and bring comfort and hope to the bereaved.

Afterlife encounters are beacons of light. They are catalysts, offering a more peaceful, loving, and compassionate world. Regardless whether they are, or are not, from the hereafter, we invite you to recognize and appreciate them for what they have been proven to be—growth promoting.

Note: To assure privacy, a minute number of individuals altered certain names and identifying details. The integrity of their stories remains, nevertheless.

Acknowledgments

This book exists because of the people who joined me in taking a stand. Wanting a more loving and accepting world, we hope to bring knowledge to the general public and comfort to those who grieve. Experience is stronger than faith, and faith is the gift the following experiencers offer to you: Adam S. Wilk, Angela Dioca, Barbara Green-Studer, Betty Davidson, Beverly Bennick, Carol Poole, Carol Dioca-Bevis, Charles Vance, Deanna Dube, Debbie Fancher, Debra Johnson, Diane Botti, Donna Allred Perez, F. Joe Davidson, Fred and Marilyn Zimmerman, Garry Roonan, George Stone, George Taylor, Harry Steiner, Jacki Mac, Jane May, Jean Vance, Jenny Vanckhoven, Jerri Wiitala, Jim May, Jo Ann Thomas, John Stephen Simon, J. R. May, Joseph Dioca, Judy Schlosberg, Linda Helton-Martin, Lori LeBlanc, Lori Taylor, Marcia Lynch, Maria Elena Tarantini, Marti Lewis, Mary E. Wood, Mary Siefer, Michael Way, Neta Sharp, Noelle King, Patti Delsoldato, Patty DePaulo, Phyllis Rose, Rosa Mendez, Sherlyne Eisden, Stan Sharp, Tammi Doherty, Thomas Kjall, Valerie Dudley, and Valerie Noss. To the people listed and to those who prefer anonymity, you all hold my profound respect and appreciation.

Beyond contributing stories, a support team diligently worked to bring this material to you. Karl Fancher was responsible for designing, hosting, and maintaining the web site Afterlife-Encounters.com. Beyond being my daily cheerleader, Debbie Fancher helped design and distribute Afterlife Encounter Surveys. Andrew Greeley, Sally Rhine Feather, Erlendur

Haraldsson, Rupert Sheldrake, John Palmer, Bob Bigelow, and Diane Bigelow were instrumental in designing the surveys.

Throughout my professional and personal life, Rhea White, editor of the *Journal of the American Society for Psychical Research (JASPR)*, has contributed her support, enthusiasm, and resources; similarly, Sonja Earthman Novo, my former supervisor at The Hospice At The Texas Medical Center, and Dr. Charles Novo have continuously provided depth. For them, I am eternally grateful.

I was deeply touched by all the professionals who contributed their time and expertise. Thank you to Andrew E. Greeley, Andrew Barone, Bruce Greyson, Carlos Alvarado, Emily Kelly, Erlendur Haraldsson, Gary Schwartz, Jannine Rebman, Jeanne Haden, John Palmer, Marsha Landers, Nancy Zingrone, Robert Morris, Robert Neimeyer, Rupert Sheldrake, Sally Rhine Feather, Suzanne Brown, Tony Muckleroy, as well as the staff at the Rhine Research Center, the Parapsychology Foundation, the Association for Death Education and Counseling, and the Pasadena Public Library.

Rekindling my childhood quest for what I had grown to think impossible, George Anderson, unknowingly, ushered me through the survival door. Thank you, George.

To agent, Bill Gladstone, and Kimberly Brabec, his assistant at Waterside Productions; and Bob Friedman, Sarah Hilfer, and all the fine staff at Hampton Roads Publishing Company, thank you for believing in this project and having the dedication to see it through.

My longtime friend Leona Lea continuously and graciously gave her support, as did my assistant and statistician, Silas Joe Thompson.

To my husband of 40 years, I give homage. Although Joe (1943–2003) was a consummate nonbeliever in the afterlife, he supported my work more than anyone, because he saw the difference between believing and not.

ONE

The Door Opens

There are more things in Heaven and Earth, Horatio,
Than are dreamt of in your philosophy.

—Shakespeare

A door to the afterlife opens, revealing a whole new world of intrigue, hope, and wonder. The possibility of heaven captures our imagination. Some people occasionally peek through the portal to satisfy fleeting bursts of fascination. Others step inside, only to discover a lasting, and sometimes all-consuming, adventure. I, however, was propelled through on my very first day of school.

"Hello, I'm Mrs. Apple, your first grade teacher," she said as she ushered each of us to our seats. When every desk was taken, she stood in front of the room with her hands on her hips. "Listen, boys and girls. Shhh, I want to tell you something." After the bustling had subsided, she leaned over and reached into a bag beside her desk. Then up she popped with a cockeyed grin and an apple in her hand. "My name is Mrs. Apple, just like this," she said, pointing to the piece of fruit. We all laughed at her animation. "I'm your teacher this year. This is where I'll sit," she said, placing the edible on her desk. "My son goes to school here too, just down the hall. He's in the second grade. Now I want each of you to stand up, say your name, and tell us something about you and your family."

A boy in the first row jumped up and down in his chair, "Me! Me! Me!" he yelled. Although he was the smallest child in our class, his enthusiasm pulsated throughout the room. "Okay, okay," Mrs. Apple said with a giggle, "you go first."

"I'm Jimmy!" he exclaimed, jumping to his feet.

"Good, Jimmy," Mrs. Apple encouraged as she sat behind her desk. "Continue."

"My grandpa died and then he came into my room and went by my bucket of—"

"Who came into your room?" Mrs. Apple interrupted, leaning forward in her chair.

Protruding his chest proudly, Jimmy answered, "My grandpa!"

"But you said he died," she inquired.

"Yes ma'am. But, but, but . . . he came to my room."

Mrs. Apple wrinkled her nose, "Huh?"

"You know . . . I'm talking 'bout his ghost," he explained.

"Oh, don't be silly," she scolded, twisting her mouth to one side.

Jimmy's eyes grew large. Dropping his head, he murmured, "But I'm not being silly. He was in my room by my bucket of—"

"Sit down," she snapped with her brows furrowed.

Jimmy sank to his chair. *Oh . . . look at him,* I thought, as I watched him trying to fight back tears. *Why was she so mean to him? And besides, I wanted to hear what happened. Why wouldn't she let him talk?*

But talk, Jimmy didn't. He did not utter a word, not for the rest of the morning or even while moving through the noisy, chattering, cafeteria lunch line. He appeared so downtrodden that I made certain to sit beside him. My numerous attempts to engage him in conversation seemed to be going nowhere, but then he leaned his shoulders toward me. "I really did see my grandpa," he murmured, keeping his eyes on his tray of food. I inserted my head between his face and plate, giving him no choice but to look at me. Flashing a half-tooth smile, I asked, "What happened?"

"Well," he whispered, "I was in my room when I saw my grandpa by my bucket of toys. He smiled and waved at me and I smiled and waved at him. Then he left."

Along with Jimmy, I relived his brief encounter, trying to imagine what it would be like to see a real ghost.

That evening, as usual, my family and I were gathered around the supper table, eating and leisurely discussing our day. Tonight was special, however, because this had been my introduction to school. My parents eagerly cast questions about the teachers and students. Their excitement fell to a hush, however, as I recounted Jimmy's attempt to describe his afterlife visitation during class and then our private lunchroom exchange. My sister chastised, "That's so weird—you're so weird—just plain old weird." Dad glared at her, then smiled at me. With that, we went on to other subjects—that is, until later.

Similar to other children, I concluded my evenings with a bedtime story. Unlike other parents, however, my dad never read stories from books. Instead, he either created spontaneous tales or narrated actual events from his life. This night Dad recounted a true story that involved his sister and her husband, Harry.

Your mother, Aunt Lu, Uncle Harry, and I drove to the Chicago World's Fair in the summer of 1933. In those days, the fairs introduced the latest gadgets and inventions. We listened to music from strange new instruments, and we tasted food we'd never heard of. There were displays, and rides, and light shows . . . well . . . we couldn't do it all if we'd stayed a week. We were having a grand old time when the darnedest thing happened.

There were these fortune-tellers lined up along the boardwalk. Your mother and Lu started giggling and teasing each other, "Go get your fortune told!"

"After you, little missy!"

"You first, dearie."

They were getting the biggest kick out of those fortune-tellers. We kept on walking along, but this one started yelling at us as we passed her, "Hey! You! Come here! I've got an important message for you!"

The girls elbowed one another, laughing, "What're ya waiting for?"

But the woman was serious . . . and was looking straight at your Uncle Harry. "Please. Please, sir," she said, "Listen to me. I've got an important message for you." Lu pulled at the back of Harry's shirt, trying to get him to turn around. She said, "She's talking to you Harry. Go on over there. See what she's got to say." But Harry ignored her and just kept walking down the boardwalk.

Then the fortune-teller yelled, "Your wife's calling you, 'Harry . . . Harry,' she says." We didn't know what to think. Lu said, "Harry, how can that woman be calling your name?" Harry didn't even look at your Aunt Lu, so she ran around in front of him. "You know her?" He shook his head *No* and kept walking. But the fortune-teller yelled louder, "Your wife and little baby are here. Their eyes and hair and skin are dark; beautiful, both of them . . . and she wants me to tell you, 'Harry, it's me, Ernestine. Harry, I'm so sorry.'" Your Uncle Harry didn't say one word—he just turned around and went back to the fortune-teller's table and sat down. Well, we had to know what was going on, so we followed him and sat down at the table too.

The woman said, "She's giving me a message—I'll give it to you. 'Harry, I'm fine now and so is Andrew. We're together. Oh Harry, I'm so sorry for what I did, especially for taking our son with me. I was wrong. Can you ever forgive me? I didn't know what I was doing. I wasn't thinking straight. I was wrong. I'm so sorry. Please forgive me.'"

I could see your Uncle Harry was shook up. He just sat there, looking straight at the fortune-teller. She asked him, "Do you have anything you want to say to her?" Harry never moved a muscle, so she said, "She's saying, 'It wasn't your fault, Harry. You didn't deserve what I did. *We* didn't deserve it. I loved you and always will. I'm so sorry. Forgive me. We're happy here, and we want you to be happy too. Please forgive me.' She needs you to forgive her . . . for yourself."

Harry stood up and walked out. I saw his eyes were glazed over, so I was worried about him, but Lu just kept laughing about how ridiculous that was. "Ha, ha, you've got a dark-eyed, dark-haired, dark-skinned baby? Is she blind? No child of yours could have dark anything!" Harry walked to the front of the fair, not even looking at us. The only thing he said was that he wanted to go home.

I drove us back to Michigan that night. We pulled into Harry's drive just before dawn. While the girls were busy taking Lu's suitcase out of the trunk, Harry leaned his head inside the car and whispered to me, "Come back at noon, but don't tell *anyone*. Lu won't be here and I've got something I want to show you."

When I went back to Harry's that day, he was waiting. He nodded and then motioned for me to follow him. We walked downstairs, into their basement. "We need to get to that trunk," he said, but I didn't see any trunk. All I saw was an old chest of drawers and boxes covered with dust. He said, "Help me," and we started trying to move the chest. I'll tell you . . . I was an athlete, tossed 150-pound weights around like they were feathers, but I thought I was going to bust a gut trying to get that chest moved. So he grabbed hold of the bottom drawer and gave it a good yank. Steel tools flew across the floor! Harry got on his knees and elbows, and reached into the very back of chest. He pulled out a key and put it in his shirt pocket. After we moved the chest and everything out of the way, I could see a blanket covering something, and when he pulled it off, there was a beaten-up old trunk. Harry kneeled down, took the key from his pocket, and put it into the lock. But then he stopped and got the blanket and spread it on the floor with the dusty side down. That's when I knew something really good must be in that trunk.

Well, when he opened it, all I saw were clothes. He picked up a woman's dress and said, "This was Mother's . . . most of these were hers." He started emptying everything onto the blanket—more clothes, a few baby things, a jewelry box, and other stuff. But when the trunk was empty, he leaned over, way to the back, and lifted up the bottom lining. There was an envelope. He picked it up, turned around, and sat down on the floor, so I sat too.

He opened the envelope and handed me a picture. He

said, "That's Ernestine, my first wife." I couldn't believe my ears. He said they were only 16 when they got married and a year later had a beautiful baby boy named Andrew. He pulled out a locket and broke down crying when he opened it. On one side was a picture of his wife—she had long, shiny black hair and dark eyes. On the other side, across from her picture, was a tiny piece of hair—also shiny and black. Your Uncle Harry pointed to it and said, "Andrew's. One day when he was several weeks old, I got a bad feeling while I was at work. I kept thinking that something was wrong at home—to go check on my wife and son. By the time I got all the way back, it was too late. . . . Ernestine left a note saying that life was too painful and she couldn't bear the thought of her child living in this world. She had killed herself and our baby. After that, I left Canada. I was going as far south as I could, because I never wanted any reminders. But I was running low on money, so I stopped here to work until I could get enough to move on. That's when I met Lu. I've never told anybody about my wife or son. All I wanted was to leave them behind, but no matter where I went or how hard I tried, I couldn't. At the fair—that had to be Ernestine."

I thought there had to be some logical explanation, so while Harry was putting everything back in the trunk I asked him if the fortune-teller could've been from Canada or knew someone who knew him. But he said they lived outside a tiny settlement—only a handful of people—where everybody knew everybody. They didn't have a funeral parlor or any of that, so he and the neighbors buried his wife and son. No one but a midwife, the neighbors, and Harry had ever seen the baby.

As we headed up the stairs, I asked Harry if the fortune-teller could've seen pictures of them. He said the only picture of Ernestine was in the locket, and it had been hidden away since she died. There weren't any of the baby. He said, "Even if that woman had heard my name or what happened, she couldn't have known what we looked like. That was them all right. I just know it." Harry and I never talked about it again, but I noticed how much he started to change.

Your mother noticed too. She kept saying, "What's gotten into Harry?" He'd always been so glum and hardly ever laughed or said anything. You see him now—he's always cheerful.

Well, your mother kept talking about Harry and about how much he was changing. Then one day we were at Lu's when he came home from work whistling. Ha! Your mother got suspicious—thought he might be up to something no good, so I told her what happened. She just couldn't believe he'd keep something like that to himself. She said, "No wonder he was always so sad."

If someone had told me a story like this before it happened to us, I'd never have believed it. Your mother and I have gone over it many times and wondered—*How could that've happened?* I don't know. Did the fortune-teller really talk to your Uncle Harry's wife? I don't know. Did your friend's grandpa really visit him? Could be. You see, Honey, no one knows what happens after we die. No one knows what's possible. But the important thing is that Harry got his life back. He wasn't haunted by his past any more.

I wanted to hear Mother's version of the story, so days later I carefully approached her, asking. "Do you remember going to the World's Fair?" Her big-eyed, "Oh yes!" was followed by, "It was Chicago, 1933." Mother told me an almost verbatim recount about the boardwalk fortune-tellers, the one calling out Uncle Harry's name, and the details of his encounter. "Your daddy and I used to wonder why Lu married Harry. He was always so sullen and withdrawn, but he sure changed after that," she said.

My parents believed that Uncle Harry's afterlife encounter catapulted him from a life of sorrow and despair to one of peace and forgiveness. As for me, the possibilities his story posed were forever etched into my psyche.

The most significant communication between people transpires below conscious awareness, in our deepest psyches. That seemed to be the case with my silent fascination with the afterlife, because schoolmates adopted me as a sounding board for

their encounters. The accounts I heard carried a similar ring—
that is, they were meaningful and comforting.

"I found this watch from Grandma!"—Jerri's Story

Jerri and I had been classmates since elementary school. By
appearance and personality, we were as opposite as a photograph and its negative. Whereas she had dark hair, skin, and
eyes, I was blonde, blue-eyed, and fair. She was an introvert and
never interested in extracurricular activities; I was extroverted
and in the middle of everything. Our similarities, however,
were our basic values. We both were remarkably involved in our
church and wanted to be missionaries. Like mine, Jerri's formative years were in the arms of an adoring grandmother.

I was delighted to see Jerri waving at me from the other
side of our high school's campus after the Christmas break. She
ran up to me. "I found this watch from Grandma! I found this
watch from my grandma!" she squealed, holding her wrist in
front of my eyes. Jerri pulled me away from the concourse and
began again.

> I have to tell you. My grandma . . . she had a heart
> attack and . . . ah, she . . . ah . . . you know . . . passed away
> before Christmas. We were all so sad that we hardly had
> any Christmas at all.
>
> But that night, Grandma came to me in a dream and
> told me to go get my present from her. She said she'd
> wrapped it and hidden it away. The next morning, when I
> told my mom and grandpa, Mom said, "It was just a
> dream." My grandpa teased me, "What? She'd better've
> gotten me something too." He was laughing about it, but
> it *seemed* so real to me. I looked and looked everywhere
> but I couldn't find any present, so I knew Mom was
> right—it was just a dream.
>
> I was looking out my window that night, trying to
> sleep, and I could've sworn I saw my grandma shining
> through the top of the trees, coming from the moonlight.
> That may sound weird, but then I heard her say, "Go get
> your present before something happens to it. It's a watch.

Look in the bottom of my big sewing box in the back of the closet, in the spare bedroom. Dump all the material out. You'll see it—it's wrapped in a red and green box." Next morning when I told my mother, she said, "Oh go on," just like that. She didn't even look up from her newspaper. But my grandpa said, "Let's go see!" He was laughing again, running in front of me, to the back bedroom closet. We took all her scraps out of the box, and sure enough, there it was just like she told me, wrapped in red and green paper. You should've seen the look on my grandpa's face—and my mom! Oh my gosh!

Jerri giggled.

Then, holding up her arm to display the slim wristwatch again, she said, "I'm so proud of it. Isn't it beautiful?"

"Oh, Jerri, it's elegant, just elegant." I answered.

Although the simple gold watch would have held little value in the marketplace, the joy it brought her was immeasurable.

This encounter, similar to the others I heard, brought comfort. Jerri's offered more, however. It provided evidence for life after bodily death. Only her deceased grandmother knew about the watch and its whereabouts; therefore, the apparition provided accurate information—known only by the discarnate.

Our small town was built on wild strawberry fields, but the annual harvesting was put aside in preparation for the upcoming high school graduation festivities. My mother, a bit of a psychic, wandered into my room, saying, "Honey, have you ever noticed that just when you're strolling along, thinking how wonderful life is, the old devil jumps up from below and grabs you by the heels? Something's going to happen." Days later, before our commencement celebration, Mother's premonition struck our close-knit community.

"Just what he always wanted!"—Christian's Story

"The day he was born," his mother explained to anyone who would listen, "I knew his name had to be Christian. Everyone still comments about how beautiful he is, especially his transparent blue eyes. I know he's my son, but he just doesn't seem to be of this world, and not just because of his looks either. He's the sweetest and most thoughtful child. He's too good to be real. I know I'm blowing my own horn, but it's true."

"It is true," everyone agreed because Christian really did seem flawless.

"He's so perfect, it scares me," she often added, defending her overprotectiveness.

Graduation night was drawing close, yet Christian had never been allowed to ride in a car with anyone except his family. When two friends stopped by his house inviting Christian to a baseball game, his mother suffered her usual panic attack. His dad, however, insisted, "Aw, it's a beautiful evening. Let the boy go for Pete's sake! Stop smothering him."

"Good grief, Mom," said Christian's sister, "Let him go. Tonight's the big rival game. Everybody'll be there."

Guilt overcame his mother's terror, so she reluctantly agreed. The threesome dashed outside, afraid she would change her mind.

Within an hour, Christian's mother heard a knock on their front door and then the words she most feared, "I'm sorry to have to tell you this, but your son is gone." Minutes from their house, a drunken driver had crashed into the side of the boys' car and Christian was thrown from the back seat. He died at the scene.

Numbed by disbelief, no one knew what to say—not to Christian's family nor to one another. A clear blue sky reminded us of Christian's eyes, the day we laid his body to rest. The Texas sun stole our tears. The crowd lingered in the cemetery after the service, then finally gathered at the foothill preparing to depart. Suddenly, amidst the murmuring of good-byes, someone yelled out, "Look!" There, like a vault from heaven, an exquisite rainbow arched in the distance and ended directly above Christian's grave. Everyone gasped. "Just what he always wanted," his sister cried out. "The end of the rainbow!"

For as long as they could recall, Christian had lived with a passion for rainbows. Glass rainbows hung in his bedroom window and mobiles from the ceiling, while his doodles and paintings adorned the walls. "I'll be happy when I find the end of the rainbow," he often sighed. "That's where I want to be." Christian's final rainbow was not lost in the moment. One of the mourners snapped a photograph, crystallizing the event, and later presented it to his family as a reminder for the comfort it brought them that day.

The phenomenon became the talk of the town. "You *know* the rainbow was a sign," said Christian's friends. "It had to be 'cause it was so still and hot that day, without a hint of moisture anywhere." Skeptics protested, "Nah . . . it was just a freak of nature." Everyone might have dismissed it, had it not been for Christian's wish to be at the rainbow's end.

The afterlife encounter was different from others I had heard about because it appeared via a symbol, was captured on film, and witnessed by many. Furthermore, whereas most encounters are never mentioned in public, the rainbow was not only discussed—it was debated. At the very least, the event broke the uncomfortable silence that often follows a sudden and shocking death.

As I filed it away in the repository of my mind, I reflected about the comfort and hope the different discarnate sightings had brought to those left behind. For me, each was touching and added more dimension to my life; however, none were my own. Then came an experience with my Grandma.

"Honey, don't you see?"—The Telephone Call

Grandma attended to my every need. She was my principal caregiver while my parents worked long hours. On my fifth birthday, however, we moved to Texas, leaving her behind. Over the years, Grandma and I forged a common dream—for me to attend a college in Arkansas, near her home. Finally our plan seemed to be realized the morning my acceptance papers arrived, but our jubilation was soon squelched. She had contracted hepatitis from a blood transfusion.

Hepatitis, in 1963, was a death sentence. Grandma was hospitalized and placed in isolation. Mandatory before entering her room: a series of painful shots. Of all Grandma's family, only my mother, uncle, cousin, and I were willing to endure the injections. No one else wanted to step inside the door, fearful of the dreaded shots or worse—the disease. Grandma needed nursing care around the clock, so we placed advertisements for nurses in newspapers, but when applicants heard the diagnosis, they fled. Finally, I said what had become obvious to me, "I must be Grandma's caregiver and stay in isolation with her until the end."

Grandma lay comatose, totally unresponsive. An oxygen tent severed her further from the outside world. I was her only entertainment—the only thing stirring within her room. Every day, month in and month out, I called out the daily menu to her and selected Grandma's favorite food and drink as if she could partake of them. I read aloud everything the nuns slipped under our door. Cards and letters of well-wishers were delivered to the hospital, all of which I repeated to Grandma, over and over, hoping she could hear and know how loved she was. I bathed her, administered her medications, cared for her bedsores, and met all her other needs. Upon her final breath, I summoned a nurse and doctor, then afterward called our family to announce she had died.

Grandma's death brought me to another crossroad. School began soon and I dreaded the thought of going to the university we had chosen. Hoping for tuition reimbursement, I pleaded my case to the dean, saying, "The reason I applied to this college was to be near my grandma."

"You'll receive a good education here," he insisted. "You may withdraw, but your money will not be refunded." I had paid cash for my tuition, which included room and board—every cent of which I had earned completely on my own. And now I thought about all those years of toiling, scrimping, and saving. I just could not throw it away, so off to Arkansas I went.

Nothing about the school pleased me. I was miserable. I flew home one weekend just to get away and there, the first night, had a dream. My grandmother came to me, speaking sweetly, just as she always had, "When you were born, I took care of you. During the first years of your life, when you were most needy, I was there—not because it was my responsibility, but because I loved being with you and I wanted to make sure you were in the best of hands. At the end of my life, you wanted to spend every second you could with me. You made sure that I was in the best hands, with someone who loved me. Honey, don't you see? We came full circle. You deserve to be happy and you—"

"No! No! No!" my mother's screams jolted me awake. Her arms were around my shoulders, shaking me as she sobbed, "Not my baby! Oh please God! Don't take my baby!" I opened my eyes to see that I was sitting up in bed with the telephone receiver in my hand. *How strange,* I thought, and then wondered, *Why is Mother so hysterical?* "What's wrong?" I asked.

"When the dead talk to the living," she cried, collapsing into my pillow, "it means the person here is going to die soon." Mother continued to sob uncontrollably, holding a handful of tissues against her face. I struggled to hear her muffled words as she began again, "The one who loved us most during our lives always comes to take us to the other side and your grandma loved you more than life itself." I put my hand under Mother's chin, lifting her eyes up to mine. "Look at me. Look at me," I insisted. "I'm fine. I'm not going anywhere. It was just a dream." I lay down beside her, but neither of us slept.

We stirred at the sunrise with no appetite for breakfast or conversation. It was mid-morning before hunger escorted us into the kitchen.

"Still worried?" I broke our silence.

"I guess not," came from her lips, but her eyes signaled otherwise. "While your grandma was alive, especially while she was in the hospital, I knew if the phone rang in the middle of the night it would be someone calling with bad news. So hearing it ring startled me. But then, when I heard you talking to her, I panicked. Who called . . . really?"

"Hmmm, well, I remember dreaming . . . and I remember the phone ringing . . . and I answered it . . ." I paused, trying hard to recollect the incident.

"I heard it ring two or three times," Mother said. "Then you started talking. I looked at the clock and wondered who could be calling in the middle of the night. When you kept talking I got up to see who it was. You were talking about the things you used to do with her—the picnics, walking across the rocks at Cold Springs, and all. But then you started talking about being in a meadow of yellow flowers and that scared me, because nothing like that ever happened. You can't go. I need you. As long as I have you, I know I'll be okay."

I wanted to bring Mother reassurance, as well as sort through exactly what happened. "I must have been dreaming about Grandma when the phone rang. I remember it ringing, answering it, and talking, but then . . . then I went back to sleep and the next thing I knew, you were waking me from a really great dream. I remember Grandma's last words—what she was saying while you were shaking me—that we came full circle. The next thing I remember is sitting in bed with the phone in my hand."

"When you answered it, who did you hear?" Mother persisted.

"I don't remember anyone at first, but then I started talking and heard Grandma's voice. Ah! I know! Maybe I was dreaming when the phone rang and it was a crank call or the wrong number, so I went back to dreaming about Grandma and imagined she was on the line. That's all it was," I concluded, wanting to put Mother's mind at ease.

"I don't know," she replied. "I've always heard that when someone dead talks to someone alive, it means that person is going to die soon."

"But I'm fine. I wish I could remember everything about it, but I do remember feeling adored and happy."

"Well, you know your grandma isn't the only one who adores you, and you're always happy," she said.

"I'm not happy at school, that's for sure!" I exclaimed. "It's like having teeth pulled every day." My mind reflected on the incident. "Does the library have books about such things?" I wondered aloud.

"I bet you'll find something when you get back to school, maybe even from your psychology and sociology professors," she suggested. Returning to the university suddenly seemed acceptable.

By the time I arrived at my dorm, snow covered the campus. I enjoyed trekking through the knee-high mounds and searching the library shelves, but within weeks I was wading through frozen slush only to find the same books I had read before.

"I'm withdrawing!" I cheered through the telephone to Mother. "I'm coming home."

"Oh, no!" she gasped. "If you quit, it'll mean you worked all those years for nothing, because all that money will go down the drain."

"I talked to the dean again, and he could give me only two reasons for staying. He said I'd get a good education and not lose my money. But, I think of it this way—I spent my money to learn how not to spend my life . . . someplace where I'm not happy."

"What an education, eh?" she joked.

"Yeah, I'm pretty sure that's what Grandma was going to tell me, in my dream . . . that I'm too unhappy here and to leave, that I have only one life to live. Money can be replaced and education found elsewhere, but not time."

I withdrew that afternoon, drove all night, arrived in Houston before daybreak, and was inside the Pasadena Public Library upon their opening, where I searched for any material relating to the afterlife.

Reading books and articles has given me a broad perspective. My most meaningful discoveries, however, came from listening to perceivers, conducting research, and my personal experiences. I have learned far beyond what Mother and I knew back then, and offer my lifetime of findings in the chapters that follow.

TWO

The Survey Reveals

In the sorrow of grief humans need to be consoled.
—Dennis Klass

Whether real or imagined, paranormal beliefs enhance mental health. Simply believing in the hereafter is life enhancing. Experiencing an afterlife encounter (AE) is a significant element for transcending loss. It, furthermore, offers a leap toward enlightenment.

While working as a hospice chaplain, the director of the Elisabeth Kübler-Ross Center of Houston, and facilitator for the Gateway Center in New York, I often heard mourners describe their encounters. Not only were they comforting, but sensing a connection with the beyond facilitated their grief process. Upon conducting survival research, however, I witnessed opposite ends of the spectrum. The phenomenon either lessened perceivers' (people who experience afterlife encounters—witnesses, observers, percipients, receivers, recipients) sorrow or caused an intense longing to have loved ones back, if only for a moment in time. The 1990s spiritual movement, with its focus on contacting the dead, brought a groundswell of attention surrounding the tremendous value of afterlife encounters, and I was concerned that many claims were exaggerated, therefore misleading. Although my main unrest centered on the bereaved, I wanted to know the effects that encounters held on nonmourners as well.

Hoping to find data surrounding the influence post-mortem visitations posed on witnesses, with the help of colleagues, I turned to published and unpublished literature. We scanned the field of thanatology (the study of death and dying), bereavement, sociology, religion, philosophy, psychology, and parapsychology, but found nothing that covered the levels of comfort or grief surrounding AEs. I therefore designed the Afterlife Encounters Survey (AES), a five-year international study for collecting data pertaining to the effects, if any, afterlife encounters held for recipients over time. Phase One measured respondents' levels of comfort during and after their encounters, then their levels of grief before, during, and after. We will explore the findings in this chapter, but first, what exactly is an afterlife encounter?

Features of Afterlife Encounters

An afterlife encounter is any sense of being connected to, or in the presence of, a discarnate entity. They fall into five categories: 1) personal (deceased relative, pet, friend, colleague, neighbor, or anyone familiar to the experiencer); 2) spiritual figure (God, Jesus, Buddha, angel, saint, etc.); 3) historical or famous figure (such as Alexander the Great, Winston Churchill, Mother Theresa, Marilyn Monroe, or Mickey Mantle); 4) unknown (discarnate entity is unfamiliar to the experiencer at the time); 5) objects and nonhuman species (telephones, computers, answering machines, animals, and butterflies, for example). Afterlife encounters appear in one of two forms—ghosts or apparitions.

Afterlife Encounters with Ghosts

Ghosts are connected to a place—therefore, each can be sighted in the same location by different witnesses. Ghosts do not display animated personalities, appear in vivid colors, emit radiant energy, or interact with observers. According to most survivalists (people who investigate the possibility that some aspect of the living survives bodily demise), ghosts are the psychical imprints of people or animals that were left in certain areas while alive, and any sensitive individual can pick up the prerecorded images and sounds. This means that ghosts hold no intentions.

I have been tracking the following case for more than 40 years, and it depicts the common features for most ghostly manifestations.

The Ghost of Fame Cleaners

My family owned a chain of dry cleaning establishments. Seven days a week, Dyer, our dry cleaner, arrived at his spotting board before daybreak and remained there until long after sunset. His family, life, and love revolved around his work. He had nothing else. My dad, Dyer's employer for some 30 years, was concerned. "He swore he'd never love again after his wife ran out on him," Dad said to my mother and me. "Look at him. He's a hermit. He'll be 70 this week and what does he have?"

"Let's invite him over for dinner," Mother said.

Dyer accepted the invitation and seemed to enjoy himself, but when Dad invited him again, he said, "Don't try to fix what ain't broke. My life's exactly the way I want it."

"Okay, just consider it an open offer," said Dad.

Seasons changed but Dyer remained the same—that is, until one approaching Easter when he didn't show up for work. Not only was that unlike him under normal circumstances, but the week before Easter was our busiest of the year. Dad raced to Dyer's apartment across the street and returned with grim news. "He must have had a heart attack in his sleep last night. He died the way he lived, peacefully and alone."

It was during the midsummer's heat, when Maria, one of Dyer's coworkers, rushed outside to greet Dad.

"Mr. Davidson! I saw him! I saw him!" she yelled.

"Who?" he asked.

"Dyer! As soon as I walked in I saw him. He was smiling, standing over there behind his spotting board working on some clothes. I smiled and waved at him, and he waved at me. I started walking to my side of the room to put my things down so I could go over and talk to him, but when I looked over there again, he was gone."

"Imagine that!" Dad joked, "Isn't it just like Dyer to leave when he thought someone might talk to him?"

Several customers and other employees reported similar experiences over the years that followed.

Then two decades brought complete personnel shift for Fame Cleaners. My parents retired to another state, and all of their employees had either moved away or died. My husband, Joe, and I purchased the business to keep it in the family, but my time was occupied as a day-trader and Joe was busy with his own company located across the alley. Easter was upon us again and the cleaners needed employees, so Joe hired two sisters who had just arrived from Mexico. Neither woman spoke English, but he did not see that as a problem, since they would simply be washing shirts as a team. The following morning, the pair was busy sorting clothes when they saw a man in their periphery. They turned to face him directly, but were stunned by his transparent-blue eyes, pale skin, and white hair. The sisters looked at one another, then back toward the intruder, but he had vanished. "Hombre! Hombre!" they yelled, running out of the building. Joe and passersby immediately searched the premises and surrounding area, but found no one. An interpreter intervened and relayed their story, adding that their fright was mostly due to the man's ethereal appearance.

Meanwhile, Joe built an apartment above the cleaners, wherein occupants of various ages (ranging from four to 40), under varying circumstances (while watching television, cooking, reading, talking, and sleeping), experienced similar but unusual occurrences. They recounted seeing a short, thin man with transparent-blue eyes, pale skin, white hair, wearing a light-blue suit—all of which mirrored Dyer's appearance during life. Numerous occupants complained, even during Houston's searing summers, "One corner of the apartment is always freezing cold." Joe relayed the incidents to me, saying, "I can't figure it out. That cool area should be as hot as hell—it's directly above the spotting board" (Dyer's former work station). Neither Joe, nor anyone at the cleaners or apartment, had ever heard of Dyer, and I did not divulge any information, thinking, *This is an excellent way to gather information, especially since Joe's a firm believer that nothing survives death.* We eventually sold the building, but continue to hear when employees or customers sight the figure of a man who meets Dyer's description.

Afterlife Encounters with Apparitions

Apparitions associate with people—therefore, each may be sighted in different locations by the same person(s). Most apparitions radiate personality, color, and energy. Some engage in conversation or touching. All, however, transpire for one basic reason—growth. They offer growth for everyone involved. In order to carry out their purpose, they appear in a form that will most likely be noticed and considered. Consequently, they manifest either directly or indirectly.

Direct encounters are often *visual*—the apparitions appear ethereal (cloudlike vapor), surreal (more real than real), or realistic (lifelike). They may be *auditory* (witnesses hear a voice, whistle, cough, or other sounds), *olfactory* (an aroma such as pipe smoke or perfume is smelled), or *tactile* (perceivers feel a physical sensation, such as a touch or coolness). Sensing a presence (a definite but unexplainable impression of being in the company of a disembodied personality) can also be classified as an afterlife encounter. The phenomenon most often includes a combination of senses, such as sensing a presence, seeing an image, and feeling a coolness.

Indirect encounters occur through a diverse range of animate and inanimate objects. Both wild and domesticated animals—cats, birds, and butterflies for instance—reportedly bring signs to surviving loved ones. Rainbows, pennies, and feathers can present meaningful messages. Devices—answering machines, baby monitors, cameras, clocks, computers, music boxes, pagers, tape recorders, telephones, televisions, walkie-talkies, and so on—serve as a bridge between worlds. Instruments designed to systematically record possible posthumous contact are used by professionals and hobbyists alike.

Let's focus on direct encounters, beginning with Katie's visual experience.

"Papa Roger saved me."—Donna Perez's Survey

I am writing for my 16-year-old niece, Katie Allred. Her grandfather (my father) died in April 2002. Katie was probably his favorite grandchild—he adored her. In June, Katie's best friend, LindyLou, picked Katie up to go out for the evening. They had gotten only about a mile down our country road when LindyLou lost control of the car on a curve. The car spun around backwards, went down an embankment, and into the woods. Katie was unharmed, but her friend was killed.

Where Katie had been sitting, it looked like someone had put their hands over her and sealed her from the wreck—we are talking about a space of maybe 24". The rest of the car, around that space, was either torn up or gone. Katie said that when the car stopped, it felt as if someone lifted her out. With woods all around her, she had no sense of direction and didn't know which way to go. She was just standing there when she suddenly saw her grandfather. He was glowing and pointing in one direction, so she went that way. Katie came out on the road and flagged down a passing car.

She told us that night, "Papa Roger saved me." Our family believes this, especially after seeing the car. Katie should not have survived this wreck—but she did, and without any injury.

In thanking Donna for participating in the study, I mentioned that encounters can occur during times of crises. For the sake of research, Donna wanted to send more documentation as evidence for the authenticity of her niece's experience.

First, she e-mailed photographs of the car, and then asked Kathy, Katie's mother, to submit a survey.

"The car was so destroyed."—Kathy Allred's Survey

My name is Kathy. I'm Katie's mom. The wreck was August 24, 2002, at approximately 7:15 P.M. Katie's dad, brother, and I arrived at the wreck before the rescue crews. We saw Katie standing beyond the wreck, with her overnight bag in her hand. On the right side of the car, the front headlight ended up against the right rear tail-light and her seat was in the trunk of the car (the seat belt was still fastened). The car was so destroyed that when the highway patrol arrived they couldn't tell what make it was. Later, the investigating officer came by our house to talk to Katie—they wanted to know how she got out of the car.

Both Katie and Will (her brother) say their grandfather is with them during the major events in their lives. I know we have angels and loved ones watching over us. As a mother, it's nice to know my children will always have extra eyes watching them while they are out there in the world. It's a relief to me, and it adds pressure on them to be good!

Because Katie recognized her grandfather's image and trusted he was there to help her, she followed his gesture. Her account demonstrates that apparitions may communicate non-verbally. Often, however, there is no communication, as Dana Owen from Arkansas explained.

"Just seeing him was all I needed to forgive."—Dana's Survey

A cousin from my mother's side of the family saw my father just minutes after his death.

Our families had been estranged since she was young, so I was shocked when I heard that she woke up at three o'clock on Sunday morning with him at the foot of her bed. At breakfast, she told her husband and children, "I looked up and saw an old man standing there, staring at me. He was radiating a peaceful golden glow. It's been over 30 years since I saw Uncle Ted, but I know that was him and that he's dead." Then, on Tuesday, they read in the newspaper that he had died at 3 A.M. on Sunday.

After all those years, she called me and described my father in exact detail. I had read that apparitions were hallucinations, so I had to wonder *How could she have hallucinated that?* She couldn't have, because the last time she or anyone in her family saw him, he weighed over two hundred pounds, had a head full of thick black hair, and a shining complexion. But during the last months of his life, he became thin, frail, wrinkled, and his hair was thin and totally gray. Plus, she described his final physical changes, which only his doctor, nurse, and I knew.

My cousin said, "Uncle Ted didn't say anything, but I somehow knew exactly who he was and that he was there to make amends. And for some reason, all the pain and anger I felt toward the family disappeared when I saw him like that. I can't believe it, but just seeing him was all I needed. I'm not mad at anyone any more. It's okay."

Now my cousin and I talk often, and she came to our family gathering this summer. Seems like a miracle.

Most percipients of visual encounters realize they received what they needed. However, some are perplexed by the lack of communication. To illustrate, let's turn to Martha Sherman and her husband, Harold.

"But he hasn't said anything."
—Martha Sherman's Encounter

Throughout 50-plus years of exploration, my greatest joy has been the people I have met along the way. Martha Sherman and her daughter, Marcia, are among my favorites. At first glance, Martha's large, almost-black eyes, drew me in like no others. "I don't understand," she began. "I've seen Harold three times, but he hasn't said anything."

To understand her bewilderment, let me introduce you to Harold Sherman. Harold, a prolific researcher and president of the ESP Research Associates Foundation, was considered an authority in the field of psychical exploration. He authored more than one hundred books, and, in 1951, co-authored *Thoughts Through Space* with Sir Hubert Wilkins, wherein they documented their long-distance telepathic communications. Keep in mind, during their experiments Sherman was the receiver (Wilkins the sender).

For his foundation, Harold hosted conferences and lectures, one of which was to be held weeks after his death. Martha's family encouraged her to carry the program through and introduce the guest speakers. The evening proved to be an especially meaningful experience for Martha.

> I didn't want to make the introductions, but they talked me into it. I was standing in front of the crowd, my knees shaking, when I saw Harold enter the back of the room. He was glowing, even more alive than when he was alive. I think he just wanted to see how many people showed up, because he just stood there looking around at the audience. He seemed very pleased to see a big crowd . . . a full house. I was so happy to see him that I relaxed and went right at it.
>
> The next time I saw Harold was in the middle of the night. Something awoke me, and when I turned over I saw an indention in the mattress, an impression of Harold's body lying on his side of the bed. I hadn't believed in life after death, but my experiences were beginning to change my mind.

Martha described her third encounter to me, and then Marcia gave me a copy of a letter her mother had written to friends. An excerpt (emphasis by Martha) is as follows:

New Year's Eve 1987

> I am going to tell you of one [encounter] because it has changed my point of view. I awoke one morning to find Harold's *warm* hand in mine. I could see his arm plainly to the elbow, as it lay apparently flat on the bed. He was wearing his favorite sky-blue sweater and he was wearing his wrist watch. It was as real as life and the *warmth* of his hand I can still feel. I want to remark here, one of his major complaints always was that he was *cold*.

I puzzled over this experience for a long time. It had come to me quite some time after Harold left and I regret continually that I didn't "date" it. Why was I holding his hand and not he mine? Why such a vivid recollection of the watch? Why no response from him? Why the arm lying flat? Was it possible that he was still resting? Was that the significance of the watch? Was the favorite blue sweater a proof of his identity and the *warm* hand the indication he was really all right? It was so very vivid and real.

While preparing boxes of Harold's material for the University of Arkansas archivist, Martha suddenly realized what she had always known about her husband. "He never rested," she said. "He threw himself from one project after another with eager intensity. He never took a vacation." On one hand, she was relieved, saying her encounter indicated that he was finally able to put his passions aside and relax. She was bewildered, however. Why had such a successful orator, one whose passion had been communicating thoughts through space, appeared and not communicated? Perhaps he was continuing his work postmortem—after all, Harold Sherman had been on the *receiving* side of telepathic messages.

During the Afterlife Encounters Survey (AES), 20 percent of the accounts were visual. Similar to Martha, participants often asked why their discarnate loved ones did not communicate. Each encounter depends on a unique set of circumstances, which we will consider in a later chapter. Meanwhile, Martha's interludes illustrated that an apparition can appear in various forms.

Of the encounters submitted during the survey, 52 percent were a combination of visual and one or more other senses. Visual/auditory encounters accounted for 13 percent. From that group, Mary Siefer, from Storm Lake, Iowa, chronicled her visitation with Amanda, her granddaughter.

"Yes, Grandma, it's me!"—Story by Mary Siefer

Our daughter Jane, her husband, Jim, and their children were always at our house for Christmas, arriving on the eve for our traditional soup supper and the church service that followed. After Amanda, one of their children, died in August of 2000, our whole family knew that Christmas would be a difficult time. My husband and I knew we had to be strong for them.

We moved to a new home in October, and I decorated it for Christmas the first week in December. In my box of decorations I found a single jingle bell tied to a red ribbon for wearing around my neck. I slipped it over my head, remembering that Amanda had made it several years before. I wore it all day, thinking happy thoughts of our 12 grandchildren and our many wonderful times.

Early the next morning, I had a beautiful dream of Amanda. I do believe I had a visitation as I remember all of it in great detail.

She was standing in our bedroom smiling at me. She was beautiful! She was wearing a silken gown in her favorite color of blue; it was crossed in front and tied at her side, and had long tapered sleeves that I could clearly see. In my dream I commented (as grandmothers do), "I can't remember that she was this tall!" She stood very straight, almost regally, with a faint glow around her. I finally said, "Amanda is that you?" She replied in a voice I well remember, "Yes, Grandma, it's me!" And to my great disappointment, I awakened.

When we were on our way to church that Christmas Eve, I told Jim and Jane about my beautiful dream. "Oh yes," I said, "I remember something else. Amanda's hair was braided—I could see it on one side." I had never seen her hair braided and thought that was unusual, but Jane replied softly, "Mother, we braided her hair in the hospital because it was so long and in the way. She died with a braid down her back." So, I am quite certain that I did, indeed, have a visit from Amanda.

Three percent of encounters recorded during the AES were a combination of sight and touch, as in the following example written by George Stone, age 69.

"He was a mean kind of man."—George Stone's Survey

I worked with a foreman for 25 years. He was a mean kind of man, never smiled or gave anybody a pat on the back for doing a good job. I guess the power went to his head. Nobody liked him. He didn't like me. He'd even go out of his way to cause me trouble.

He died six years ago, and about a month after, he started coming to me in dreams. But he seemed different, like he wanted to make up for everything. I read that we must forgive those who do us wrong, so I asked the holy spirit to come into my heart, and I sent love and forgiveness to that man. A week later I was lying on my side watching TV when I felt the pressure of someone's hand on my shoulder, and at the same time I saw a glow from the corner of my eye. I moved my eyes over and there was a bright light and just above it was my deceased foreman. He was smiling, showing just his bottom teeth. He looked so very much alive. I'd never seen him smile before. It was a wonderful experience.

But what happened four years afterward amazed me. The foreman's brother-in-law died and I went to the wake. While there, I saw three of my foreman's brothers. We were all talking in the hall when I noticed that every time his brothers smiled, they showed only their bottom teeth, just like he did in my encounter with him. That really convinced me of life after death.

George Stone's afterlife visitation brought him two milestones. During his reunion with his former boss, George learned to forgive. Four years thereafter, his encounter brought him personal evidence for survival of bodily death.

Let's now consider the sense of presence. Have you ever been alone in a room, and then at some point sensed another person? Upon looking around, you discovered that, indeed, someone had entered the door. Biologist Rupert Sheldrake conducted studies wherein experimenters stared at the back of subjects' heads.[1] Most sensed the stares and turned around to look at the experimenters. A biological function for all living human and nonhuman animals, Sheldrake designated the phenomenon "seventh sense."[2]

Afterlife encounters involving the sense of presence carry similar qualities—therefore, perhaps the connection between the living and discarnate should be termed "eighth sense." Regardless, many participants in my study, similar to Sheldrake's, recounted feeling a sense of presence and then turned around to discover they were being observed. Whereas five percent sensed a presence only, 41 percent reported other modalities in accompaniment. Lori, who experienced her account at the age of 16, narrated her episode.

"That's exactly what he was wearing."
—Lori's Apparitional Encounter

Moving away from my family, friends, and hometown to go live with my father was especially difficult. I missed everything I loved, especially Gary, my best friend. He was like a brother to me, and to this very day I can still see him smiling, laughing, and chiding me about the hazards of smoking.

One night in late July, I received a phone call from my older sister saying she had bad news for me. "Someone died," she said. My heart skipped, pounded in fearful anticipation. "Now don't you cry," she said. But I already was crying. I heard distress and sympathy in her voice, and I knew—*knew*—I had lost someone close and special to me. "Gary Piper died. He had an accident at work," she said.

My mind instantly flashed back to the last day of school. He ran up to me, panting slightly. "Hey Lor, have you seen Maggie?" I smiled into his blue eyes. I knew how much he cared for Maggie. They had been dating for quite some time and he was head over heels for her—his first touch of love. "Sorry, Gary, I haven't seen her," I said. Before I could tell him I was moving, he took off running down the hall, shouting over his shoulder, "Thanks anyway, Lor. If you see her, tell her I'm looking for her. See ya!"

I thought I'd see him again before we moved, but I didn't. We had no chance to say goodbye, and now he was gone from me forever. Loss and emptiness filled me that night. The tall, skinny, curly-headed youth that I had shared so much with was gone. I hadn't even said goodbye to Gary, and I was not able to attend his funeral. I was desolate, heartbroken, hurting—unable to let go of my friend and of my pain.

The hardest part was knowing I had to let go, but I didn't know how. How could I? We had no chance to say goodbye. Gary was the first person I ever knew who died, and I didn't even get to go to his funeral. Trying to distract me from my pain, my father asked if I'd be interested in a job. I knew I needed a diversion, so I agreed to mow the lawn at a local United Baptist Church. I didn't mind physical labor, especially during autumn.

One particular day, however, I felt the hair on the back of my neck tingle. I sensed someone was staring at me. I stopped mowing, looked over my left shoulder, and discovered that I was indeed being stared at. It was Gary! I looked at him standing there watching me. He was wearing blue jeans and a T-shirt, unlike anything I'd seen him wear before. Seconds felt like years, as we gazed at each other. But then I thought, *This can't be Gary—he's dead!* I whipped my head around, then instantly turned back again for another look, but he was gone. The street was empty. I frantically searched all around for signs of another person. I thought, *Whoever that was couldn't have disappeared in a second.* But he had.

A friend from my hometown came to visit me shortly afterward, and when I told him about my experience, he looked at me in amazement. He said, "I saw Gary the day of his accident and that's exactly what he was wearing." He also said, "Gary was buried in a United Baptist Church cemetery."

That night I had a dream. I was sitting on a black leather couch in Gary's office, waiting for him. Gary walked in, sat beside me, and we talked for what seemed like hours. At the end of my dream, we held each other and I finally got to say goodbye. My worldview changed after my encounter. To me, it proved survival—survival of Gary's spirit and love for me. Because he loved me so much that he gave me what I needed, a hug and time to say goodbye. More was to come, however.

I went to visit Gary's gravesite, but he didn't have a headstone. I wandered around the graveyard, whispering, "Gary . . . where are you . . . where are you?" A leaf came floating from the sky. No trees were overhead, so it seemed the leaf was from nowhere. I watched it gently drift, drift, drift. Finally, it landed and I walked over to get it—and there, on that exact spot, was Gary's grave.

My healing from those experiences is amazing. My broken heart was able to mend. I never heard from Gary again, but then why should I? He gave me what I needed back then, and for that I'm very grateful.

Lori's encounter began with a sense of presence and developed further because she was open to the experience. Her account suggests another feature of AEs—which we will explore in depth later—postmortem manifestations bring perceivers what they need. Meanwhile, let's move to the next modality.

Three percent of AES respondents experienced a physical touch or some type of movement. From this group of participants, many felt their disembodied loved ones lying beside them in bed, just as they had during life. Michael, from California, described his sensation.

"I could feel her next to me."—Michael Way's Survey

I worked unusual hours and took a long nap in the early afternoon. When my cat was alive, she would jump up on the foot of the bed and sleep with me. After she died, she continued to do so. As soon as I settled into bed, I felt it jiggle, then I'd feel her next to me. It was comforting to know she was still around. The experiences continued on an irregular basis until I changed beds many years later.

From the 950 encounters reported, pets accounted for 11 percent. Approximately one-half of the animals were not alone. They often appeared with deceased family members, even when the people had died long before the pets were adopted.

Discarnate animal companions bring unconditional love, acceptance, joy, and trust. They lighten our hearts. As a result, pets sometimes serve as a bridge between worlds. By appearing first, they create a light and relaxed atmosphere, setting the tone for human contact.

Olfactory manifestations accounted for 2 percent of the surveys. Jeannie, a wife and mother in California, felt tremendously comforted by her encounter.

"You smell sooo good."—Jeannie's Encounter

While I was in the hospital for surgery, my husband received a phone call from someone who referred to himself as Pocco. Since he didn't know anyone by that name, he told me about the call. I got the chills because my high school boyfriend, Gary, was called Pocco by some of his friends. I thought maybe Gary was trying to find me, but I couldn't imagine how he found my last name. Thinking he wanted to reach me, I started looking for him.

Several years later, I stumbled across a site for social security on the Internet and typed in Gary's name. It came up, along with the date of his death—February 10, 1998. I almost fell off my chair. That was the same time as my surgery and the phone call. I was so stunned and sad.

Gary and I hadn't talked in ten years, and I had always wished I'd meet up with him again because we parted with hurt feelings. Now it was too late. I wondered if Gary had tried to call me while taking a final sweep through life. He never married or had children, so maybe he had come to me.

Then last winter, something unusual happened again. I work for a company that makes portable data storage, so it's a very sterile place with an elaborate filter system. It even has plastic curtains around each area. I was sitting inside a cubical, wondering about Gary. So I said to myself, "Gary if you're with me, give me a sign." A few seconds later, I smelled donuts so strong it was like being inside a Krispy Kreme donut shop! I couldn't believe it! Gary had worked as a baker for a large baking company and every time he'd pick me up, I'd say, "You smell soooo good." He'd laugh and say, "You're strange," then he'd go home and shower off the scent. It was our little joke.

Gary always said that we were soul mates because he was ten years old when his dad died and I was ten when my mom passed. I thought he was a little weird for talking like that; after all, that wasn't the norm for a guy his age. Now I know what he meant—he will be watching over me. At times, he's on my mind, then other times he's far from it—I wonder if he's with me during the times I'm thinking of him.

Because apparitions appear in a form that witnesses will notice, they sometimes manifest indirectly. Let's now explore indirect encounters.

Indirect Afterlife Encounters

Indirect encounters are limitless. They include a wide variety of objects—from the delicate mechanisms of a music box to the cast-iron motor of an automobile. Apparatuses such as answering machines, monitoring equipment, and computers serve as conduits for communication as well. They occur through animals, domesticated and undomesticated. Let's begin our examples with Jane and her daughter Amanda.

"Not to worry—you just had an Amanda visit."—Story by Jane May

The first Christmas after Amanda died, I was shopping at K-Mart when I came upon some small heirloom dolls. Since I constantly searched for Amanda's face everywhere, and since she always looked like she had a doll's face, I naturally searched for her face among the dolls. I found one with long, blonde curls, dressed in green with green eyes that came pretty close to looking like her! It was a music box that played "Somewhere Over the Rainbow," from one of Amanda's favorite movies, and the doll moved to the music. Since Amanda had been a musical theater actress, it seemed perfect that it could both "sing and dance," so I bought the music box, brought it home, and placed it on a shelf in Amanda's room.

Apparently this was a good move. Not long after Christmas, Meredith (Amanda's sister) walked into the bedroom (she had shared it with Amanda). With thoughts of Amanda on Meredith's mind, she shut the door, walked to the shelf with the doll, and stood looking at it. To her amazement, it began to play for her! Startled, when it stopped playing, she tried to make it play again by slamming the door, jumping up and down, and bumping the shelf. Nothing prompted it to play again, even when it was rewound and allowed to play down to see if there was residual "play" that could be prompted by some action. She reported this event to my husband and me half reluctantly, as though we might think she was imagining things. We said, "Not to worry—you just had an Amanda visit."

One night a few months later, I was changing the beds in the girls' room for company, when thoughts of Amanda never coming home again overwhelmed me. I started to sob as I worked, and the doll spontaneously burst into a few bars of its song for me. I was instantly comforted.

We didn't hear from the doll again until Meredith's birthday in June. Meredith was at work in Houston when her coworkers surprised her with a birthday cake. As she blew out the candles, she wished to hear from Amanda. At home a few minutes later, J. R. (her brother) was in his room and I was in the study when we heard the doll's music box start playing. It pinged out nearly an entire verse of the song while J. R. and I raced into the girl's bedroom to watch it. Again, an Amanda visit, we figured. When Meredith called I told her she had gotten her birthday present from Amanda and explained what had happened. She was thrilled to find out that her wish and the doll's spontaneous song were at approximately the same time.

One night, over a year later and just a day before the second anniversary of Amanda's passing, I awoke and couldn't go back to sleep. I moved to Amanda's room, hoping a new location would help, and lay in bed there thinking of the many things I had to do. One of those

"things" was to write our story of the music-box doll for
Dianne. As I thought about it, I realized that we had not
heard from the doll in a very long time and wondered if
we ever would again. I tossed and turned and finally got
up to get a drink of water. Upon my return to the room,
I shut the door, climbed into bed, settled down to try to
get some sleep, and the doll pinged a few notes of its song
as if to say, "Don't worry, Mom, I'm still with you!"

We look forward to many more visits from Amanda.
It's a reassurance that all is right with the world because
the soul really does live on.

Jane May, similar to most perceivers, did not need validation that her indirect encounters were from the hereafter.
Those who question the validity, however, can begin by examining the source. First, could the music box's playing have a
natural cause? The May family thoroughly tested it under various conditions—they slammed the door; jumped up and down;
bumped the shelf where it rested; and even rewound it,
watched it play out, and then listened for residual movement.
Second, has the encounter occurred more than once? Yes, on
four different occasions. Third, have more than one person witnessed the encounters? Again the answer is affirmative—three
people heard the melody and observed the music box playing.
Next, has it operated upon being prompted? Within minutes of
Meredith's wish to hear from Amanda, two people on the
other side of town, not knowing Meredith's desire to hear from
her sister, witnessed the music box playing "Somewhere Over
the Rainbow." Last, has it played during significant times?
Several seasons passed before Jane e-mailed that her music box
continued to play, only during special occasions, and it usually
played most of the song.

Beyond examining the initial source, the group as a whole
can be investigated. I visited an international wholesale and
retail music box company.

"Can a music box play by itself, without someone turning
it on?" I asked the supervisor.

"No, it can't," she answered.

"Does your sales staff ever hear one playing when customers are not in the building?"

"Sometimes," she replied. "Every once in awhile, they hear one after a buyer replaces it on the shelf or in the box, but never more than a note or two."

I looked around at the enormous quantity of items on display, trying to gather the exact question to ask next. She grinned, saying, "It's a standard joke around here . . . if a customer complains about a music box spontaneously playing part, or all, of its song, then we know they have a resident ghost. The mechanisms of a music box can't play more than one or two notes unless it's turned on by someone."

From a dainty doll to horsepower on wheels, indirect encounters offer healing in many forms. Lori and her mother, in the following story, were taken aback by their experience.

"It's impossible for an engine to restart by itself."—Lori Taylor's Story

My father, Joe Conti, unexpectedly passed away from a heart attack in October 2000. My mother, sister, and I were devastated. We were blessed to have this wonderful man as our husband and father because he took such good care of us and held our little family together.

Dad had always been my car advisor. Even if I loved one particular car, I wouldn't make a deal unless he gave it his seal of approval. The year before he died, I found a beautiful Toyota Camry at a large dealership. We took it for a test drive, and Dad gave it two thumbs up. After I bought it, he told me how much he liked it many times. It was a great car in mint condition and never gave me a problem.

About three months after Dad died, I picked Mother up one morning on my way to the cemetery. I had visited his grave numerous times, but this was Mother's first visit. We drove to the section where he was buried and parked. I shut the engine off, took the key out of the ignition, and went to Mother's side. I looked around, glad to see there was no one in sight, that we'd have our privacy. We were taking the long walk toward Dad's grave when all of a sudden I heard an engine start up behind us. I looked back because I knew *nobody* else was there minutes ago. I was shocked! It was *my* car! It had started up all by itself! The engine had stopped, smoothly and completely, so this was not a case of reignition, and I did not have a remote control starter.

I thought my car had a problem, so I ran back and got inside. The ignition was still in the off position with no key in it. As my mother stood there witnessing the whole thing, I tried to shut the engine off but it wouldn't. There was nothing I could do but let it run. We quickly walked on to the grave, talked to my father, then drove back home. This time, when I turned the key to the off position the engine shut off just as it always had. That incident had never happened before that day, and it never happened again.

Since then, I have sold the car to someone I work with and he tells me that the engine has never done that with him. I'm convinced that my father started the car. Maybe it was a welcome sign for my mother—that he was with us at the cemetery. It may seem like a subtle incident, but it took a lot of energy for my dad to start that car for us.

People want to believe in the afterlife, but I never thought much about it. I only thought about the physical world. When I heard stories, I thought maybe there was some truth to it, but it never really hit me hard until I lost my dad and had the experience with my car. There were several other incidents that I could not explain, so I threw myself into reading about the afterlife. It has been the only thing that has helped us through the grief. And it was the combination of reading, and actually feeling he was trying to visit us at times, that got me hooked on it. I have been changed by this. I would give anything to have my father back but through this, I have opened up to a whole new awareness. I, like many of us, have many questions and so much interest that I wish I could devote 24 hours a day to it.

Upon receiving Lori's survey, I wanted to explore the possibility that the engine could have started under its own power. I therefore visited two large Toyota dealerships, an automobile repair shop, and an engine machine shop, all of which dealt with Camrys. I spoke with owners and mechanics whose consensus was, "It's impossible for an engine to restart by itself once it totally shuts off. Someone had to start the car." As I was leaving my final consultation, I pushed the issue by explaining the circumstances. Much to my surprise the owner exclaimed, "Well then, it had to be the ghost, because a car can't start on its own!"

Let's now turn to encounters through devices, such as answering machines, room monitors, and computers. The first example was originally attached to a survey submitted by Angela Dioca. Upon my inquiry, her dad, retired and living in Florida, turned to his journal and e-mailed the specifics.

"Your wife left a voice message last night."—Joe Dioca's Story

On April 25, 2001, I had a procedure done with an experimental device called an Angiojet and Magic Stint to support a deteriorated artery in my heart. Doctors scheduled my follow-up appointment for May 15.

The next week, on May 1, my wife, Ellie, suddenly died. Then, on Monday, May 10, ten days after her death, I received a call from my cardiologist's office. The receptionist said, "Joe Dioca?"

"Yes," I confirmed.

"We're changing your appointment to tomorrow morning," she said.

"But I already have an appointment scheduled for May 15."

She said, "We updated it because your wife left a voice message last night (Sunday) asking that the doctor see you sooner. She said you don't look well."

During my examination the next day, doctors found that I was having life-threatening arrhythmia, which had to be treated immediately. I was so distraught over Ellie's death that I had not realized how close I was coming to having a heart attack had she not rescheduled my appointment. It brings me comfort to know that Ellie was watching over me, loving and protecting me.

In my follow-up with the Dioca family, Joe and his daughters assured me that no family member or friend could have called the doctor's office. Angela further confirmed in her e-mail as follows:

> Regarding my dad's phone call, there is no possible way anyone else could have made it. The only people who even knew about his appointment were Carol, Sean, Dad, and myself, and we were all blown away, as was the poor girl at the doctor's office. They even tried to retrieve the message but it had been erased. Also, we were all so grief-stricken that we never would have done that to him. My mom was always watching out for my dad (still is)!

The Diocas' account highlights a common feature of recorded encounters—after the messages have been received, they disappear. There are exceptions, however.

A skeptical colleague was researching survival-related incidents when she returned home to hear a message from her deceased husband on her answering machine. Although the message contained something only the two of them knew, she immediately made copies, insisting it was a cruel prank. Determined to locate the culprit, she solicited the help of every agency she could think of—local telephone company, police department, etc. "I'm going to get to the bottom of this," she told them. When all investigations came up empty, she hired one of the most successful private detectives in her state. "No problem," he said. "I have sources, so I'll have it resolved within two days and if not you won't owe me anything." She drove to his office, showed him everything examined thus far, and played the recording.

"Are you sure he's not out there somewhere?" he quizzed. "I mean, did you actually bury your husband?"

"Yes—years ago," she answered. For more than two weeks, the detective feverishly explored every possibility. My colleague shared the results.

"In the end he was baffled. He showed me the great lengths he'd gone to in his investigation. But he had no explanation for how the message could have gotten to my recorder, except to say, 'This did not get on your answering machine by an incoming call.' He confirmed that the message was not from this world, but what I liked was that it answered questions for me. I was concerned that even if there is life after death, my husband wouldn't be everything now that he was when he was here . . . and if he isn't, then I'd still have lost the love I had. I hoped he'd still be totally him. And the message left on my answering machine confirmed that he is. It was beautiful and significant."

Encounters via telephones and answering machines are usually brief, often limited to a few words, but the comfort and meaning they provide are immeasurable. Monitoring devices can be another means for connecting indirectly, as Debbie Johnson attested.

"That was Mom."—Debbie Johnson's Story

My mom passed away on August 9, 2002. A month after, on September 11, I was watching TV in our bedroom, while our baby, Kyle, was fast asleep in his. My husband and I have a monitor in our room, which has six red lights formed in the shape of a crescent moon. The bottom light glows when someone talks in Kyle's room. This night, our house was still—the windows were closed and the air conditioner running.

About 12:30 A.M., I heard Kyle wake up. He was talking in his normal baby way and the monitor was registering one red light, as usual. Then I heard him start laughing, and moving his arms and legs, as if he was playing with something or someone. All of a sudden every light on the monitor lit up and loud static came through. For 45 minutes, Kyle sounded restless, seemingly engaged in conversation. I thought it was odd that even though not a peep came out of him at times, the monitor lights kept going crazy!

Through it all, I had a very odd feeling that we weren't alone. Kyle had just turned one, so I just knew my mom was visiting him in her own way, to wish him a happy birthday. After 45 minutes, the static and lights stopped, the monitor went back to normal, and I went into Kyle's bedroom. He was under his covers, sound asleep. A basket of his stuffed animals, which had been standing by his dresser, was knocked over and toys were scattered across the floor. Kyle couldn't have gotten out of his crib by himself, so I knew he didn't do it. That scared me, so I went back to our room and told my husband. He said, "That was Mom, probably dropping by to check on us and to wish Kyle a happy birthday." He was her little angel, and now she is his.

What moved me the most that night was that my mom, in life, never did things on a whim. Her death was totally unexpected, and I was devastated. I know she'd never ever leave me alone at such a difficult and sad time. She always gave her love and time, in abundance, to all her children and nine grandkids, so why would that end? I don't believe for one second that it has! I feel my mom around me often, and I'm really glad for that! I really believe a mother's love is undying.

In our high-tech world, computers are readily replacing human beings in the job force. Are they a threat to mediums? Reports of computers acting as conduits flourish. People claim they have received help with everything from relationships to bank accounts. Thomas, age 51, worked as a mental health professional before becoming a university librarian in Örebro, Sweden, near Stockholm. In a number of ways, his indirect encounter held special meaning for him.

"It's a strong message."—Thomas Kjäll's Survey

Mother and I had a warm and close relationship. Early in the summer of 2000, at the age of 79, she was diagnosed with pelvic sarcoma. The report of no cure was conveyed, as she had heart trouble and was not in condition for surgery. I called Mother every day and visited often. I accompanied her to oncologists, and, together with my sister, contacted doctors, alternative healers, therapists, and home service. My girlfriend and I spent a great deal of our free time helping my mother and father with practicalities in their home.

Mother's health worsened and she was hospitalized in October. I applied for a social security benefit called "close relationship care," which gives citizens almost six months' leave from work with a reduction of salary. During the last six weeks of Mother's life, I stayed with my father so I could visit her every day, all day.

Very early one morning, the nurse was sure Mother would die, but she held on until I entered her room about nine A.M. I said, "I'm here," and within the hour she peacefully passed away. I think she didn't want to leave before I got there. I was glad I could be a support and comfort for her like she had been for me.

The next day, I was in deep grief and sorrow. I turned to my computer and the Internet, reading articles about the afterlife. A special conversation Mother and I had several weeks before her death started coming into my mind, so I put my hands in my lap to think about it. Suddenly, the text in the article began to fade away. In its place, a portrait of my mother, which I had stored on my computer, grew forward on the screen, then a beautiful picture of a flower appeared, then the portrait of my mother, then another flower, and so on. This continued for about four or five minutes. My hands remained in my lap—not touching the laptop!

I see the "computer-encounter" as comfort for me in my grief, and also as a greeting from over there. It's a strong message for life surviving death. I am very thankful for having had the experience and thank my mother for giving me these personal answers to lifelong questions. It's an important issue.

Thomas's encounter occurred before his eyes. In most cases, however, the devices were unattended and the messages

discovered later. Judy submitted her survey wherein I noticed
something unusual, seemingly out of the ordinary. Although we
deleted several sentences for privacy, the remainder appears below
as I received it via my Internet site www.afterlife-encounters.com.
Do you spot anything peculiar?

"You Light Up My Life."—Judy's Survey

David was a beautiful child with a sparkling personality. He was my youngest child of five, and I often told him
that he'd always be my baby. David was seven years old
when we discovered he had juvenile diabetes. It was a cruel
and unrelenting disease that took him in three years. All
the while, David was such a brave little boy. Everyday he
wore a smile on his face and kept his sense of humor. He
was my joy! Debbie Boone's song "You Light Up My Life"
came out about that time, and I told David that it was my
song to him because it was so fitting.

How true it still is—that song, "You Light Up My
Life"—for what a son I have! You see, David still brings me
comfort and love. He has never left me all alone. I have
had many afterlife encounters with him over the past 21
years—since he left this world at age ten, in July 1981.

The night his body died I saw his face. The day of his
funeral, I dreamt we were walking to this big door, but
beyond was a heavy fog that only David could walk through.
Every word I write is *true!* Over the years I wrote everything
down as it happened because it helped me so much. As you
might realize, David still helps me as the years go by.

In January 1998, 17 years after his death, what happened to me was a lot more than a dream. It was truly real
and I believe nothing like it will ever happen again. I was
lying on my bed with my eyes closed, and all of a sudden
I found myself with a group of people and someone who
said he was my spirit-guide. There were other spirit forms
talking amongst themselves. I looked up at the sky, at how
beautiful it was, and thought, "So this is heaven and David
is here somewhere." Then David appeared before my eyes.
His back was to me and he wasn't alone. His grandmother
was with him. My spirit-guide said to David, "Your

Mother is here!" David turned around and looked right at
me with a big smile on his face. His hair was golden. As
he was walking toward me, his spirit had such a bright
golden glow that it almost hurt my eyes. He looked
directly at me and my heart felt such joy! I hadn't felt so
happy in such a long time. I wanted to hold him in my
arms, but my spirit guide said, "You cannot touch him.
You have to go back because it's not yet your time." As I
was coming back, my guide said to me, "Keep praying.
They're not wasted words. Pray for grace." I have been
truly blessed and I am most thankful because every word
is very true!!!
       david

Glance over Judy's survey. Notice the names—only one
begins with a small case letter. It did not seem likely to me that
a mother would fail to capitalize her beloved son's name.
Furthermore, its location in the document seemed unusual—it
is not included with the text, but appeared more in the fashion
of a signature.

Since people from almost every continent were reporting
their e-mail-encounters, I contacted Judy, asking her to resub-
mit her survey, which she did. This time no signature appeared.
I therefore responded, "Except you signed the original."

"No, I didn't sign it," she answered. "It ended just like this
one. Why?"

"Look at your original," I invited, "and tell me what you
see—the name at the bottom."

She e-mailed the following day, "I looked and there is no
name at the bottom." Judy insisted that her last words on the survey she submitted via the Internet were "every word is very true!!!"

"I'll send your entire survey to you as I received it," I wrote,
"because the name 'david' appears at the end." The following
is her response:

Hi Dianne,
       I received your copy. Yes! There it was, signed by David.
It thrilled my heart! He is with me. You can see yourself

why I feel truly blessed. I am a very honest and truthful person, please believe that. I repeat again, I didn't sign David's name. I believe that with God and with an open heart and mind, all good things are possible. My daughters asked me to print some copies for them to keep, so I did. Since David's death, I have been telling my daughters the same things I told you. Perhaps it's David's way of giving them a sign. They always asked me why they hadn't dreamed about him. I told them I was his messenger and now David has given us all a message of comfort. Thank you for sending it to me. I know you must be really busy.

Love, Judy

This is one of many encounters that I cannot explain. For verification, let me say that I could not alter the surveys. Upon receipt, I printed each survey that was submitted through the web site and saved it to file. Karl Fancher, independently, saved all of the surveys on a compact disk. The printed originals and disk will be archived for future reference at the University of Virginia—with the exception of respondents who requested anonymity.

We will explore encounters captured by recording equipment in a later chapter—therefore, let's now consider messages perceived indirectly through wild and domesticated animals.

Valerie Dudley is an executive assistant for a venture capital firm that invests money for high-net-worth individuals and institutions in Manhattan. While working in her loft-type office, overlooking the great divide—Sixth Avenue and Avenue of the Americas—she happened upon the Afterlife Encounters Survey and immediately submitted her account.

"Now Dad, did you send this cat to me?"—Valerie's Story

My dad was regarded as the best commander in his battalion and an outstanding captain in the U.S. Army. But to me and the people closest to him, he was an entertainer, poet, and a songwriter. When he played his guitar and sang, almost everyone stopped to lend an ear. I was listening to Dad on cassette tapes while writing his memoriam for *The Roanoke Times*. Father's Day was only days away and my upcoming trip to Virginia added to my missing him. "I just want to hug him or be hugged by him," I said to myself repeatedly, crying my eyes out. I curled up in a ball, wrenching in pain, and lay there praying that I could get a hug from my dad.

After finally falling asleep, I had the most vivid dream I have ever had. I was a little girl again, we were in the same house I grew up in, and Dad appeared exactly as he did back then—young, handsome, and well dressed. I will always remember my encounters with him in that dream.

In my first encounter I said, "Daddy you're here! You really are here!" With that, I ran up to him like a child does with a parent, and I literally clenched my arms around his waist and would not let go. He just smiled at me.

Still in my dream state, the second encounter began when I awoke to find Dad standing in front of the closet. He was taking off his tie very quietly trying not to wake me, almost serene like. I said, "Daddy you are still here . . . you're still here." He said to me, "Go back to sleep, honey." I could still cry at the thought of it—he was so comforting. I got out of bed because I literally knew I had to get all I could of him before he was gone again. I peeked out of the bedroom into the hallway and saw my handsome dad in the same clothes walking by, so I jumped in front of him and said, "Daddy you're really still here . . . you're really still here." I still couldn't believe he was there. I grabbed him again around his waist and held on for dear life. I could feel him hugging me. Neither of us would let go.

I will never ever forget the physical intensity of that hug. Today I believe he came to give me what I so desperately called out for—a hug. I got what I asked for and so much more. I realize it wasn't just a dream—spirits often visit us in dreams because it's the easiest way to communicate.

Several days later, on Father's Day weekend, my dad gave me a different kind of surprise. I drove to Virginia where my mother, sister, and I visited the cemetery. Mom was in such deep grief at the gravesite that my sister casually said, "Daddy, why don't you come back as a cat for Mom?" I, the logical daughter, said under my breath, "Dad, ya know she's a little weird." I could hardly wait until the next morning, Father's Day, when I could go back to the cemetery to have my very own private time with just my dad and me.

Early before daybreak, I was finally on my way to the cemetery for our special date. I actually spoke out loud before I got there, "Dad, maybe you could give me a sign that you're there. It's going to be just me and you."

The visit was immensely emotional once I arrived. I wanted to surround him with my love so I attached a large laminated copy of his memoriam to a wooden marker and drove it into the ground. On his headstone, I placed a Snickers bar in special remembrance. When I was 19 and still living with my parents, I came home late one night and went into the kitchen for a snack. Just as I opened the refrigerator, I heard a very harsh voice say, "Valerie."

"Yes?" I answered.

"Did you eat my Snickers bar?" Dad asked.

At that point I realized he must have wanted that candy pretty bad to wait up and question me about it. So I replied a very hesitant, "Yes."

He said, "I had my mouth set on that." I laughed to myself, although he didn't find it funny at the moment. Later, my brother told me that Dad had hidden it in the refrigerator and searched feverishly for it all night, so it became a joke that brought all of us laughs many times.

So there I was, at the cemetery before the crack of dawn giving him Snickers. Within the next minute, a half-dozen crows came swarming, perching themselves on nearby wooden markers. Out of nowhere, a white cat suddenly appeared. I couldn't believe it. I said, half jokingly, "Now Dad, did you send this cat to me?" The cat walked over, stood right in front of his grave, and stared at me. I stared back, mesmerized by what I was seeing; then it scurried away seemingly to just disappear.

A strange coincidence? My dad was a beautiful soul

with a humorous personality. He did wonderful things for others just to make them smile. Knowing my Dad's sense of humor, I truly believe he somehow sent this little friend to me to show me that what I thought was silly talk from my sister could actually be possible. And he wanted to thank me for making a special trip on this special day.

I never had the need or desire to care about this kind of thing until the unexpected loss of my dear father. My encounters provide me with such a profound sense of hope and comfort that I'd like to share them with others who are grief stricken. Maybe they too will believe there is really something else out there.

Science has found that psychokinesis (PK—mind over matter) exists. Human beings can maneuver objects mentally. Another scientific finding—one consciousness can influence another. Perhaps future research will prove that consciousness survives bodily death and can sway living beings, including animals. Meanwhile, we continue our exploration with Marti Lewis, who narrated her indirect encounter.

Marti's career as a marketing manager spans two decades. She facilitated partnerships between a discount club and elementary school, helping the school raise funds for education. In March 2002, she was honored by being selected as Business Person of the Year by the Chamber of Commerce of Middleburg Heights, Ohio (a large suburb of Cleveland). Marti, however, celebrated her family most—her husband, daughters, and failing parents (for whom she was the principal caregiver). A difficult four-year period culminated with a welcomed relief—an afterlife encounter.

"Sister, what about my mother?"—Story by Marti Lewis

My mother read cards, a 52-card deck, not tarot, and I was her biggest critic. Mother was very good. Professionals came to her—even a doctor who lived in Hawaii called her every month for his reading. I would not allow her to read for me, even though I knew how accurate she was with other people.

Two months after Mother died, I was attending a Catholic charismatic conference where the speaker was talking about the afterlife. He said that anyone who was into the occult or fortune-telling would not enter heaven. During the intermission, I went outside with a sister of the Incarnate Word community. We were standing on the blacktop, with no greenery in site, when I looked at her and said, "Sister, what about my mother? Will she be banned from heaven? She loved God." At that moment, a gorgeous monarch butterfly began to flutter around me, hovering around my head and hands, until it finally landed on my shoe. I thought about my 28-year-old daughter, who equated the symbol of a butterfly with my mother, so I stooped down and opened my hand. The butterfly alighted on my palm. I gently tightened both of my hands around its wings, wanting to hold it forever. After I opened my hand, the butterfly lingered. I turned to the Sister, who said, "Marti, the butterfly is a symbol of the resurrection. Your mother is just fine." With that, it soared out of sight. I was convinced it was a visitation—my mother assuring me that she was with God.

Since then I have lost my dad and three wonderful friends. I'm sure you understand the reason for my insatiable interest in afterlife encounters, and it felt good for me to think about these things.

Marti's story was especially touching to me because she found compassion, acceptance, and support within her religious community. When encounters are not shared by their perceivers and validated by listeners, they become disenfranchised, which we will consider in the final chapter. Now let's continue focusing on the features of postmortem visitations.

Multiple Afterlife Encounters

Seventy-eight percent of survey respondents experienced more than one encounter. Valerie Noss offered excerpts from her journal wherein she recorded numerous direct and indirect accounts with her son, Bruce.

"There was another man in the house with us."—Story by Valerie Noss

Bruce was my only child, so we were extremely close. I talked to him while I was pregnant and he made up for it once he was out of the womb, often saying remarkable things out of the blue.

Until the age of five, Bruce enjoyed an imaginary playmate named Michael. His playtime and conversations were so real that I almost felt that if I looked hard enough I'd see Michael too. Then one day he asked, "Are angels real?"

I said, "They could be."

He said, "I thought so, because I saw one."

Flabbergasted I asked him, "What did the angel look like?"

"Like an angel," he answered.

On another occasion he said, "Who's the man who lived with us when I was a baby?"

"It was just us," I answered.

"No," he insisted, "there was another man in the house with us!" From the time Bruce was born until he was four months old, we lived in his deceased grandfather's house.

In another conversation, he asked apprehensively, "Mom, have I died before?"

I said, "No, Honey, of course not, but why are you asking?"

He said, "I remember it."

"What do you remember?" I asked.

"I remember a time when I couldn't breathe anymore and died. When am I going to die again?"

I told him, "Honey, you aren't going to die until you're 80 and a very old man with grandchildren." He looked at me with a lot of concern and said, "I don't think so." All that came from a five-year-old child! I was afraid Bruce would repeat our conversations in kindergarten and his teachers would think something was wrong with him, so I didn't encourage him. I regret that now.

My son, at age 25, was overcome by cancer on the morning of February 17, 2002. At 1:00 A.M., he had seizures and fell into a coma. I was resting on a cot beside his hospital bed, when, at 4:00 A.M., I heard rustling. I looked over to see Bruce getting out of bed (fully dressed) and leaving with a woman. I couldn't see her in detail because the only light in the room came from the small television screen, and also because Bruce was behind her, which blocked my view. But I knew she was a woman, shorter than he, and wearing white. As they reached the door, they vanished. I looked over at his bed again and saw him still lying there in the coma, but I knew something was different even though his body continued to labor with each breath. Although his heart stopped at 6:45 A.M., I knew Bruce had already left. I also knew that I wasn't meant to see them—my son thought it would hurt me too much to watch him leave.

Bruce has been gone for seven months, and I have had many encounters with him. I have felt his unmistakable presence, which was very comforting. Things have been manipulated: the refrigerator door opened, the car radio turned on, and a candy box in his room fell off the shelf. One night while I was using Bruce's computer in his bedroom, his wristwatch (which was on the bed stand a few feet away from me) fell to the floor with a bang. It must have been Bruce telling me to put his computer in its case, because he had requested me to do that while he was still alive, but I never got around to it. He has given me messages in dreams, and when I awoke I actually felt as though I had spent time with him.

As you have probably detected, at the heart of afterlife encounters lie comfort, love, and hope. Whereas growth seemed to be the overwhelming theme underlying every account, we now have data to support that conjecture.

Survey Results

Phase 1 of the Afterlife Encounter Survey began on August 22, 1998, and ended on August 22, 2002. Respondents were asked to measure, on a scale from 10 (tremendous comfort) to 0 (no comfort), the levels of comfort they felt during, immediately after, one year after, and then the number of years since their encounters, and the comfort they currently felt. The section that followed focused on grief. Respondents were asked if their AEs occurred after the death of a loved one, and if their answers were in the affirmative, they were asked to measure their levels of grief prior to, during, immediately after, days after, one year after, three years after, and then their current level.

Degrees of Comfort

From the 596 survey respondents who experienced encounters, 98 percent reported their incidents brought them comfort to some degree, and the comfort did not diminish over time. Eighty-two percent scored their levels of comfort between 10 and 8 during their encounters, 81 percent immediately afterward, and 84 percent one year thereafter. Of the participants who reported 20-, 30-, and 40-plus years had elapsed since their experiences, most rated them on the highest scales as well.

Eight percent of participants were not bereaved or were well past mourning at the time of their accounts, and they too rated them favorably. For example, 19 years had elapsed since her grandmother's funeral, yet Debra found tremendous comfort in hearing from her. Then a message from her recently deceased stepfather confirmed her feelings.

"Go tell Debbie."—Debra from Wisconsin

I have had encounters with my grandmother who passed away in 1974. Between sleep and wake, I hear her voice saying "Debba" just the way she always called me.

When my stepfather died, my mother stayed with us for the week after his funeral. I woke up one morning and sat at the kitchen table with her, wondering how I was going to tell Mother that her husband had come to me in a dream to say good-bye, and that he didn't want to die but had to. When I told her, she became very pale, saying, "I dreamed about him too, but I told him I was afraid. I said, 'Go tell Debbie.'" His appearing to me confirmed for us that people on earth who are grieving can be comforted by their departed loved ones.

The survey documented that encounters bring comfort over an extended period, for mourners and nonmourners alike. Whereas most respondents scored their visitations on the highest levels, 13 marked them low (4 to 0) and 14 found them not comforting. I discovered three basic reasons for people reporting discomfort.

Lack of understanding about postmortem personas was most often associated with discomfort. At the time of their episodes, 10 percent of AES participants were between the ages of 3 and 17, many of whom encountered their deceased parents. The children who were frightened sensed their discarnate parents as disciplinarians, there to reprimand them in some way. The children who were not fearful believed their parents were protectors or ambassadors, there to help.[3] Peppy's adventures demonstrated the point.

"Mama says you'd better be good!"—Peppy's Story

My parents came to America from Italy in the early 1900s. They had high hopes for a better life, especially for the children they planned to have. They settled in the company town of Dawson, New Mexico. Dad worked as a coal miner, and Mama gave birth to five daughters and three sons, one right after the other. We were living the good life until my dad's doctors found a fast-growing cancer. Back then, there was no treatment. Dad knew his family would have to leave Dawson after he died, because everyone who lived there had to be on the company payroll. He wanted us to still live a good life and make it on our own after he was gone, so he bought a grocery store and farm just outside of town. He stocked the 88 acres with milk cows and the big red barn with farm equipment. Our new cement block house had four bedrooms and a walk-in pantry.

After Dad died, it was a hard life, filled with chores to do all the time. But the family pulled together around

Mama. Then she got sick and died too. Now it really was a different and difficult life. We kids held on to one another. It was just us now, except for one thing—one thing that really helped.

After Mama's funeral, each of us kids started seeing or hearing her spirit around the house. It was a good feeling to know she was there looking out for us. None of us said anything though, until Mary, the oldest, about 19 or 20 at the time, started talking about Mama being there for us. Mama eventually settled in the pantry. We'd feel her in there and would go in to talk to her when we needed to.

I guess we boys must have been a handful, because Mary started saying Mama's spirit was there to keep us in line. Then every time we gave the older kids a hard time they'd say, "I'm going to tell Mama what you did!" or "Mama says you'd better be good!" I loved my mother more than anything, so to think I might've done something that would've disappointed her brought me to my knees. I still fall to my knees if I try to go into that room. It's overpowering, even after 60 years.

The farm had long been abandoned when Peppy escorted me to the house and pointed out the room where the pantry stood in the far corner. He crumbled to the floor on his knees, sobbing, unable to approach the storage area. I then, independently, met with each of his surviving sisters. "It wasn't just the boys," the youngest explained. "If Mary thought any of the kids were getting out of line she'd threaten to tell Mama. And she'd punish us younger ones by making us stay in the pantry." After six decades, their experiences were still difficult for them to discuss. The impressionability of childhood remains through time.

According to the survey findings, adults reacted with the same mind-set during their encounters with authority figures— that is, those who speculated the apparitions were there to disapprove felt uncomfortable or frightened. They did not understand that discarnates carry no judgment or negativity of any kind.

Another cause for discomfort was death anxiety. Some perceivers, especially skeptics, were frightened of anything related to dying or visits from the grave. The following survey was submitted from Cordoba City, Argentina, by Maria Elena Tarantini.

"He looked healthy and *very real.*"
—Maria Elena from Argentina

I'm writing this on behalf of my 65-year-old mother who doesn't speak or write English. My eight-year-old nephew, Pablo, died in an accident on June 22, 1999. My mother (his grandmother) was devastated. The fact that she didn't believe in life after death was terrible for her. She was the most skeptical person I've ever known.

Almost a year after Pablo's death, Mother came to me in a state of shock. "I saw Pablo! I saw Pablo!" After I calmed her down, she said that around four A.M. she was sitting on the bed getting ready to get up and go to the toilet when she saw him standing at her bedroom door. He was smiling at her, and there was a luminosity around him, even in the jeans and blue and green sweater he was wearing. He looked healthy and *very real.* She couldn't talk to him, or even try, because she was scared to death, so she pulled the covers over her head and started to pray. She stayed like that for hours and didn't even go to the toilet. When she looked again, he wasn't there anymore.

Now she regrets not having paid attention to him in case Pablo wanted to say something. She believes he is somewhere, but she's still reluctant to totally accept that death is not the end. I have no doubt that she had an afterlife encounter with Pablo, but then I have always believed it was possible.

After thinking about her sighting, the grandmother wished she had been hospitable and, to this day, remains curious as to what her grandson wanted—which is typical for most perceivers who were initially frightened.

The third reason respondents placed their encounters on

the lower comfort scales was the issue of grief. For these recipients, perceiving their deceased loved ones caused an intense longing to have them back again, either during their visitations or immediately thereafter.

According to the Afterlife Encounters Survey (AES) results, the accounts that initially scored little or no comfort dropped from 5 percent to 1 percent over time. Perceivers who were initially uncomfortable declared that their encounters became increasingly beneficial as they gained understanding about the phenomenon, shed their grief, or both. In fact, many hoped or prayed for visitations later—approximately one-half succeeded, all of whom were tremendously comforted by their experiences.

Upon final analysis, afterlife encounters rendered considerable and persistent comfort for 98 percent of AES participants. Let's now consider the grief section of the questionnaire.

Grief Was Affected, One Way or the Other

Whereas 65 percent of AES participants listed their grief at the maximum levels (10-8) prior to their visitations, only 4 percent remained at the top of the chart by the third year of bereavement. Encounters were a positive influence, most mourners declared.

A small portion, however, scored them unfavorably, explaining that their sorrow and longing intensified. Upon close examination of the cases wherein grief was exacerbated, most individuals experienced their AEs through mediums and felt as if they had lost their loved ones twice. Four respondents said they were almost as devastated after their discernments as they were at the moment of their losses. Believing they must depend on another person for future contacts, they felt helpless and hopeless. In contrast, recipients of firsthand encounters believed they could have more in the future, and further experiences would be more positive since those previous had taught them about the phenomenon and facilitated their grief process. Thus, the spontaneous versus mediumship issue pointed to humankind's core psychological theme—fear of loss of control.

The majority of survey respondents cited their afterlife encounters as a positive factor in coping with grief. Although their sorrow was not extinguished, it was lifted from time to time. Many, similar to Mary Wood, found their visitations offered something beyond mourning.

"Hush, little baby, don't you cry."—Mary Wood's Story

My beautiful son was born on May 31, 1988. One of the nurses in the hospital said she didn't like working with the babies, but as she was handing Justin to me she said, "There's something special about this one." As he grew I realized how special he really was.

Justin was beautiful inside and out. He was warm and friendly. It was said many times that he was everyone's friend. I think Justin actually liked himself, which is rare. But he wasn't arrogant by any means. You might say he was spiritually advanced. He had an adventurous side, which made him fun and interesting. He loved sports, played the clarinet in the school band for two years, and then football. After that, he joined the wrestling team and brought home a medal from his first tournament. I was so amazed at how he would just jump into anything. He came home one day and said, "Do you want me to get into chorus?" I said, "Yes, that would be great." So he did.

We were so close that now I think my unconscious knew something was going to happen. We were making plans to do special things together—something told me I needed to spend extra time with him. On Valentine's Day we, as a family, went out to celebrate. I bought him a card and wrote a note to him inside about how much I loved him.

It was April 3, 2002, when I asked Justin to empty the dishwasher, and as I started off to bed he said, "I love you, Mom." I answered, "I love you too, Justin," not knowing those would be our last words to each other. He went out that night with his friends.

The next morning my husband heard his cell phone beeping. It was the hospital. They said Justin was in critical condition. I ran to look in his room, where I thought he was sleeping. I tore his bed apart, but he wasn't there. I lost it at that point. I knew our beautiful child was gone.

Our whole lives together passed before me. I could remember everything that happened and how I could never stay mad at him for any length of time. And I thought about the accident that took him. The boys were on their way home, not three miles away, when they were hit by a tanker truck. My son was in the back seat with no seat belt. The other two boys fully recovered from their injuries, but I wasn't lucky enough to keep my precious child. From what I was told, Justin's head hit the floor of the car and the police were unable to revive him.

Maybe he saw what his life would be if he survived, what it would be if he didn't, and then decided to go home. I'm 43 and had seen several parents bury their children. I couldn't even imagine what it would be like and I didn't want to. The only way to know this pain is to experience it.

On the day we lost Justin, I was standing in the kitchen looking out of the window and kept hearing his voice saying, "Mom, Mom, Mom." It was as if he was getting mad that I couldn't hear him. I didn't know what to think. Then that night my daughter and I were sleeping in his room—well, we were lying there with our eyes closed trying to sleep—when we heard a music box. It was playing "Hush, little baby, don't you cry," and then a bell rang three times. I said, "Jessica, did you hear that?" "Yes," she said. We were too sad to become really excited, but we thought it was a sign from Justin.

I have to tell you, I started learning fast what spirituality is. I kept saying over and over, "I need to know if Justin is okay. Is he safe? Is he being cared for?" He began answering my questions, I was open to hearing the answers, and I wanted to share what I learned with everyone. I started reading every book I could get my hands on. Most of them fell into what I already believed, but before losing Justin it was just a belief. I didn't really put a whole lot into it. But now it was a knowing. My entire outlook on what happens to us when we leave this world became so different.

I felt that I had to make my family understand, so I told them everything. At first, they thought I was just in deep grief and didn't know what I was talking about. But I kept talking and telling them to read the books. My mom read some of them, and then said the things I had been saying made sense. I just had to let them know that Justin remained in our lives. I wanted them to believe it.

It's been almost one year since Justin left this earth. I miss him and cry often. At times I feel like I can't go on, but I have to go on with what I have left—and that's knowing my child lives. Justin continues, and my love for him grows stronger with each passing day. We are forever connected. He is still my son, and I am still his mother. Through all of this I realize how much we humans need each other. Because of this I have become closer to God. I think He is in our hearts, and if we listen He will help us to see that everything will be okay. We'll all be together again.

Most survey participants recounted that just thinking about their encounters gave them a reprieve from mourning, and the consolation they received extended beyond bereavement. One study[4] suggested that the aftereffects of the phenomenon can be similar to the effects of near-death experiences—powerful and transformative. AEs offer the living a spiritual transcendence. To illustrate, let's turn to high school principal, Dr. Jim May.

"I just saw an angel on your shoulder."—Story by Jim May

Throughout the weeks that I sat in the hospital faced with the very real prospect of losing my beloved 20-year-old daughter to a bizarre and mysterious illness, I spent a good deal of time in reflection. I read every word of the New Testament of the Bible, something that I had never done before, and began with the Old Testament, retracing the same material that I had covered many times before in my ambitious attempts to read the good book in its entirety. I'm not sure just what happened to my belief system during that time, but somehow it shifted slightly.

The chaplain of the hospital had become a trusted

friend. It was he whom I saw, walking up that hallway with a nurse to talk with us in the waiting room, as Jane and I sat in a state of stunned shock shortly after we had been whisked out of Amanda's room—she had gone into cardiac arrest with us by her side the third day of our stay. I did not know who he was then, but assumed he was a doctor. His gentle smile assured me that things were all right. "She's okay, for now," he said. Somehow at that point, I felt that my prayers had been answered and that the petitions I had offered and the deals that I had made with God had been agreed to. Despite the sobering reality of her condition, I felt a strong sense that Amanda would endure.

Having just experienced that trauma, I recall shortly thereafter a nurse tapping me on the shoulder as I walked down the hall in a stupor. She was an attractive African-American lady with long dreadlocks. "I just saw an angel on your shoulder," she said, smiling. I fell into her arms and hugged her and through my tears thanked her for giving me that hope. Did she really see an angel or was that just her way of offering me comfort? If she did see an angel, who was it?

Throughout the summer we experienced many points of hope, despair, horror, and ultimately resignation. Amanda was not going to recover and if by some twist of fate she did, her quality of life would be a cruel imprisonment. Her body had suffered through so many indignities that it became clear to all that we had to let her go.

School was beginning in the fall, so I returned home to pick up the pieces of our shattered existence and to try to resume my responsibilities as a high school principal. The call that I received from Jane on a Saturday hit me in the belly as I sat in my office plodding through the haze that was my state of mind. I needed to fly back to Cincinnati to be with Amanda at the end. Even as I sat with her through the weekend, I still maintained a glimmer of hope, but by Monday morning it was apparent—the struggle was over. We had to prepare for her exit. Amanda had been on an extreme level of blood-pressure-elevating medicine, so we decided to reduce it to normal and let nature take its course, after everyone who needed to be there arrived.

Finally, the chaplain was there, as were people who had become part of our extended family, which included her boyfriend, nurses, college students, and teachers. The chaplain gave a beautiful prayer and just as he came to "Amen" Jane softly said, "She's gone." A sense of divine intervention overcame me and I emotionally cried out, "Praise the Lord!" Knowing that it was inevitable, I was hoping for a fitting departure and the timing of it had struck a resonant chord with me.

We had Amanda's body cremated. There was no hesitation as to what to do. She was not a person tied to a particular place and the idea of cleansing or purging the infection by fire gave us a sense of comfort; besides, that way we could keep her ashes with us always.

The first night home with Amanda's ashes, something very unusual occurred. It was about 3:00 A.M. and I awoke sensing a strong urge to go out into the living room, where we had placed her ashes on the fireplace. As I sat there in my grief and sense of profound loss, I thought that I saw a beam of light bounce off the walls. I waited and it occurred again. I woke Jane so she could experience this with me or help explain it. As we sat on the couch together, swirls of light circled the room, dancing along the walls. Could it be a car's headlights turning the corner? If so, how did the lights go all the way around the room? And we would have heard a car. For over 20 minutes the lights continued to swirl and dance around the room. Jane suggested that it might be heat lightning, since it was an August night, so I walked outside to see if that might be the cause. Off in the distance to the south was lightning, but when those distant thunderclouds lit up there was no reflection on trees or anything else. Neither of us could explain it; however, for the first time in months we felt peaceful and calm. We were able to go back to bed and sleep soundly.

At that time, my reading and reflection was essentially religious or traditional grief literature. The paranormal had never been something that I discounted as ridiculous, but I had not experienced it; thus I had no certain belief. I have always kept an open mind.

My work was both a blessing and a burden. On the one hand, it diverted my thoughts away from my loss and going to work gave me a support system besides my family, which was struggling to keep things together. On the other hand, the onerous responsibility of being the principal of a large suburban high school is a burden even in the best of circumstances, and after being absent the entire summer there was much to be done, and I felt numb and foggy and defeated. One morning on my way to work with my heart and mind feeling very heavy, traffic stopped. I found myself looking out onto a beautiful pastoral scene with cattle grazing in a sunny meadow against the backdrop of cobalt-blue storm clouds, framed by the most stunning perfectly formed rainbow. In my mind, I heard Amanda's voice. "Don't worry, Daddy. Everything's going to be fine." Wish fulfillment? Maybe. Maybe not. From that morning on things began to look up for me in a very real sense. I felt more involved, more integrated, more effective. I wouldn't go so far as to say that I had my edge back yet, but it was a definite start.

We held three different memorial services for Amanda in three different parts of the country. By the time we flew back to Cincinnati for the third and final one, I was to the point of functioning pretty well. Because she had been Broadway-bound as a musical-theater student at the University of Cincinnati's College Conservatory of Music, the service was a performance and a celebration of her life. My wife and I were asked to come up to the stage to say a few words, which we did. I wanted to acknowledge the efforts of all those who had been so supportive of us. I made a special point to acknowledge the chaplain and worked in the anecdote about the perfect timing of his Amen with Amanda's last breath, quipping that she was theatrical to the very end. It seemed natural to describe the last breath one takes in the process called respiration as expiration. I used the word expire, and then caught myself. I replaced it with the word transformed because I did not get the feeling that Amanda was really gone, but had rather changed forms.

After the ceremony, one of Amanda's friends came up to me with a very fixed stare and told me, "I have to tell you something." She went on to describe how, just as I made that statement, a very pink feather wafted down from the top of the apron at center stage behind me. The color was interesting in that all of the CCM students were wearing pink ribbons on their shirts in honor of Amanda. The feather prompted much discussion in the audience at the time. "Did you see that?" "What was that about?" My son and daughter saw it as well. Everyone immediately determined that it was Amanda's doing. When some of the witnesses went to get it from the stage afterward, it was not to be found.

Later that fall, I had "a visit" from Amanda. One night I had dreamed that I was in a meeting with teachers in a classroom and there, sitting in one of the desks, sat Amanda, as pretty as ever. Dumbfounded and overcome with joy and confusion, I blurted out, "But Amanda . . . I thought you were dead!" In a giggling voice reminiscent of the rabbit in the old Trix commercials she responded, "Oh Daddy, I'm just dead in the physical world." Then she came over, crawled into my lap, and nuzzled up against me. I awoke with a start and a sense of joy.

I shared this experience with my wife, who was quite jealous that she had not been visited that night. However, she shared with me some of her experiences that were similar. Jane had awakened one night to a smell that seemed "shoved" up her nose! It was a woodsy, citrus fragrance and she checked out my medicine cabinet to see if it was an aftershave of mine. It was a familiar scent, but hard to place. Finally, she searched the attic and pulled out one of Amanda's childhood books—a scratch and sniff Bambi book with forest smells. There it was—the woodsy, citrus smell! I was fascinated by this and had done enough reading on death-related literature to recognize this as clairsentience. Now it was my turn to be jealous because I had not experienced it as Jane had.

That first Christmas was going to be a very difficult one, we all knew. We had been making the annual trip north to see our families since the girls were very young.

Our little ritual, as we turned off the turnpike toward our first visit, was to sing, "Over the river and through the woods, to Aunt Alta's house we go." This time, just as I made our well-known turn, it hit me. Up from my chest and rushing into my nose was the smell that Jane had described. Jane then said she smelled it, and later so did Meredith (Amanda's sister). We all very matter-of-factly said, "Hello, Amanda. We love you."

Amanda had been a spiritual seeker years before her death and while she had not rejected Christianity, neither was she bound to the doctrine that characterizes so many mainstream Protestant faiths. Her library contained many thought-provoking books, which I have benefited from tremendously. I am now an avid reader and explorer of nontraditional belief systems.

In *Hamlet*, Shakespeare has him explaining the appearance of the ghost of his father to his friend, "There are more things in Heaven and Earth, Horatio, than are dreamt of in your philosophy." Perhaps this best describes the shift in my beliefs. I cannot explain my encounters nor do I expect anyone else to explain them. Consciousness itself is a very ethereal and inexplicable thing. While some of these experiences may be the result of overactive sensory impressions, all of them cannot be.

Something "strange" happened in each event I have described. As I share my experiences with others and they share theirs with me, I think *There must be something to this*. I have come to accept them as normal. Amanda is still very much with me—not just in my mind, but as a spiritual being outside and alongside my own being that is evolving, searching, and growing. The pain of grieving has been replaced with excitement about discovering other dimensions. We still cry, but for different reasons—not from loss, although it still hurts. We now cry out of joy and love for the blithe spirit that is our Amanda.

Beyond spiritual transcendence, Dr. May's afterlife encounter suggested another common aspect that we will explore in a later chapter—the most educated population perceive posthumous visitors.

A final overview of the data collected during the AES points to the short- and long-term positive influence of the phenomenon. The effects proved so strong that 99 percent of perceivers welcomed more discarnate experiences in the future. Although I have long been an advocate for the benefit encounters propose, the number of respondents who consistently scored their comfort at the highest levels surprised me. And the survey held other surprises as well.

Because the study focused on the levels of comfort and grief surrounding AEs, I speculated that the only people who would complete the survey were those with apparitional experiences. However, 231 surveys were submitted by respondents who had never experienced anything close to an afterlife visit. Most questioned why they had not, and expressed their strong and extended longing to do so. As a result, the AES offers data beyond the benefits of afterlife encounters—it supports postmortem existence theories, which we will explore in the next chapter.

THREE

Addressing the Survival Issue

Sometimes these experiences are accompanied by physical effects that seem to be connected and that cannot be considered as hallucinations.

—J. B. Rhine

Prehistoric cave paintings depict humankind's early beliefs about life beyond physical death. Symbols evolved into hieroglyphics, which provided the first form of written word—explicit documentation, inscribed on the interior walls of tombs and scrolled across coffins. Life continued in the Great Beyond, the ancients were certain—so certain that their daily lives were consumed by preparing for spiritual continuance. With our earliest ancestors, we share a common thread—the belief in an afterlife.

Today, some three-quarters of Americans believe. Approximately one-half the population in the United Kingdom, Spain, Finland, and Italy, and two-fifths in Norway and the Netherlands follow suit.[1] Philosophy and religions worldwide are based on the concept of immortality. What does science offer? It provides an enormous body of work—evidence that spirit, consciousness, personality, or some part of living beings continues after the body ceases to function. Let's explore the latest studies and then respond to skeptics' claims.

Researchers have long considered three criteria by which

encounters are deemed evidence for postmortem survival.[2] To those, we will add three.

Six Conditions Deemed Evidence for Survival Beyond Bodily Death

1. The apparition stated information that was unknown by the person who experienced the encounter (the perceiver, percipient, witness, receiver, recipient, observer).
2. The encounter was collective (concurrently experienced by more than one person).
3. The apparition was unknown by the witness at the time but later identified.
4. The apparition reported a *current* event that was unknown by the perceiver and later verified.
5. The apparition autonomously manipulated a physical object.[3]
6. The apparition exhibited a purpose that was extraneous to the percipient.

The First Condition

New York City overflows with myriad entertainers whose names go unrecognized. Beverly's is among them, but then her focus was on supporting the troops while they served our country. As she performed at home and abroad, a stack of outstanding volunteer awards mounted. The birth of her two sons brought additional meaning into her life. Her most joyous years were short-lived, however. Beverly was suddenly left a single mother, working two jobs as a sales clerk and struggling to find time for her sons. As the boys grew, it became obvious that both held their mother's spirit of giving and work ethics, but Tommy displayed her talent as well. Beverly offers an encounter that brought unknown information—information that was timely and needed.

"If we only knew where he was murdered."—Beverly's Story

Tommy was born on January 16, 1962. He was a strikingly beautiful baby and grew up to be extremely hand-some—movie star material. Most people were in awe, say-ing he took their breath away, but more because of his personality than his appearance. Tommy was shy, and very, very humble and kind. He always had a radiant smile on his face that lit up every room he entered. He was a peace-maker and clown for family and friends. His sense of humor was so great that he'd dance around our house with exaggerated movements and facial expressions just to watch us roar with laughter. He loved family holidays, trips, and activities.

Never losing his childlike innocence, he played ball with young kids and opened the fire hydrants for them on hot days. He loved animals. He often brought injured dogs and cats home, nursing them back to health. But if he found a dead one someplace, he'd feel such sorrow that he'd tenderly bury its body. Every night, Tommy read his Bible, often falling to sleep while reading it. He was such a gentle soul that in thirty-three years, I never heard him speak an unkind word about anyone. No matter what peo-ple said or did to him, he forgave them.

A carpenter by trade, Tommy seemed to have hands of gold because he could just look at something and build it. He did all of his own auto repairs, from putting in new engines to sunroofs, and helped neighbors and friends do the same. There was nothing he wouldn't do for other people, even strangers. He went out of his way to help. Everyone who knew Tommy loved him because he was such a kind and gentle man who cared and respected everyone. We were all shocked to hear that such a gentle soul—Tommy with a soft spot in his heart the size of Texas—could be murdered.

It was Saturday night, February 4, 1995, and Tommy was getting ready to meet his friends. New York was in the middle of a major snowstorm, so Tim, my other son, and I warned him not to leave our house. We just sensed some-thing terrible. As Tommy was walking out, Tim and I looked at each other in fear and despair, "Something very bad is going to happen tonight," we said. We both felt Tommy was going to be killed. We were nervous wrecks, couldn't sleep, and when we hadn't heard from Tommy by the next morning, we frantically started calling hospitals and police stations. Then our darkest suspicions came true. Homicide detectives called, "We need to come over to speak to you," they said. Tim and I knew Tommy was dead.

An hour later, they arrived and officially told me, "Your son Tommy was killed. We found his body in an abandoned van, about 60 feet from Brooklyn's 88th precinct. He was in the fetal position, knees tucked into his chest, behind the front seat on the passenger side of the van." But they didn't know the murderer or the actual murder scene. There was no blood outside the van and not enough inside for Tommy to have been killed there. He was murdered elsewhere, then transported to that site. The police investigators said, "If we only knew where he was murdered, we could get witnesses."

They also told us that Tommy fought for his life. His body had multiple defense stab wounds, and they found bloody smears outside the van as if he had run around and around it trying to escape. Detectives knew he didn't die there, and they needed to find where the murder took place.

Timmy and I cried out loud, looking up toward the ceiling, "Tom, who in God's name would do this to you? Who? Who? Who would do such a thing?" The chandelier overhead started blinking, very bright and very fast, and it continued minute after minute. We all, including the detectives, keep watching in amazement—looking at one another, then at the light, then at one another, and so on. The chandelier had never done that before, but Tim and I forgot about it, being in such sorrow, and then family started coming in from all over the country for Tommy's wake and burial. "Surely," we said, "the homicide department will find where he was murdered, by whom, and for what reason."

Five days after Tommy's death, however, detectives said they were in the complete dark—just as stumped as they were on Sunday. I prayed to my son that evening, "Help us. Help us find who did this." Early that morning

I was awakened by Tommy's voice calling me, "Wake up. Wake up." It sounded as loud and clear as if someone were standing beside me. I sat up straight to see where he was, but he was not there for my eyes to see. He said, "Mom, go to Washington Avenue and St. John's Place. You'll find my blood still locked in the snow, covered with ice. Go immediately. It's going to get warmer and the ice will melt, so you must go now before the evidence is lost. Look for my blood in the snow . . . just like a dog when he wets in the snow . . . it turns yellow . . . my blood is locked in the ice and snow. Go before it melts."

I immediately sprung up, got dressed, and rushed to tell my family who were still staying with me. "You're crazy with grief," they said. No one wanted to go and they tried to intervene, but there was no stopping me. My mind was made up. I said. "If you don't drive me, I'll go by myself." They drove, reluctantly. When we approached Washington Avenue and St. John's Place we saw a small mountain of red snow that had been shoveled near a pay telephone. It was blood—a lot of it—large amounts, as if someone had been critically wounded or murdered there. Drops the size of half dollars trailed from one side of the street to the other. I called homicide detectives and told them to get to that location . . . that I had received a tip. I couldn't tell them my dead son had told me, because they would have thought I was off my rocker. They would not have believed me, but this way they came. Right off the bat, detectives found three eyewitnesses to the murder, witnesses who even described the van that was driven away with my son's body in it.

Homicide detectives questioned people around the area of Washington Avenue and St. John's Place and found witnesses who identified the murderer. "Light did it," they said. Ah! I made the connection. That's why the lights on the chandelier blinked every time we asked, "Tom, who in God's name would do this to you? Who? Who? Who? Who killed you? Who would do such a thing?" Tommy kept blinking the whole chandelier, telling us the nickname of his murderer—Light. The chandelier had never done that before and has not done it since.

The eye witnesses stated on paper that the guy, nick-named Light, robbed Tommy of his jewelry and identification, then chased him around and around the van, repeatedly stabbing him. He finally stabbed my son through his heart to end his life, threw his body in the van, and sped off.

Detectives said the killer drove Tommy four miles away from the crime scene, thinking *No witnesses, no case. Police will find an abandoned body and van, but won't be able to find out where, why, or who did it.* If Tommy had not come back to tell me where he was killed, no one would have ever found out.

About four months later, on a pleasant day in June, Baby (Tommy's dog) and I went for a walk. Baby is a very strong, healthy six-year-old Staffordshire Terrier (pit bull). We were strolling down the block, passing the empty lot where Tommy parked his car. I had nothing on my mind in particular. We were just mulling around. I was looking at Tommy's Scout Jeep and thinking to myself, *What a shame . . . the jeep Tommy had so much fun in is just sitting there getting dirty.* All of a sudden, out of the blue, Baby went berserk! She started pulling on the leash so hard that it almost yanked my arm out of its socket. My whole body twisted around. She was pulling, barking, and yapping, trying to get to someone in the direction of the corner, which was about 30 feet from where we were standing. My eyeglasses were on a chain around my neck, so I couldn't make out who was making Baby go bananas. I could see a male dressed in blue standing there looking at us, but without my glasses he was not defined enough for me to see who he was. While Baby tugged to get to him, I stared for a minute. He was a young man, wearing a pale blue shirt and dungarees, about the same size and with hair color the same as Tommy's. Bells went off in my head. I thought, *Who is this?* My heart raced, and I got a funny feeling inside that told me, *Put on your eyeglasses and look . . . really look.* My hands trembled, but I wanted to see who was standing there watching Baby and me so intensely, so I put my glasses on, focused, and saw him clearly. The figure was my beloved son, Tommy.

He was smiling at me with his beautiful teeth and smile. His blue eyes, beaming with joy, looked straight at me. His face was aglow against his powder blue clothes. He was beautiful. Not saying a word, he kept smiling at Baby and me. He was so happy and alive.

And I was so overtaken with joy that my heart jumped. "Hey Tommy!" I yelled. He was there—right in front of me. I thought, *What happened? Was his death a dream? Or is he back now?* I was confused, but then I thought, *Get over to him and talk so you can sort it all out.* In the next instant, I realized, *He's wearing his new dungaree outfit.* Tommy had bought it and was proud of his purchase, but he never got a chance to wear it. *The outfit is still in his dresser with tags on, but he has them on now,* I thought. My heart skipped beats and I felt like it was going to burst with joy, relief, happiness, and love. My son was back, standing there, smiling. Baby yanked me, pulling me to get to her beloved master.

Tommy kept smiling, then started a slow turn. My feet started running fast to get to him, but as we took our first steps, Tommy, in slow motion, turned away and started to glide over the sidewalk. His feet must have been an inch or so off the pavement because he continued to move in a floating motion, with us following him. We ran—ran as fast as Baby could pull me—almost off my feet we were racing so fast. Three blocks we chased after him. My chest was on fire. Tommy continued to glide at a slow smooth pace, inches off the sidewalk. Baby started pulling faster than I could run. My feet were barely hitting the ground.

That dog is 80 pounds of pure muscle and I'm a fast runner, but we couldn't gain an inch on Tommy's slow-motion, rhythmic, glide. He remained about 30 feet in front of us, regardless of how fast Baby pulled me. I saw that no matter what, we weren't, and wouldn't, gain any headway. Like a bolt of lighting through my head, I realized, *We are not seeing the earthly Tommy, but Tommy as an angel spirit.* We continued our mad chase to catch my Angel, my Tommy.

I thought about what someone had told me a very long time ago, "Never take your eyes off an apparition, even for a second, or it will disappear." I said to myself, *I can't seem to catch up to Tom, but I mustn't take my eyes off of him for he will surely vanish.* I was trying to keep my eyes on him and not trip on the crooked sidewalks. Tears started running down my cheeks from focusing on him and trying not to blink. I had always been athletic and was still a good fast runner, but my heart was beating so hard that it seemed my chest was on fire, ready to explode. We continued the chase, nevertheless. As we got to the third block, four schoolgirls from St. Edmund's Parish took up the complete width of the sidewalk, giggling and pushing each other. Tommy glided past and around them with the greatest of ease. As they approached me, I was scared to pass them, because I didn't want to take my eyes off him. I feared the conse-quences. I began passing them, but with the girls taking up the entire walk, Baby's dragging me, and a little bumping going on, it was impossible. I lost a second's eye contact with Tommy and in doing so—poof! He vanished.

He was nowhere in sight, but there was nowhere for Tommy to go! A long straight sidewalk was in front of us, with no one on it. To one side of it, an empty lot stood with a six-foot-tall fence all the way to the end of the street—no house or building for him to enter. The other side was a street filled with speeding traffic—six lanes of cars and trucks. In the blink of my eye, Tommy had disap-peared without a trace.

Baby and I stood there with our mouths open, hearts pounding out of our chests. That dog, a fast and mighty runner, had pulled me faster than I had ever run. She had been in such jubilation, trying desperately to get to her master, but we just couldn't. Baby kept turning her head, in search for Tommy, as she panted with her tongue hang-ing far down out of her mouth. My chest was burning and my eyes were weeping from the strain of it all. But I knew what it meant.

Tommy wanted Baby and me to see him. That visit was his ultimate gift, a blessed event that I'll never forget. He came back to give me his sweet and gentle smile, to let me know he was happy and at peace. He knew I needed that because I missed him and grieved so.

Some people will consider this a fairy tale, or an optical illusion due to tremendous grief, but I know differently. Yes, I suffered deep grief, but I wasn't, and am not, crazy from it. I know who we chased and so did Tommy's dog. My beloved son appeared to me during my deepest sorrow to ease my incredible pain. I want to assure other bereaved mothers that there is a hereafter, and there is life after loss. I'm proud to share my experiences with other families who are reaching out for answers. When we open our hearts and minds we can open the gap between heaven and earth. Our loved ones can let us know they are at peace so we can find peace. Even when they do not verbally communicate, they are here to aid, comfort, and give hope. They come back for a reason—to share heaven with us.

Tommy was a kind, sweet, sensitive, and loving son, whom I miss with every breath I take. When times get rough, I think of him and his horrible ending and the pain he must have suffered; then mine is nothing. And I remember heaven's gap, where my son crossed to contact me. That's how I go on.

Beverly's encounter meets the criteria for a witness receiving previously unknown information and later discovering it to be true. The specifics in this case were documented in police records, but most important, had it not been for Beverly's afterlife visitation, the circumstances of Tommy's murder would have melted with the snow.

My files contain many reports whereby apparitions directed their surviving loved ones to large amounts of hidden cash. Whereas those encounters met the first condition, greater evidence for postmortem existence occurred when the discarnates appeared to a third party. Patti DelSoldato's account was one example.

"Okay, I'll tell him."—Patti DelSoldato's Survey
I was sleeping when I felt someone watching me. I awoke and there was a friend who had recently died. I

asked, "What are you doing here? You're supposed to be over there."

She said, "I know, but I've tried to get in touch with Nick to tell him to thoroughly look through the house, that I had money hidden all over . . . in cans and even in the ceiling."

I said, "Okay, I'll tell him."

"Oh, you're something. Thank you," she said and left.

Her son Nick was a real skeptic, so I thought it over for a few days before calling him. I finally got the nerve.

"Your mother came to me in my sleep," I said over the phone.

"Oh yeah? What did she want?" Nick asked. I told him.

"That's just like my mother . . . always worrying about money."

He'd already found some in a can, but then he started digging for it. Nick came back to me, saying, "I can't believe my mother didn't believe in banks!"

Patti was puzzled. "Why me? Why did she come to *me* instead of her son?" Nick was not open to the concept of life continuing beyond death; therefore, he would have dismissed a posthumous manifestation. This brings us to Charles Vance and the second condition.

The Second Condition

Charles Vance's account meets both the first condition (receiving information previously unknown by the perceiver) and the second. The second condition that researchers consider as evidence for life beyond bodily demise is collective—the apparition was concurrently experienced by two or more individuals.

"I've left something inside that wall."—Charles's and Jean's Experiences

George Taylor, a friend for more than 40 years, knows death and grief firsthand. Therefore, when we happen upon one another, he champions my work with the bereaved by offering meaningful quotes and anecdotes. George caught me by surprise, however, when he told me about his best friend, Charles Vance. It seems Charles, one of the most driven and successful businessmen in Houston, was visited by an apparition. The apparition, a seemingly modest man during his lifetime, revealed to Charles where he had secretly hidden an astonishing amount of money.

"Oh George," I sighed in disbelief, "*Murphy?* The guy who owned that little hole-in-the-wall vacuum cleaner store? He had a lot of cash stashed? Who'd believe that?"

"Well, he did—thousands and thousands of dollars!" exclaimed George, laughing.

"*Murphy?* How can that be? My mother used to send me into his store for cleaning bags when I was a kid. Are we talking about the same Murphy, the guy who turned the front of his little frame house on Strawberry Street into a vacuum cleaner shop?"

"That's him."

"I can't believe that," I said, wondering if George had misunderstood his friend.

George laughed again, "Here . . ." he said, tearing the corner off a sheet of paper. "I'll write Charles's phone number. Ask him about it yourself."

"I'd like to hear the story from him, but I don't want to call," I said, shrugging my shoulders. "I'd feel like I'd be invading his privacy."

Months of curiosity and further urging from George brought me to call Charles. "George told me about an encounter you had with an apparition," I began. "And I'm wondering if you would consider telling it to me?" Before I could explain the circumstances, Charles burst out, "I can't believe George told anyone about that! I can't believe he'd do that!"

"George knows about my work and that grieving families are comforted by stories like yours," I justified. "I've heard so many about hidden money, but yours is really intriguing to me. For one thing, I knew Murphy and he didn't seem to have a dime, so my curiosity is the personal side of it. More important, though, is that I think it could help people. You're a prosperous business-man—not the type of person most people associate with such sto-ries. And from what George told me, your encounter is evidence for life after death—the apparition told you something that no one alive knew, the message wasn't for you, you weren't a relative of Murphy's, and you weren't grieving. That makes your account more valid. George thought your story would help someone along my way, but I'd need your permission to repeat it."

"Hmmm, well . . ." Silence filled the telephone. Then he began, "I don't talk about it to anyone. It's just something that happened. . . . Murphy told me there was money and there was . . . but . . . if it could help someone . . . well . . . that would be nice."

"I think it could, but I'd like to hear it from you," I said.

"I'm on my way to a meeting, but I won't be so pushed for time after the holidays, so call me then and I'll tell you," he said. With that, we wished one another a Merry Christmas.

After two attempts to speak with Charles proved unsuccess-ful, I decided to give up. But then a torrential spring storm blew in, grounding me for the day. It was late afternoon when something prompted me to call him immediately. An employee of his company had suffered a violent assault that morning, and as with most people who feel the whisper of death brush by, Charles wanted his life to mean something. We agreed to meet at his business that evening.

He towered above me, and his smile, handshake, and greet-ing were every bit as monumental. "If I can help one person, I will," said Charles, ushering me across the parking lot and into his building. From the back of the room, a remarkably chiseled woman rose to her feet and directed me through the maze of desks until I reached her. "I'm Jean, Charles's wife," she said, grasping my arm. "Let's go into his private office."

Jean's offer, "Can I get you a glass of iced tea, lemonade, or something?" felt like a trusted friend's welcome. We were settling into the sofa when Charles rushed through the room, dropped into the armchair behind his desk, leaned forward on his elbows, and began his story.

I met Murphy when I was 17. I did some repair work at his store after school, the way other kids did back then. Murphy and I formed a special relationship over the years. He was my mentor, my best friend, my father-figure. He told me about the problems he'd had so that when I had problems he could help solve mine with me. We were real close—real close. I learned a lot from him about business and life.

Murphy was one extreme or the other—he was either totally religious or he was not. He either partied and drank a lot, or he was religious and he didn't do any of that. But even when he was not religious, he talked about the afterlife. He'd get on these discussions with me, Jean, and his wife Lorraine. He'd say, "When I die, I'll let you know if there's something over there. I believe in God, I believe in an afterlife, and I'm a really mentally strong person, so I'll contact you. If there really is a God, I'll come back and tell you." I'd say, "Yeah, yeah, yeah."

As time went on he got real religious. Every time Jean and I went by his house it became a preach-a-thon and that was uncomfortable for me, so we stopped going. Many years went by that I didn't see Murphy. Then one day he came by my office and said he was healthy and felt good, but was going into the hospital for some corrective surgery. Two days later he died. He must have sensed he was going to die, because we had not seen each other in so long, yet he came by to see me. Jean and I went to his funeral, paid our respects to Lorraine, and all that.

Then almost one year to the day after he died, I had this dream. I was dreaming about something when in the middle of the dream . . . it was like a film burning in the center . . . that's the only way I can describe it. Can you remember being in a movie theater and seeing the celluloid part of the film burning through, then the bright light coming through the center? That's what this was like. I was having this dream when the film burned through the middle. It started little bitty and went just like this. . . . [Charles overlapped his left hand over his right to reveal a small opening in between; then he pulled them apart until his thumbs and fingers touched just enough to form a

large hole in the center.] Through the middle, the burned
out part, came a really bright, bright, bright light. It was
so, so bright it woke me up in that dream. Then the light
started dimming and everything started coming into
focus, and there stood Murphy in front of a small house,
a meticulous house with vivid colors and a picket fence.
He looked like he was in the prime of life—young, healthy,
vibrant, and so calm and at ease. He looked so good, I
mean, good, good. He was leisurely dressed and looked
about 35 years old, perfect weight—just a perfect Murphy.

Then he said, "I've made it. I'm here. Tell Lorraine to
look in the hall, at the dead end, just south of the bedroom
to the right of the light socket. I've left something inside
that wall. Be sure to give her that message. Also tell her to
keep the promise we discussed at the table." Then I noticed
a sign in his yard with real vivid colors and flowers that read
At Peace with Jesus. After that, the hole closed and I woke
up in a cold sweat, wondering *What the hell was that?*

It stayed on my mind continuously for days, which
was unusual for me. I've always known that I dreamed, but
I've never remembered any of them. Even if I wake up in
the middle of one, I forget it immediately because it seems
insignificant. But this dream was so significant and so
vivid. In fact, to this day, so many years later, I can still see
the vibrant leaves and petals on the plants, and all the colors, and every vivid detail. And he was so perfect, so matter of fact, like, "I'm here," so simple.

Finally, after a few days, I had to talk to somebody
about it, so I said to Jean, "Hey, this is weird but I just
have to tell somebody. . . ." Afterward, she said, "I'm going
to call Lorraine."

"Oh, no, please don't do that," I said to her. "I don't
feel comfortable talking about it or telling anyone. It's just
something crazy. I don't know why I dreamed it, or what
it means, or anything." But while I was gone from the
house, she called Lorraine. Lorraine's response was, "Well,
why doesn't the son-of-a-bitch contact me?"

Charles laughed out loud, shaking his head from side to
side. "She sure was upset that he hadn't been to see her." Jean

sat up straight, raised her hand, and interjected, "Wait! This is Charles's story and I want him to tell it, but . . ." and then she elaborated.

I didn't call Lorraine until Charles had that same dream four or five more times. He kept telling me, "I keep having this *same* Murphy dream. He keeps coming to me in the exact same way and I don't know what to do to stop it." I told him, "Let me call Lorraine." Charles would say, "No, no, don't call her—she'll think I'm crazy." But I'd tell him, "Look, this is important. It must be something Murphy wants you to do or he wouldn't keep coming to you like this, and he's coming to you more often, so he must really need this message to get to Lorraine. If you'll call and let her know about your dreams, maybe they'll end. Murphy will have what he needs." But Charles was apprehensive about calling her; after all, we hadn't seen her since the funeral and to call her out of the blue after a year with this dream, would she think we *both* were crazy?

But then I saw how much it was bothering Charles, and how desperate Murphy was becoming. It seemed really important to Murphy that we get the message to Lorraine, so I called her. I said, "Look, I've got something really weird to tell you. I hope you don't get mad, but I think you need to know." After I told her I said, "We've moved and this is my new telephone number in case you want to call me. We're not trying to jump back into your life or anything. We just wanted to tell you about this dream." And that was it. I didn't expect to hear from her.

But soon, she called back and said, "Oh my God! You'll never believe this but I just dug into the wall where Murphy told Charles to look and I found a whole lot of cash—*thousands and thousands* of dollars." I couldn't believe my ears, so I said, "You're joking, aren't you?"

"No, believe me. I'm serious," she said. "I found a lot of money. Listen, I was having the house remodeled next week, and I had no idea about the money inside that wall so it would've been . . . well . . . it wouldn't have been secure. I couldn't believe it, so I called my daughter who lives in Florida to tell her about the money and how I found it. She said she'd been having dreams of Murphy too and then she described the identical house with the same florescent colors that don't really exist. It was all three-dimensional, beautiful, and a sign in the front yard that read At Peace with Jesus."

Lorraine's daughter told her the very same things that Charles had told me.

Leaning back in his chair, Charles peered off to the side. "All of it was just so vivid," he said. "I think about it all the time."

"Had you ever seen the message At Peace with Jesus around Murphy in any way?" I asked. "Oh no! Never!" Charles answered, leaning forward across his desk toward Jean and me. "To this day, I've never seen anything like it. And the daughter . . . Lorraine described the sign that her daughter saw, and it was the same one, in the same place, just as I'd told Jean. And we both saw Murphy standing on the walkway with the sign to his left. I've never seen anything like that and I don't know the daughter. She was from Lorraine's first marriage."

"It was just so amazing," sighed Jean. "Lorraine was definitely put away by it. We all were. I mean . . . two people, same story, same house, same sign, all the same details, and lots and lots of money none of us had any idea was there . . . exactly like Murphy told both of them."

Charles said, "Murphy was such a private person that no one knew he had money. There was no way I knew he had cash like that. And when Lorraine called Jean back, she said she had no idea he had it either, until she found it stashed inside the wall. I've spoken to her several times over the phone since this happened, but I just can't talk to her face to face. This isn't something that I can talk about. We've never told this story to anybody but George and—"

Jean interrupted, "Well, Charles gets embarrassed about it, and he definitely didn't want to tell Lorraine, because he thought it was just a crazy dream."

"Right!" he jumped in. "I thought it was crazy. I mean, I'm not a religious person. I believe in God, but why me? You know? Why would something like this happen to *me*? I'm a strong person, but Murphy had the strongest personality of anyone I've ever met and so religious."

"Oh!" Jean exclaimed. "He was a spiritually strong person all right! He never knew the word *no*. He thought anything was possible."

"And I'll tell you," asserted Charles, "I never, ever, had any kind of experience like that in my life. It sure gave me the belief that anything is possible . . . things other than what we know can happen."

We all sat, reflecting. Then Charles circled back. "Murphy had promised Lorraine that he would give her a sign after he died, and he did. But she was upset because he didn't give it *to her*."

"Yeah, Charles had one other dream after that," said Jean. "Years later, while we were going through a stressful, stressful, time in our lives, Charles woke up one morning and said he had another Murphy dream, but this time Murphy said, 'Listen to me! Everything is going to be okay. Don't let yourself worry and get stressed over this, because it'll all work out all right.' When I called Lorraine and told her how upset we'd been and that Murphy came to Charles with this message, that's when she said, 'Well that son-of-a-bitch has never come to me and told me a thing!' She was serious about it."

Charles laughed again, saying, "I don't know why he doesn't." Then, pointing to a large collage of photographs on the wall behind me, he said, "There's a picture of Murphy with Lorraine, Jean, and me. I've not dreamed of him since, but I know that if I ever have a real problem to solve, he'll help me. He'll be here if I need him."

"I'm so glad Charles talked to someone about this," said Jean, patting me on the back. "I'm Catholic and we don't usually discuss such things, but I think this helped him."

"Well, at first I thought I was just lucky to dream about Murphy," Charles reflected. "But then, when I saw how excited

Lorraine was . . . I mean . . . she didn't know there was any money either. She said he switched banks just to get half a percent more interest on their savings account, so who'd have guessed he kept thousands of dollars in cash buried inside a wall? No one," he said, shrugging his shoulders. "After Lorraine found the money . . . well . . . it no longer seemed like just a lucky dream." Laying his hands on top of his desk, palms up, Charles said, "I think, *What are the odds in that? They're staggering.*"

"But more than seeing Murphy and more than money being inside that wall, what keeps me in awe, over ten years later, is the vision. I can't describe the colors and the clarity. Everything was so perfectly vibrant—every color, every leaf, the steps, the picket fence, the house—everything was so crystal clear, and I normally don't see well! It's something I can't forget." Charles again motioned to the collage on his wall, "As many times as I've looked at that picture I can't remember the details, but to this day I remember every detail of that site, that vision, that scene, or whatever you call it. It really is something you don't forget."

"Murphy's daughter had been having the very same dreams but ignored them," Jean said. "I think Murphy kept coming to Charles instead of Lorraine because he knew Charles would pay attention."

Although Jean had never been involved with apparitions, at some level she understood. If family members dismiss the visits, are unaware of them, or are acutely grieving, then discarnate loved ones turn to couriers to expedite their messages. Whereas encounters by courier contain an element of immediacy, encounters by proxy are more leisurely. This brings us to Debbie's story, which meets the third condition.

The Third Condition

An apparition who was unknown by the witness at the time of the encounter, but later identified, is considered evidence for disembodied existence.

"Please tell my dad not to feel guilty."—Debbie Fancher's Story

"Easy on the eyes," my colleague described Debbie. "And on the psyche," I added. Debbie, a dedicated high school Spanish teacher, spent many evenings and Sundays at church, singing in the choir. We met after her dad died, while I was working at the hospice, and became good friends.

It was three months into what promised to be an exciting new millennium when Debbie called saying, "I have the blues." She was depressed about leaving the teaching job she loved, but her reason was certainly less than depressing. Having just given birth to a daughter, she wanted to stay at home during the baby's first three years, as she had with her son. The newborn, diagnosed with severe acid reflux, required medication around the clock.

"Hmmm," I said, "I wonder why you're feeling blue? It couldn't be leaving your job, giving birth, caring for a sick baby, and suffering from a little sleep deprivation could it? Nah—that couldn't be it." Debbie's giggle reverberated in my ear.

"Ahhhh, I know, I know . . . this too shall pass, but I just want it to hurry up!"

Summer had almost slipped by before I received another phone call from Debbie.

> I had the most vivid dream Tuesday night. I saw this beautiful girl with wavy blond hair, piercing eyes, and a peaceful smile. The background looked like a beautiful landscape painting, and she looked like an angel standing there with the wind blowing her long hair. But what caught my eyes were her eyes. Then . . . and this happened so fast . . . she said, "Please tell my dad that I'm okay and not to feel any guilt." I instinctively knew who she was. She didn't even need to tell me her name.
>
> I woke up sweating and very bothered. I hope I'm wrong. I don't want that dream to be true—who she is or that she is dead. I know someone I can call, a friend, to see if it's true, but I keep thinking, *How can I do that without sounding totally off the wall?* I've thought about that vision all week.

The alarm in Debbie's voice brought me to ask, "Who do you think she was?"

I'm afraid the figure was the daughter of our new school principal, Dr. May. He seems like a very nice person, but I don't really know him or anything about his personal life. Except, I did hear one story at the end of the school year. Another teacher, the head of our foreign language department, told me that one of his daughters was sick with some kind of bacteria that was invading her bloodstream, and being the germ freak that I am, I thought, *Oh my God! How can bacteria be prevented from entering the bloodstream?* I said a prayer for her and then went about my business taking care of my children.

Then this summer I heard Dr. May's daughter had been in the hospital for over two months. But with just a bacteria infection, I thought, *Surely a healthy young girl will overcome that.* Sunday morning at church, my friend, who happens to be his secretary, told me that his daughter was still in the hospital and not responding to treatment. She told me her name was Amanda, so I put her on the church prayer chain again and moved on to deal with my baby, who I'm still having to medicate around the clock.

I didn't think any more about it, but then . . . my dream . . . maybe I'm just suffering from sleep deprivation. . . . I hope so. . . . I mean I never saw his daughter and she's probably okay by now. I don't know, but her eyes and her message . . . I keep going over it . . . wondering *Why? Why would her dad feel guilty? If she really has crossed over, it's from some bacteria in her bloodstream, so why would he feel guilt? And even if all that's true, I don't know him, so why would she come to me? And I'll never even see him again, so why would she give me a message to give to her dad?* I keep thinking that her effort was in vain, and that's really bothering me. So tell me, what's going on here?

"I don't know," I replied. "But can you ask the other teacher if the principal's daughter is doing better? Maybe the image was *not* her."

It was Thanksgiving before we talked again. "How have you been?" I asked. "Did anything ever come about from your vision?"

"Oh, let me tell you. Well, it's too weird to talk about over the phone. Can you come over? I can tell you all about it, and Mother would love to see you again too."

When I arrived at their home, Debbie's mother greeted me with the same welcoming spirit as her daughter. "I told her about the dream," Debbie said, putting her arm around her mother's shoulder. "And when I told her what happened after that, she was visibly shaken."

"Yes, I was," replied the elder.

"Let's sit down and I'll tell you about it," said Debbie, motioning for me to sit next to her on their living room sofa. "It's just so weird and so hard to believe," she sighed.

The vision I told you about happened on a Tuesday, right? Well, the next Sunday, when I saw my friend at church, she told me that the principal's daughter, Amanda, had passed away on Monday. I looked at her thinking, *Oh my God, what am I going to do? How am I going to tell my principal that his deceased daughter came to me in a dream to tell him she was okay and not to feel guilty?* I didn't say anything to my friend because I didn't know how. After thinking about it though, I felt overwhelmingly good—the fact that I was able to communicate with someone I'd never met or seen before was validating for me.

I wrote Dr. May a sympathy card and tried to say that he would see her again. I can't recall exactly what I said in it. [Debbie paused.] No, I don't remember, but I knew that telling him about the visit wasn't a good idea, partly because I didn't want him to think I was a fruitcake, or worse—trying to mock his tragedy. I was sure that her wish for me to tell her daddy she was fine would never happen. For one thing, I didn't plan on ever working at that school again. I just couldn't see me going back. And even if I ran into him someplace, I could never get the courage to tell him because I don't know his belief system. So how could I ever tell him?

I agreed. "Some people consider the topic taboo, and your principal could be one. Besides, Debbie, you know how vulnerable newly bereaved people are. Hearing about encounters can be offensive if they aren't open to the subject." We strolled out to my car, with Debbie wondering aloud about her experience, especially why a stranger would appear to her.

The year of 2001 brought an early fall, but it was a late night when Debbie called. "I have to tell you something," she said. We agreed to meet on Wednesday, but Tuesday, September 11, interceded. Along with millions of other horrified people, I watched the unfolding events and called Debbie. "I have to postpone our meeting," I said. "I can't reach anyone at Gateway (the grief center where I worked in New York) so I'm flying up as soon as I can get a flight."

"Wait! You remember my dream—my vision of the young girl? That's what I wanted to tell you about, and now it's really important for you to know so you can take it with you. Can you come over now?"

"Actually, I can, since everything's shut down today," I answered.

Through her glass-front door, colorful images flashed from the big screen television. Although Debbie and her mother hastened to greet me, our salutation was very different from the usual merriment. We were drawn to the broadcasts, but our time was limited so we forced ourselves to turn the volume down and settle in. Uncharacteristic for her, Debbie measured her words.

I'm so glad you could come over today because I really wanted you to hear this before you go. I decided it would be fun to do some substitute teaching at my son's elementary school and the high school where I used to work. I don't know if it was divine intervention or just what, but instead of getting calls from his campus, I only received calls from the high school.

So one morning, as I was driving over there, I got a strange sense of the girl who came to me in my vision. It's difficult to explain. It was as though she was telling me, "Okay . . . now's your chance to tell Dad." I kept dismissing it, thinking, *There is no way! I can't do that!* [Debbie sighed, shaking her head from side to side.] Dianne, I really couldn't. As much as she wanted me to, I just wanted to forget about it.

Then several weeks later, I saw her dad, our principal, in the hallway. I didn't know what to say, but I wanted to say something comforting, so I said, "I'm so sorry to hear about your daughter." I was shocked and relieved when he said, "She's still with us—literally." So I told him, "I have a story I'd like to share with you." He said, "See me in my office later where we can talk." I'm not sure how long it was before we met, but when we finally did, it seemed that Amanda made sure I knew it was okay to tell him about her, that her father was receptive to hearing about it. So I shared my dream encounter with him. He seemed touched, and even confirmed that my vision came one day after Amanda had died. He said that she had made her presence known to them too, and then he told me some of his family's stories, which were really incredible.

I know what an incredible girl Amanda was and that she still is. I'm honored to have briefly met her after she left this earth, and I can only imagine what she was like when she was here. I wondered why she came to me, and now I think I know the reasons. She knew I was open to it. And she knew that her afterlife existence would be validated by the fact that I didn't know her or even what she looked like. I think she made special arrangements for me to see her dad again so all this could be confirmed.

I wanted to tell you so you could take this story with you because people are more open to these things than we probably realize. A lot of people are hurting right now and you can bring them comfort. Even though you don't talk about it, you carry what you know inside of you and people get it.

With that, we hugged and I was on my way, along with more evidence that consciousness lives beyond bodily death. The next time Debbie called, spring flowers were blossoming along with her afterlife encounter.

Everything came to light for me while I was at school the other day. I was leaving my classroom after first period, and in broad daylight I suddenly saw an image that was identical to the girl in my dream. She was there, walking down the hall! I stopped frozen. My mouth must have been open no telling how wide because the head of the foreign language department, the teacher who originally told me that Amanda was sick, asked, "What happened? What's wrong, Debbie? You look like you've just seen a ghost!"

"Oh . . . I . . . I . . . think I have," I said.

I was so glad that teacher was in the hall too because I didn't know what to think. I mean I knew the image wasn't a ghost, but it just startled me since she looked like Amanda, the girl in my vision.

So I asked, "Who was that?" She said, "Oh, that's Dr. May's daughter." Looking at me, not knowing why I was so flabbergasted, she said, "She looks just like her sister who died." I said, "I know . . . I know." I kept thinking, *Oh, okay, okay . . . that's her **sister.*** The teacher kept looking at me strangely, so I said, "Can we go sit down someplace because I'm shaky and I need to talk about this. You'll probably think I'm crazy, but . . ."

After we sat down in her office, I told her about my vision, and I was surprised because she got really teary-eyed and said, "I believe you. Listen . . ." and then she told me about something similar that happened in her family. It was an amazing story.

I can't exactly describe what seeing the sister was like for me. It was eerie, but in a good way. Can you remember me telling you that if I saw a thief in front of me, I wouldn't be able to pick him out of a lineup? I can't ever remember what anyone looks like, so I've never been able to describe people. I think about the vision and I know how she appeared, but I could never describe her exactly. I can say, "She had full blonde hair with beautiful waves, dancing eyes, sweet smile, and radiant skin," but to be able to put the words to explain her perfectly, well, I'm just not a descriptive type person. I wanted to be able to tell her family precisely, so when I saw Amanda's sister it was great, because I could just point to her and say, "Okay, this is what she looked like."

I'm sure the family copes with Amanda's death by knowing that she's still with them and always will be, but this they knew long before I shared my dream.

Debbie's inability to describe Amanda was not unique. Words can never duplicate an image. Whereas another visual representation may suffice, language falls short. Debbie wanted me to see Amanda's sister—therefore, she arranged a meeting with Meredith, her parents, and brother. The family verified the date of Amanda's physical death, the guilt her dad felt, and that the sisters were almost mirror images. "Meredith and Amanda looked enough alike that some people—teachers and students—at their high school never realized there were two of them. Meredith got congratulated for her dance performances (which were Amanda's), and Amanda got complimented on her art pieces (Meredith's). They just smiled, thanked the person, and then shared the good news with the other later!" The May family voiced their appreciation for having experienced an encounter by proxy.

The next account also meets the third condition—the apparition was unknown by the recipient at the time but later identified.

After the tragic death of her daughter Heather (September 25, 1990), Geri Wiitala began experiencing afterlife encounters with the 17-year-old. Since that contradicted her fundamentalist beliefs, Geri found herself deeply entrenched in a religious struggle. She began a spiritual quest to find answers, which eventually led to her book *Heather's Return*, published by A.R.E. Press in 1996. While on book tour, Geri accumulated many encounter stories, one of which stood out as evidential.

"Oh my God! That's Kelli!"—Story by Geri Wiitala

I finished giving a presentation for the Death, Dying, and Grief class at a local college. It had been a wonderful evening and the young students were eager to ask questions and discuss their own experiences. As the crowd began to leave, a middle-aged woman approached me. I had noticed her during the lecture because she was older than the other students and kept solemnly nodding during my talk. As we greeted each other, she smiled and told me she would like to share something, but she did not feel comfortable talking in front of the others, so we sat to the side.

She said that her brother and his wife were at home with their son Ryan, age four at the time, when his wife was called to work unexpectedly. Since he was immersed in writing his dissertation, he asked her to drive the boy to a neighbor's house until supper. She agreed. As he stood in the window waving good-bye, watching his wife back out of the driveway, he saw his little boy throw open the back door (this was before seat-belt laws). Ryan fell out and the car rolled over him, crushing him to death. "We were all devastated," she said.

"And are your brother and his wife still married?" I asked, knowing that some marriages do not survive the death of a child.

"Yes," she said. "They had something happen to them that enabled them to work through their grief. About two weeks after the accident, my brother (an atheist) was sitting in his living room, wrestling with grief and guilt. His sobbing was interrupted by a strange humming sound, so he looked up and saw a funnel-type thing coming down out of the ceiling. Out of the funnel, dropped his son and a little girl, whom my brother didn't know. He yelled, 'Ryan! Ryan! I can't believe it's you!' Ryan said, 'I was sent to tell you that I'm okay, and that I'm with my friend Kelli.' My brother asked him why he had to die, and said he wished his mother hadn't been driving the car because he was stronger than she, and the burden should be on him.

"Ryan said he didn't know why he had to die, but that he was really okay, and that his mother would prove to be the stronger of the two. He said, 'I have to say goodbye, but don't worry because I'm with my friend Kelli, and I'm happy.' With that, they went back into the funnel, then up and out through the ceiling.

"My brother told his wife (also an atheist) and rest of our family. We were curious and kept asking, 'Who's the girl? Who's Kelli?' Peace started taking over our family again. And just like Ryan said, with time my sister-in-law proved to be the stronger of the two. But the story didn't end there.

"Several weeks after my brother's experience, a man and woman knocked on his front door. They said, 'We just moved into the neighborhood and heard about your son. We're bereaved parents too. Please come over and have coffee with us.' My brother and sister-in-law had been recluses since Ryan's death, but the couple were also bereaved parents, so he hesitated at first but then accepted their invitation.

"When my brother walked into the living room of the new neighbor's house, he was startled. He pointed to a large picture and blurted out, 'Oh my God! That's Kelli!' The neighbors looked totally stunned and said, 'How could you know our daughter, Kelli?' They had just moved there from the Midwest and Kelli had been dead for three years. So my brother explained what had happened, and that he and his wife and all his family had wondered about this girl, Kelli. Finally, we knew."

His afterlife encounter proved to be very encouraging for everyone involved, and it brought questions. Since we have no provable explanation, we can only speculate. Speculation is interesting and thought-provoking, so when the woman asked what I thought about the encounter, I said, "It seems to me that your brother was given a gift by his deceased son appearing. It helped him manage his guilt and grief. I think that Kelli was even a greater gift. He didn't know her, so his account is more credible because he found out who she was. Bereaved parents are sometimes viewed as delusional in their grief. Some of them doubt their own experiences themselves. The Divine knew that Kelli's parents were moving into the neighborhood and sent Ryan with her as verification that they survived death. Do I know this to be true? Of course not! But it is valid speculation."

His encounter reminds me of an account in *Heather's*

Return when Heather came to Judy—someone none of us, not Heather nor my family, had ever met before. Most members of my family were jealous because Heather visited with Judy instead of them—after all, they loved her so much. My sense is that the Divine was trying to reassure me (a very Doubting Thomas) that Heather was really alive and existing in a different form.

Now I realize that these so-called paranormal experiences are more normal than I had originally believed, and they fortify my belief that when the body dies the spirit truly does live on and can communicate with loved ones on this earth.

To further illustrate an encounter with a figure who was unknown to the receiver at the time, let's turn to Kathy, Katie's mother from an earlier account.

"LindyLou's grandma passed away."—Kathy's Survey

Monday night/Tuesday morning after the wreck that killed LindyLou, my daughter's best friend, I dreamed I saw her. LindyLou was in a place that was so peaceful, with lots of bright light. She was wearing a pale blue toga and singing hymns with an older lady who was dressed in the same type of clothes. I didn't know who the woman was, but I sensed it was a relative because she and LindyLou resembled each other. LindyLou told me that she was happy, then said good-bye—smiling that smile of hers. When I woke up that morning, I told Katie and my son, Will, about the dream. Katie said, "LindyLou dearly loved doing that, and you described her grandma, but she's still alive." About an hour later, a friend of Katie's called saying, "LindyLou's grandma passed away during the night or early this morning."

People have a way of explaining these things away, but personally, I think our loved ones try to send us messages that they are at peace and happy, and that we should live our lives to the fullest.

Encounters with unknown postmortem personalities, such as Debbie, Geri, and Kathy reported, are compelling evidence for life continuing beyond physical death. Survivalists commonly surmise, "Afterlife encounters depend on strong emotional ties," but these three examples are in contradiction. The witnesses had no prior connection to the deceased, and the discarnates interacted with new people, in new environments, and under new circumstances.

Skeptics insist that the first three conditions are not evidence for postmortem existence. Why? They claim that every word that has ever been spoken and every thought that has ever been conceived remains in the universe—therefore, afterlife encounters are the result of the living tapping into the past. While working at the National Institute for Discovery Science (NIDS) and serving on their board of directors, I was fortunate to have investigated survival with some of the most highly esteemed scientists in the field. I questioned each of them, "How do skeptics explain encounters wherein the long departed discuss current events—events the receivers didn't know but verify later?" Their collective answer can best be regurgitated by one of my mother's sayings, "Some people love arguing with the signboard and taking the long way home." I, therefore, offer a fourth consideration.

The Fourth Condition

The fourth consideration for a nonphysical entity surviving death: The apparition reported a current event that was unknown by the perceiver, and the information is proven accurate thereafter. John Simon, a former New York City taxi driver, submitted his survey, which meets this condition.

"Call my mother in Queens."—John Simon's Story

We were young, building his 1946 Harley, when my best buddy said, "I'm gonna die on a Friday the 13th."

"How do you know that?" I asked, surprised at such a statement.

"I've always known it," he said. "Don't know how I know, but I just know." Years passed before I recalled those words.

February 13, 1978, my friend burned to death in an arson fire at the Chelsea Hotel on West 23rd Street in Manhattan. The grief I felt was enormous. You see, just two weeks before, he'd confessed to me a terrible crime he'd committed. I was shocked, but I listened as he spontaneously blurted out his transgression against God and man. His confession put me in an awful quandary. *Should I go to the police?* I kept asking myself. By the time I'd just about made up my mind, he was dead.

Six months into his afterlife, he came to me in a lucid dream. I couldn't see him because my visual field was the blackest of black. No nothing—like a pure black velvet screen. I heard his voice and felt his presence though. He said, "I'm in hell!" That was all. It was enough! He faded away, and I woke up shaking.

Another six months passed before he returned. In this dream-encounter, I saw him. He was smiling, and waved at me as he stood next to a headstone. I'd never seen the stone, nor did I know his had been set. He gestured toward it, then I heard his thoughts, "Call my mother in Queens and tell her I love my headstone." After that, he told me, "I'm no longer in Hell. I'm going to school now!" When I woke up, I drew a picture of the headstone, complete with curly-cues, shape, and color. Then I called his mom. I was shocked to hear his stone was laid the previous day. I immediately called in sick (at my job as a New York City cab driver) and drove out to the cemetery. Sure enough, my sketch matched his new headstone to a tee.

About 18 months later, he returned one more time, in the same manner as his first visit. I saw only blackness, but sensed him and heard his voice. "This is my last visit," he said. "We won't meet again until you cross over." He told me he was fine, still going to school, and then asked, "Is there anything you wish to know?" Here he was, in a unique position, able to access universal knowledge and records, but I couldn't think of a thing, until finally, I asked him, "Will I ever win the Lotto? Will any of my small-time gambling ever pay off?"

"I'll check," he said.

I had a strange sense of being put on hold for five to ten seconds before he was back with negative news, "No."

I asked, "Why not?"

My friend answered, "Karma."

I asked, "How did you manage to get out of Hell?"

"I got out the moment I forgave myself!" he answered. We said our good-byes, and then he faded away. I've not been visited by him since.

The Fifth Condition

An apparition manipulating a physical object independent from the witness is the fifth criterion for evidence of survival. Although the phenomenon has been widely reported in literature, some parapsychologists speculate that the perceivers, not the posthumous personas, moved the objects by psychokinesis (PK—mind over matter). Several stories presented thus far seem otherwise, however. Jane May's music box played under many different circumstances, for example. Let's now consider Tammi's encounter.

"It isn't broken anymore."—Tammi's Survey

On August 26, 2000, I was blessed with a beautiful baby boy whom I named Colton James Boeskool. He weighed 5 pounds 8 ounces and was 19 1/2 inches long. Everything about him was perfect, right down to his ten little fingers and ten little toes. Colton was such a loving and warm child. He always seemed to have a smile on his face and just flowed with love. He had the most precious blue eyes, blonde hair, and a smile that was contagious.

On July 24, 2002, tragedy shook our family. My baby boy, Colton, at the age of 23 months, accidentally drowned in our backyard swimming pool. He was rushed to the emergency room, where doctors and nurses worked on him for 45 minutes, but couldn't save his life. Colton was such a loving soul and will be sorely missed by all who knew him. Most of all, he will be so missed by his mama, daddy, sister, and brother. I miss him so much every day that I just wish I could turn the clock back. I would give anything to have him here with me.

But since his passing, Colton has given me so many wonderful signs that he's still here with me in spirit. I would like to share one story with you. It will always remain in my heart, for it shows how much he loved me.

A couple of months after his accident, I woke one night out of a deep sleep, ripping the necklace from my neck. It was a special necklace because it had charms with the birthstones of each of my children. It was my lifeline to them and I treasured it so much that I never took it off. I had no idea why I ripped it off, so I got out of bed, turned on the light, and to my dismay, saw that I really had. I was so upset that I started to cry. The incident made my grieving for Colton a little stronger, but I knew that there was nothing I could do about the necklace right then, so I put it on the nightstand next to my bed.

My mom came home from her vacation the next evening and went in my room looking for me. She noticed my necklace lying on the nightstand, so she went over and picked it up. She immediately saw that I had completely broken it in two places and knew I'd be upset about it. As soon as I got home a few hours later she told me she saw it upstairs and wondered how I had broken it. I told her the story, saying I thought I must have acted out in a dream.

The following morning we were in my room talking, making plans to go to the cemetery to see Colton's new headstone. I asked, "Can we stop and buy a new chain for my charms?" Mom said, "Of course we can." I got up, conversing with my mother, and walked to my necklace lying on the nightstand. As I picked it up, I stopped dead in the middle of my sentence.

"What's wrong?" Mom asked.

I held the necklace up to her, "It isn't broken anymore," I said. "It's fixed."

Mom asked, "Are you sure it's the same necklace?"

I said, "Of course it is. I haven't touched it since I put it on my nightstand, and the only other person to touch it was you."

She said, "I know it was broken because I held it in my hand, and I saw where the chain was broken in two different spots."

I knew immediately that my little boy Colton had fixed my necklace. He knew how important it was to me, and he knew how sad I was about breaking it. He mended it to make me happy again and to let me know that even though he isn't here with me in the physical sense anymore, he's with me in spirit. My heart was so overjoyed that he could do this for me. I cried and cried tears of joy and sorrow—joy that my baby boy's spirit is alive and here with me, sorrow because I miss him so very much. This story really did happen and will always remain in my heart from now until I, too, pass over.

The Sixth Condition

The six consideration whereby afterlife encounters provide evidence for survival beyond physical demise is when the apparitions exhibited a purpose that was extraneous to the perceivers. Linda, from Ft. Worth, Texas, offered her survey as an example.

"Find the truth about how I died."—Linda's Survey

I didn't believe in the paranormal much and have spoken with very few people about what happened to me. On November 6, 1961, Wayne, my fiancé, was killed in an accident at the age of 20. Thirty-five years later, in 1996, I underwent chemotherapy and several surgeries for a rare form of cancer. During one of the surgeries, according to the doctors, my heart stopped for three minutes, and although I do not recall anything medically, I remember having a wonderful dreamlike experience. I was in a beautiful place and Wayne was there. In appearance, neither of us had changed. He told me to find out the truth about how he died, that his military record was not accurate, and he gave me names of four men who would know. Then he said, "I'm not dead. I've just passed on to another level. I've never left you." He knew all about my life—about my children and everything that happened to me since 1961.

After my initial encounter, I felt Wayne's presence again, pushing me to find the true facts about his death. I began searching for the people he said were involved. I had met a few of his old buddies, but none of the men he mentioned were among them. One by one, I found all four. Each, separately, gave me the same details that Wayne had about how he was killed. So I located his sister, who, from his military records, requested a copy of his autopsy. It did not include any of the information Wayne and his comrades had given me.

I don't hear or see him any more, but I know Wayne is with me at times, especially when I face health problems. His presence has totally taken the fear of death from me. I wake up in the mornings, feeling the warmth of sunshine all around, even when it's dark and midwinter. I feel very positive about life and look forward to each day with a secure feeling. My entire attitude about life has changed. I'm a much more loving mother and wife.

Credible research and anecdotes provide reasonable evidence that the living exist after bodily demise. Furthermore, science has proven that energy is eternal—and consciousness is energy. Dogmatic skeptics, however, continue to ignore or discount valid research findings.

Webster lists two definitions for the term skepticism. The first is thoughtful inquiry; questions, doubts, or considerations. Healthy skepticism—to consider all possibilities—is wise. The second definition, however, is derived from early Greek philosophy: to deny the possibility of any real knowledge. Dogmatic skeptics cynically assert their opinions without proof to support them. The synonyms are as follows: arrogant, self-opinionated, dictatorial, and authoritative. As Rupert Sheldrake pointed out, "The most zealous behave like vigilantes policing the frontiers of science."[4]

Dogmatic skeptics remind me of the patients at a psychiatric hospital where I worked as a psychotherapist. Although they were intelligent, educated, and successful members of society, a significant portion suffered from one major dysfunction. The medical director explained, "Their obstacle is that they don't want to vary from their pathology. They see things only one way—their way—and they have no desire to change." Inflexibility and seriousness are pathological. Being a fanatic, about anything, is less than mentally healthy.

Devout skeptics refuse to consider the enormous volume of work that science has to offer. Let's consider their perspectives, and then view some contrasting data.

Dogmatic Skeptics Claim

Skeptics insist that people who report afterlife encounters are suffering from one or more of the following:

* Alcohol abuse—perceivers were under the influence
* Drug-induced—substance-caused hallucinations
* Mentally ill—perceivers were deranged
* Repetitive imaging—perceivers developed the images
* Emotional state—crisis prohibited or altered their perception
* Deliberate fraud—claimants sought attention, fame, fortune, or power
* Deceived—perceivers were tricked
* Inaccurate reporting—witnesses unconsciously exaggerated the truth
* Mistaken identity—living individual resembled the deceased
* False memory—personal reflections changed over time
* Illusion—people misinterpreted or misperceived normal events
* Grief stricken—mourners exercised wishful thinking
* Expectations—the bereaved expected visitations from their dearly departed
* Hallucinations—afterlife encounters lack longevity

The first claims are so irrelevant that they merit only brief mention. Certainly, some people who reported apparitions or ghosts were under the influence of alcohol or drugs, but they are in the minority. As for the mentally ill, hallucinations, recounted by psychiatric patients, are very different from AEs. Generated by negativity, hallucinations produce frightening images and sounds that cause adverse reactions, such as panic or anxiety. Skeptics further allege that afterlife encounters develop—that is, perceivers repeatedly imagine an apparition, with each building on the previous. In actuality, most sightings are startling and single events, forever crystallized in the moment. Further allegation claims that receivers were in an emotional condition, which ignores the fact that most were unquestionably in a homeostatic state—enjoying a favorite pastime or sleeping. Fraudulent, deceptive, and inaccurate reports are inevitable, but minimal considering the mass numbers collected. Invented accounts, unfortunately, are chronicled; however, most are detected by survivalists because they deviate from the norm (characteristically, apparitions float above the floor, their feet are not seen, they do not open doors to enter or exit, and so on).

More plausible claims include mistaken identity. A common feature of the grief process is mourners mistaking living individuals for those departed. Nonmourners experience similar circumstances. A sales clerk, for example, spotted her brother's young bride exiting an adjacent store, but learned minutes later that her sister-in-law had been killed in an accident earlier that morning. The clerk rushed to her brother's side, telling him about her vision. The following month, however, during a support group meeting, she told members, "He was so grateful to hear that Jana was walking and looked good that I don't want to tell him . . . but . . . I met the girl I thought was Jana. She'd just started working at the dress shop across from me about a week before my sister-in-law was killed. She looks so much like Jana that I would've bet money that was her." In cases of mistaken identity, most witnesses realize their error at some point.

Memories change, skeptics explain. Indeed, details surrounding personal events normally shift over time. Afterlife encounters, however, may be an exception. Members of support groups and individual clients often shared their accounts with me, and then later brought their journals or diaries. Their oral descriptions usually mirrored their written statements.

Similarly, many AES respondents had recorded the specific details of their visitations in their journals. I compared those entries, written years prior to their surveys, and found few differences. Encounters seem to crystallize in the moment.

Skeptics insist that AEs are illusions. In some instances, they are correct—people can misperceive or misinterpret external events. Illusions are "false conclusions drawn from correct data."[5] The first consideration with any paranormal event is: Could it have been an illusion? We initially seek a natural source. In Jane May's story about the music box doll, we first asked, *Could the music box's playing have a normal cause?* The May family thoroughly tested it under various conditions: they slammed the door, jumped up and down, bumped the shelf where it rested, and even rewound it, watched it play out, and then listened for residual movement. Next, after Jane e-mailed, saying the music box continued to play most of the song during significant times, I consulted with managers from the most prominent music box outlets and they ruled the cause transpersonal. With normal circumstantial explanations excluded, we are left to explore paranormal possibilities, and who knows what may be revealed? We have discovered that dogs hear high-pitched sounds that our ears cannot. Insects see colors that we do not. Carbon monoxide exists, yet our senses are incapable of detecting it. Could skeptics, who unequivocally conclude that an afterlife encounter is simply an illusion, be experiencing one themselves?

Apparitions, skeptics further allege, are the result of mourners' wishful thinking, longing, and expectations. However, non-mourners receive discarnate visitations. Moreover, 30 percent of perceivers do not believe in encounters beforehand.[6] Furthermore, of the AES participants who experienced postmortem personalities, 82 percent were not longing for anything of that nature. Of the respondents who had never experienced an encounter, 89 percent reported an intense and extended longing. Grief, expectations, desire, longing, or wishful thinking does not necessarily play a role in spontaneous accounts.

When we have successfully countered other perspectives, the most devout skeptics turn to the outdated elapsed-time theory.

Accordingly, discarnate visitations extinguish over time—therefore, they are simply hallucinated by the bereaved. Early researchers Gurney, Myers, and Podmore conducted the first large-scale study in 1886. Gurney and Myers diagrammed their findings, which illustrated the period between death and encounters was most often within 24 hours, then decreased rapidly (within days), and slowly declined until they were too minimal to chart by the one-year point. Gurney, however, noted that a large portion of their study included newly bereaved participants; therefore, their findings were not a true representation of the phenomenon. Myers stressed "if once we face the supposition that an apparition may be the result of some kind of energy exercised by a descendent whose body is unquestionably dead, we have no logical ground for denying that he may exert a similar energy many years after death."[7]

Myers's words "many years after death" echoed in my ears every time I heard someone exclaim, "I saw her—and she died years ago!" Then, during Phase 1 of the Afterlife Encounter Survey (AES), participants reported some 20, 30, 40, and even 50 years had lapsed. For George Stone, a 70-year-old school crossing guard in Canada, it had been almost six decades.

"She was my playmate from 58 years ago."—George Stone's Survey

I've been crossing kids at the same place for a long time. A few years ago, after they all had crossed the road, I was about to go home when I saw another kid coming down the hill. So I waited. As she came closer, I noticed she was dressed different from the others. She was dressed like kids back in the 1940s. When she came close, I knew who this little girl was. She was Mary, my little playmate who died 58 years ago.

Mary was as solid as me, and her face was shining. I was so shocked that I could not speak. After a while, I said, "Hi." She spoke back to me, and asked, "Will you be here tomorrow?" I said, "Yes." I did not want to let on that I knew her, but she wanted to make sure I did, so her mother appeared beside her. Mary's black hair was fixed in ringlets, so I asked, "Who did your hair?" Mary said, "I did." I heard something across the road and looked to see who it was, and when I looked back, Mary and her mother were gone.

My seeing and talking to Mary changed my life. I think Mary came to show me that there is no death—that we live on in a better life. I'm more spiritual than I ever was, and more kind and loving toward others. I'm not interested in the *things* of this life now. I just want to help people, as many as I can, and then be with my loved ones when it's my time to pass over. End of story. George.

George's account was one of many that suggested the early published findings did not accurately reflect the experiences. I therefore turned to Erlendur Haraldsson, a longtime researcher with the Department of Psychology at the University of Iceland. Dr. Haraldsson e-mailed me the results of his large-scale survey conducted in the 1980s (unpublished), wherein he measured the interval between death and afterlife encounters. From his 350 cases, 39.4 percent occurred within one year. And from those, the first 24 hours accounted for only 10.5 percent. However, 16.1 percent took place between one and five years, 6.8 percent from six to ten, and more than ten years elapsed in 13.9 percent of the cases. These figures seemed to depict the phenomenon more accurately.

Wanting contemporary data surrounding the elapsed time issue, I designed Phase 2 of the AES and webmaster Karl Fancher posted it on my web site, afterlife-encounters.com. Almost 1,200 people from 19 countries scored a total of 1,978 accounts. Whereas 53 percent occurred between the moment of death and the first anniversary, 47 percent manifested well beyond the one-year point.[8] On one hand, the survey resonated with those previous surveys—it did not collect a true profile of the phenomenon because a disproportionate number of participants were newly bereaved. Nevertheless, it revealed that many years often elapse between death and discarnate appearances. Visits from the Great Beyond escape the grasp of time—they occur when perceivers need them most.

Why are cynics so unyielding? Fear. Death, dying, and the afterlife have been taboo topics in many cultures, and some individuals still recoil at the thought of glimpsing behind the door. Then charlatans and the ill-informed come along and create further blocks that prevent many from peeking through the portal. On one hand, skeptics propel research. They are the catalysts behind many discoveries, and for that we can be grateful.

However, those who never venture from their self-centered rigidity fail to see how they affect people outside their world—that is, until theirs is shattered. Sigmund Freud proclaimed himself a skeptic, as was the fashion for intellectuals in his field—most denied any interest in transpersonal psychology for fear of being labeled superstitious. The death of Freud's daughter, however, caused him to realize his shortcomings and regret his utterances. Unfortunately, he had already disenfranchised his patients who believed.

No one—*absolutely no one*—has the right to take another person's experience from them. The only hope some mourners have left is the remembrance of experiencing their dearly departed, and to obliterate that in any way is unwarranted. And skeptical insistence is baseless, because the truth is that no one can say unequivocally whether or not we continue beyond physical demise, but more evidence leans toward the affirmative.

A committee of psychical researchers in 1894, after 17,000 people had been interviewed, suggested their study was evidence for the continuity of life and possibly communicating with the dead.[9] They nevertheless advised readers to draw their own conclusions. Gary Schwartz and his panel of investigators, a century later, repeatedly stated throughout their experiments and literature, "Let the data speak." Similar to those before me, I am offering the information I have gathered along my journey and invite you to evaluate it in your own way.

Will scientists ever conclude that some part of living beings survives death? For many people, the question of survival is irrelevant. They believe in and appreciate afterlife encounters for what they are—comforting, enlightening, and transforming. Who are these people? Do believers and perceivers hold a common profile? Who is most likely to experience the phenomenon? The answers appear in the next chapter.

FOUR

Profiles of Typical Perceivers

Of course I believe in ghosts. Doesn't everybody?
—Red Skelton

Every population has recorded postmortem events. Early surveys in England, France, Germany, and the United States revealed that approximately 12 percent of their compatriots had experienced at least one account.[1] Later studies indicated that 42 percent of Americans reported "contacts with the dead."[2] Who are these individuals? Why do some people have encounters, but not others? The answers emerge from three profiles.

The Social Profile

The most extensive systematic study, The Unusual Events Survey, representing a general sample of Americans, was conducted for the Bigelow Holding Company in 1991.[3] The survey was administered face to face, between poll takers and 5,947 participants. To verify the data, an interview with each respondent was conducted from Roper's central telephone facility. Respondents were diversified in age, race, occupations, income, political interests, social status, education, religion, and geographic locations throughout the United States.[4]

According to the results, 11 percent of those polled reported they had "seen a ghost." From the collection of almost 6,000 people, pollsters categorized participants according to their similarities and discovered the "Influential Americans" group reported the greatest number of AEs—16 percent. Influential Americans, according to Roper, are trendsetters, community leaders, committee members, and government advocates. They are socially active, college graduates, middle-aged, wealthier than the norm, and married with children. These findings supported and extended the surveys conducted during the 1980s, which determined that highly educated individuals were more likely to experience, and believe in, afterlife encounters.[5]

What's in a Name

Perceivers often exclaim, "I must be going insane!"

"If so," I reply, "you'd be in good company because some of the most brilliant and celebrated people across the globe have revealed their accounts." Socrates; Winston Churchill; Pope John Paul; Abraham Lincoln; Benjamin Franklin; Henry Ford; Oliver Wendell Holmes; Mark Twain; Robert Louis Stevenson; Victor Hugo; Carl Jung; Edgar Cayce; Nobel Prize winner Thomas Mann; Danton Walker from the New York *Daily News*; publisher Edward Bok of *Ladies Home Journal*; and England's greatest physicists Sir Oliver Lodge, Sir William Crookes, and Sir William Barrett are among the names you may recognize.

Movie, theater, and television personality Red Skelton confessed that many of his performances began with a pantomimist from centuries past (Grimaldi) whispering directions in his ear. His passion since childhood—collecting stories about afterlife encounters—culminated in his book *Red Skelton's Favorite Ghost Stories*, first published in 1965.

That same year, physician, psychiatrist, and professor Elisabeth Kübler-Ross became famous for her Five Stages of Loss Theory. A standard story she narrated to her workshop participants involved a woman she met while working at the University of Chicago Medical Center. After a long day of instructing students at the hospital, Elisabeth was eager to return to her office.

As she entered the elevator, she noticed a lady who seemed familiar. "Do you mind if I walk along with you?" the woman asked as the doors opened. *Who is this?* Elisabeth wondered. They conversed along the way, with Elisabeth becoming more curious about her identity, but not wanting to ask. Then, stopping to open the door to her private office, she invited, "Won't you come inside so we can continue?" She studied the lady's face, voice, and gestures, trying to recall where she had previously met this person. Finally, the woman leaned forward and asked, "You don't remember me, do you? I'm Mrs. Schwartz."

"Oh, yes! Of course!" Elisabeth exclaimed, realizing the figure was her former patient who had died of cancer the year before.

She thought, *Are my long hours causing me to hallucinate? I need to get something tangible for myself, and if this is a genuine apparition, I want something to show my colleague.* Passing a sheet of paper and pen to the apparition, she asked, "Will you write a note for the chaplain? I'm sure he'd like to know you were here. And be sure to sign your name so he'll see it was from you." The hospital chaplain was delighted upon reading the note and hearing Elisabeth's story.

More recently, former president Jimmy Carter and first lady Roslyn were strolling along the grounds of their estate, participating in a televised interview. The Nobel Prize winner commented about a black dog that he and his family often saw in the yard of their Georgia home during the 1950s. Carter turned to the interviewer, adding, "One day I told Sonny to go out and pet it, but when he reached his hand down, the dog disappeared." The journalist asked, "You're joking, aren't you?" Both of the Carters assured her they were serious. (By the way, some cultures believe that black dogs, in spirit, protect and defend those who work for the highest good of humanity.)

Beyond witnessing apparitions, the most educated believe afterlife encounters are possible. Thomas Edison was bridging heaven and earth, but died before his planetary telephone was complete. California Senator Leland Stanford, founder of Stanford University in Palo Alto, California, designated a great deal of money for continued research after his death.

During the *Columbia* memorial service at the National Aerospace and Science Administration (NASA) on February 4, 2003, Captain Kent Raminger, United States Navy, Chief of Astronauts, spoke to his fallen comrades "Rick, Willie, Mike, K. C., Laurel, Dave, Ilan . . . I know you are listening. . . ." Many listeners worldwide understood and agreed.

Public disclosures support research findings—findings that have repeatedly indicated that the brightest and boldest experience, and believe in, postmortem manifestations. Another common profile arose from my work.

The Personality Profile[6]

During my years of working with the bereaved and investigating afterlife encounters, it seemed one personality type reported apparitions. Wanting to test my observations, I turned to the most administered personality test in the world, the Myers-Briggs Type Indicator (MBTI).

According to the MBTI, each person's makeup is a combination of four opposite personality types—Extrovert or Introvert; Sensor or Intuitive; Thinking versus Feeling; and Judging or Perceiving. I speculated that people who were Extroverted/Intuitive/Feeling/Perceiving witnessed disembodied personalities more than their counterparts.

To understand my theory, let's begin by comparing the groups. First, the Extroverts and Introverts. Extroverts focus their attention on the external world, especially people. They are energized by the accompaniment of others and continuously scan outside themselves for stimulation. On the other hand, Introverts focus internally. They find the accompaniment of other people draining, thus avoid external stimulation. Wouldn't it seem likely that extroverts would detect apparitions in their environment?

Comparing the Sensing versus Intuition group, Sensors trust their past experiences and five senses. Intuitives look to future possibilities and rely on their intuition or gut reaction. Therefore, wouldn't intuitive people discern nonphysical entities?

When it comes to the Thinking versus Feeling group, Thinking types decide with their heads. They are the skeptics, remaining detached from other people. Feeling types, however, decide with their hearts. They are trusting, make decisions spontaneously according to the circumstances, and consider everyone involved. Feeling types display their emotions so easily that, to Thinkers, Feelers are too gushy and welcoming. Doesn't it seem that Feeling-type personalities would encounter disembodied loved ones most often?

Last, the Judging versus Perceiving types differ in time and flexibility. Judgers are inflexible. Almost everything they do is decided, planned, organized, scheduled, and controlled. Perceivers, however, enjoy change and adapt to it effortlessly. Lingering in exploration, they appreciate whatever unfolds. Doesn't that suggest the Perceivers would perceive the unusual?

Grouping the typologies together, doesn't it seem that most recipients of afterlife encounters would be a combination of one personality type—Extrovert/Intuitive/Feeling/Perceiving? That was my theory, but it rested on speculation; that is, until I administered the MBTI to 68 individuals. Participants varied in education, employment, age, gender, geographical location, and interests. They were from the general population and bereaved. The results?

The data did not totally favor my hypothesis. The findings indicated that the first group (Extroversion/Introversion) contributed only slightly, and the last (Judging/Perceiving) held no statistical significance.[7] The middle two groups, however, emerged as significant.

Participants who were a combination of Intuitive and Feeling accounted for 96 percent of the encounters. Not one of their polar opposites (Sensors/Thinkers) reported anything considered paranormal. The overwhelming results indicated that personality traits play a role in discerning the hereafter. The study concluded with good news. Through awareness and practice, those who desire discarnate visitations can become more Intuitive and Feeling.

The Spiritually Engaged Profile

Jose, a former hospice patient, expressed the third profile poetically, "You know, Arcangel, I'm just becoming spirit now." We come from the Light and as our days on earth draw to a close we prepare to return. Spiritually engaged, the terminally ill commonly witness pre-death encounters. In fact, it is so common that hospice staff and volunteers consider AEs a signal that death is drawing nearer and increase the frequency of their visits. The phenomenon is not only for the terminally ill, however. To illustrate, let's turn to Gary, a young widower.

"Don't bother."—Gary's Story

I was washing my car, getting it ready to trade in, when I saw my wife standing there as plain as day. She said, "Don't bother. Just enjoy your family and friends because you'll be with me soon." But that doesn't make sense. I'm in excellent health, and life is finally good for me again, so why would she appear and say that?

Gary and his new red car were still sparkling on the morning he stopped by my office on his way to work. He described how vivid and frequent his encounters were becoming, and questioned, "I wonder why?" His image and words are now crystallized in my mind, for it was midafternoon when his employer telephoned, "Gary was killed in a freak car crash this morning. Police said he didn't even know what hit him." Regardless of the manner, as death nears, people spiritually engage.

Is there another profile for perceivers? Mourners have long been considered the most common. Let's therefore turn to studies on the topic.

Grief and Afterlife Encounters

The grieving population, supposedly, experience more postmortem sightings. One research project, however, divided participants into two categories—those who were bereaved within the past five years, then those who had never lost a loved one or the loss exceeded five years. From the two groups, only recently bereaved siblings measured slightly more incidences compared to those nonbereaved.[8]

My investigations resulted in similar findings. The bereaved recounted a larger portion of incidents with the Hereafter because they needed, remembered, and treasured them more than their counterparts. As an example, Joe Dioca, retired and living in Florida, narrated one of his visitations.

"She's still my inspiration."—Story by Joe Dioca

Ellie worked as a family counselor for the Salvation Army's Department of Social Services. One of her greatest delights was to bring families back together. Everyone loved her. She had such a charismatic personality that her presence lit up a room.

She was not just my wife for 43 years and the mother of our three children, she was my sweetheart, soul mate, best friend, confidante, and my inspiration for living. Ellie was the love of my life, and I adored her, treasured her, and protected her. I cannot remember an argument or disagreement between us that lasted more than ten minutes. She always insisted on a hug and kiss any time I left the house—regardless of whether I was leaving for work or just going to the corner store. Everyone who knew us throughout the years considered us to be one because we were almost always together. My children referred to their mother and me as Peanut Butter and Jelly.

Ellie went to the doctor for a blood clot in her leg on May 1, 2001, but he didn't think it was severe, so sent her home. Four hours later, she suddenly fell into my arms. The clot had broken loose, gone to her heart, and she was having a cardiac arrest. I tried so hard to save her with CPR (cardiopulmonary resuscitation) until paramedics arrived, but I failed.

The evening Ellie died in my arms is etched in my mind and heart. I relive it over and over again. What a horrible ordeal—to have a life that you cherish and love slip right out of your arms forever and to be helpless to stop it. I still wake every morning and look at her side of the bed, hoping she'll be there, hoping it was all a bad dream. We were so close that her death nearly destroyed me, but she helps me survive.

I visit the cemetery, where my encounters with her are difficult to explain. One morning I brought three beautiful pink roses and placed them in the vase on her grave. Then I walked over to sit on a marble bench about 50 feet away. Just as I sat down, I noticed one of the roses actually lifting up and out of the vase, so I jumped up and rushed to grab it before it hit the ground. But the second I reached the grave, a bolt of lightning came down and literally destroyed the bench I had been sitting on and the tree that shaded it. The lightning was so close to me that it burned the right shoe off my foot! It was as if Ellie called me closer to escape the lightning strike.

So you see, her visits help me survive. She's still my inspiration for life. Although it seems as if part of me went with Ellie, part of her comes here to be with me. I feel very strongly that life and true love do not end at the grave but continue into eternity. Love can never be severed. I know that when my time of calling comes, my Ellie will be there with outstretched arms to give me that hug and kiss I so long for. Our grave marker says it all, Together Forever.

Joe is among the majority—65 percent of widows and widowers report encounters with their departed spouses. So comforted by their visitations, many try to evoke more.[9]

How do leading bereavement specialists respond to the concept of postmortem manifestations? I have noticed a dramatic shift over the years. Prior to the 1980s, most professionals avoided the topic—however, if they mentioned it, they were careful to use the term "hallucinations." Then, they replaced "hallucinations" with the phrase "perceived contact with the dead." Gradually, qualified veterans in the field included afterlife encounters along with other normal circumstances of mourning and designated the phenomenon significant. The most prominent specialists today acknowledge, "We can't use the term *perceived* any longer because many contacts seem more than simply perceived." Informed healthcare practitioners validate encounters for what they can be—functional, revitalizing, and transforming. To demonstrate the therapeutic value of AEs, Angela presented her account.

"A calm came over me."—Angela's Survey

After my mom passed, I was totally overcome with depression, grief, anxiety—you name it, I had it. I cried all night, begging Mother to come and get me so I could be with her. I saw no point in life anymore. I could not imagine getting married without her, having a child without her, or living a normal life without her. This went on week after week. I went to Mother's grave during my lunch breaks, where I sat and cried.

It normally took me hours to fall asleep, but one night as soon as my head hit the pillow I felt something like a trance. I couldn't move or open my eyes. I was lying on my side, aware of where I was, but felt frozen. Suddenly, I knew my mom was in the room. I did not see her. At first I just felt her presence, and then I felt the side of the bed go down as if there was someone sitting on it. Then I felt Mother lean against my cheek, and I heard her whisper in my ear, but I couldn't understand what she was saying. From that moment on, a calm came over me. I slept soundly and woke up refreshed the next morning.

For the first time, I didn't cry on my way to work. I visited Mother's grave at lunch time and sat there with such a feeling of calmness. It was the weirdest thing! I can't explain it exactly, but I felt as if a weight had been taken off me. Although I long to see her again, I know she was there. She knew what I was going through and came to comfort me. To this day, my encounter with my mother gives me hope and a tremendous amount of support.

It seems evident that rather than experiencing the greatest portion of encounters, the bereaved simply recall and cherish them. To determine the most likely candidates for receiving visitations, we first consider three profiles—social, personality, and spiritual. Then, if we consider manifestations as otherworldly, the phenomenon is not totally dependent on perceivers. The highway between worlds runs both ways, which brings us to who is most likely to be encountered as well as when and why.

FIVE

Heart Strings

What if you slept?
And what if, in your sleep,
you dreamed?
And what if, in your dream,
you went to heaven
and there plucked a beautiful flower?
And what if, when you awoke,
you had the flower in your hand?
Ah, what then?
—Samuel Taylor Coleridge

Afterlife encounters transpire during various states of consciousness—while percevers are sleeping, dreaming, daydreaming, in reverie (between sleep and awake), preoccupied, or fully alert. Emotional climates vary as well. Witnesses may be feeling jubilation, boredom, or in crisis. Regardless of mental and emotional conditions, postmortem sightings occur when perceivers are in transition. Their basic purpose is to render aid during transitional periods, and the discarnates who appear are those who can best fill that purpose. At the heart of afterlife encounters lies "when," "why," and "who appears." Let's begin with when they arise.

When Do Afterlife Encounters Occur?

Early studies suggested that when and why postmortem manifestations arose were synonymous. Accordingly, perceivers were in crisis, which caused them to perceive the unusual. My studies contradict that claim. Afterlife encounters occur during two different transitional periods.

Transcending into the Hereafter

Physical death is one transitional period. Discarnate figures help the dying to disengage from this world and enter the next. Those who loved us most, whom we loved in return, greet us with open arms. Apparitions we would never expect can appear first, however, as in the following two instances.

"He was sitting where you are."
—Albert's Pre-Death Encounter

Albert was one of my favorite hospice patients. A veteran of World War II, he married in 1946 and moved to a small coastal town where he and his wife lived a quiet life with their daughter. Most important to Albert was his independence, in which he basked for more than five decades. Now cancer invaded his body, and physicians at the Texas Medical Center strongly advised him to enter a hospice program, especially since his only surviving relatives were his daughter, son-in-law, and their two young children. To appease them all, Albert moved into his daughter's home and signed on with our hospice, but then he refused most of our services. In order for admissions to submit the necessary insurance forms, he agreed to meet with one person from each department (physician, nurse, home health aid, social assistance, and chaplaincy). I was Albert's designated chaplain.

At first glimpse, Albert reminded me of my father-in-law. Surrounded by World War II books and perched in a lounge chair one step from the big-screen television, he was engulfed by his passion—football. The season was just beginning, so our conversation revolved around our favorite teams and who we thought would win that weekend and Monday night. Much to my surprise, he invited me to return the following week.

The moment I stepped inside their front door on Tuesday

afternoon Albert called out, "Sorry about that—all of *my* teams won." It was easy to see that an askew grin was a precursor to his dry wit. We looked over the television guide, deciding which upcoming games would be the most exciting to watch and picked our winning teams. Then, as he tossed the guide next to his stack of wartime books, I pointed to one and said, "My father-in-law was a tail gunner." Reminiscences flowed from Albert. Finally, as I was bidding him farewell, he asked, "Can you come over every Tuesday so I can gloat over my winning picks?" His invitation was more than just football. We both knew that. Albert had found an attentive ear.

As his cancer progressed, he became less animated and tired easily. The hospice provided a hospital bed, which his family placed directly in front of their television. With each of my visits, his conversation turned more toward his perils during the war, the death that had surrounded him, and the terror he felt while thinking *I could be next.*

It was Friday, the eve before the football playoffs began. I arrived at my office early as usual, but then received an unusual telephone call. "This is Albert's daughter. Dad demanded that we move him into the guest bedroom last night. We tried to talk him out of it, because we all want him in the family room with us. Besides, the TV back there is so small he can't see the games."

In preparation to leave this world, people with terminal illnesses typically disengage from their normal interests. Albert, however, had not displayed any previous signs of withdrawal. He was still caring for himself—bathing, shaving, eating, walking, and so on. His sudden demands signaled that something was shifting for him. "He also insisted," she added, "that I call you first thing this morning and tell you he needs to see you today." Asking for anything was totally uncharacteristic for Albert. Considering his radical changes, I dashed across town to their home.

"Oh, thank you," Albert's son-in-law yelled out, stopping his car at the foot of their driveway as I arrived. "Go on in. He's waiting for you." I was alarmed when I saw Albert in the rear bedroom, laying flat on his back with one side of his bed-rail locked in the up position. But then, turning his head, he looked at me with a cockeyed grin that reached all the way to my heart. *What on earth,* I wondered. Albert motioned for me to hurry. "What's it like over there?" he asked before I reached him. Standing by the sliding glass doors that led to their garden patio, his daughter spun around and stepped outside.

Sensing we were in for an in-depth conversation, I sat in the bedside chair and asked, "What do you mean?"

"You know . . . over there . . . heaven or whatever you call it. What's it like?"

I probed, "Ahhh . . . I'm not sure. Why, Albert?"

"I saw someone," he replied, turning his face toward the ceiling. "He told me to ask you to come over here first thing this morning."

"Who did you see?" I asked.

"My uncle," he replied. Albert rolled to his side, toward me, and pointed two fingers.

"He was sitting right there where you are. He told me not to be afraid of . . . you know . . . that I'm going to die. I told him, 'I can't help but be scared.' He said to ask you what it's like over there . . . that you've been there."

I was taken aback. I wanted to hear more. "Tell me about you and your uncle. Were you close?"

"Well, I didn't think we were, but now I see that we were pretty close. He was upset when I left for war, but proud too because he had been a soldier himself. He died while I was overseas, so I never saw him again. It was good to see him sitting right there"—Albert lifted his hand and again gestured—"where you are, in that chair." We remained quiet, with me hoping that he would not circle back to his question. But then Albert repeated, "So what's it like?"

"I don't know . . . I mean I'm not sure," I answered.

"My uncle said you do, that you were there."

Intrigued, I asked, "What did he say, exactly?"

"He said you were there and know what it's like. I'm scared and don't know what's ahead, so tell me."

"Oh gosh, I never talk about it," I said, wishing I could avoid disclosing my near-death experience.

But then, again unlike his normal personality, Albert said, "It would mean a lot to me." Who could have refused?

I kept it brief, saying, "Something happened to me after surgery and I stopped breathing. I just know what it was like for me, but it could be different for you."

"I'd like to hear about it," he persisted.

"I rose into a tent of pure golden light. Only good was over there . . . love and acceptance . . . that sort of thing. No pain or suffering of any kind."

"Okay," he said, smiling, willing to let the subject drop.

I was relieved to be off the hook, but I was fascinated by an apparition giving Albert such private information about me. "What did your uncle look like?" I asked.

"My uncle," he answered, tilting his head to the side.

"I mean, was he younger or older than you remembered, or different in some way?"

"No, he was exactly the same except he was so bright that I was wishing I'd had my sunglasses on. He told me I had nothing to fear."

"Do you believe him?" I asked.

"I'm beginning to," he said with an affirmative nod.

Terminally ill patients commonly experience pre-death encounters as their departure time grows near; therefore, hospice staff take note and increase the frequency of their visits. I began going to Albert's home twice every week wherein he described several visitations with his deceased wife. Then, on the Friday after Christmas, I noticed Albert was casting a certain countenance—a remarkable peace, calm, and joy. Once we were left to ourselves, he whispered, "I got a late present. Grandma. She was here. I forgot what that kind of love was like. She stood at the foot of my bed with her hands reached out for mine. She wanted me to go with her."

"Are you about ready?" I whispered in return.

Albert grinned. "Just about," he answered, nodding. He asked me to stay until nightfall. I did.

Dawn was yet to break when Albert's daughter called. "Dad just died!" she exclaimed. "I mean, he just up and went! He walked to the door of the family room and blew me a kiss. My husband and I watched him toddle on back to his room, and then we looked at each other and got up running. But by the time we got back there, Dad was already in bed, dead. We still can't believe he just up and went like that. He stayed in control the whole time. He did it exactly the way he wanted to. He did it his way." Indeed. Albert died in character—quietly and with those who loved him most.

I have never sat with a dying patient who was not in the accompaniment of an apparition as their time grew near. *No one ever dies alone.*

"It was the hand of God."—Babe's Story

Dying of lung cancer, Babe requested a visit from one of the hospice chaplains. As I entered her home, she motioned for me to sit next to her on the sofa so I could hear her whispers. Propped up on pillows, she struggled to utter, "Dianne . . . what will God do with an old sinner like me? I've never been to church. After my husband walked out, I worked two jobs on the docks just to buy food and clothes for my kids and put a roof over their heads. I had no time for myself or anything except my family. I started smoking before I knew better, and ran wild for a spell too. What will happen to me when I die?" Before collapsing into her pillows, Babe held on to ask, "God knows that I never meant no harm to nobody, but what does He do with folks like me?"

As she lay staring at me, I kept thinking, *You did the best you could.* Finally, she raised one hand only a bit, and pointing a finger my way she forced out the words, "You know . . . I did the best I could."

Over the next few weeks, we talked a great deal. Babe's sense of humor and inner strength were much larger than her five foot body, which was weakening rapidly. "I have to live until next month because my son will be home from Holland," she wheezed. But her surviving until then did not seem possible, and in fact, I was called to her side the next day. Babe was actively dying, and no one expected her to make it through the evening.

Early the following morning, I was once again summoned to her home. "Dianne! Hurry! Come here!" a hearty voice exclaimed as I entered the door. I could hardly believe my ears and eyes—it was Babe. Speaking with ease, she began, "In the middle of the night I felt my lungs collapse. I tried so hard to catch my breath, but I couldn't. I knew that was *it*, but I hadn't seen my son yet, so I started yelling for help, not out loud, you know. I was begging, 'Please, please, oh please, I can't die yet.' Then, I saw something right here," she gestured to her left side. "A giant hand appeared, went under my back, and lifted me up, underneath my lungs. A big whiff of air went in, like this," she gasped in demonstration. "The hand kept pushing my back up and then letting it go back down again until I started breathing on my own. It was the hand of God. He saved me. He granted my dying wish," she said, pausing to smile. "God knows that I lived the best life that I could, and now I know that He will welcome me home."

Stabilized for several weeks, Babe was able to visit with her son after his arrival from Amsterdam. In her final few days, she visited with her dearly beloved discarnate grandmother who, she said, anxiously waited. With her earthly and celestial family gathered around, Babe died peacefully.

Life-Continuing Transitions

Pre-death encounters facilitate the dying as they make their transition to the other world. Life-continuing visions help the living continue in this one.

Life brings many transitions. During these periods, life-continuing encounters offer comfort, love, encouragement, guidance, or help in some way. They can be congratulatory, occurring during weddings, baptisms, and other celebrations. Similarly, AEs bring meaningful support during rites of passage, as J. R. testified.

"It's one of the greatest things."—Story by J. R. May

Amanda, the younger of my two sisters, died during the summer of 2000 after becoming ill with a bacterial infection. Since then, our family has had many supernatural encounters with what we believe to be Amanda communicating with us. The one that remains the most special to me was on the morning of my audition to Houston's High School for the Performing and Visual Arts.

I was taking a shower and thinking how greatly my life would be altered if I went to this school. I wanted to be an actor and get a great education, so going there would be a tremendous opportunity if I could get accepted as one of the 30 theater students. I knew about the school because both of my sisters had gone there—Amanda for dance, Meredith for art. "It's one of the greatest things that could've happened to me," I remembered each of them saying.

Then, as I was walking back to my bedroom, I saw a white rose lying on the carpet as though it had been carefully placed in the doorway. Immediately I recognized that this was not normal and yelled for my mom and dad, who came running. We debated where the rose had come from and how it got there. My mom was sure it had not been in the hallway when she entered my room to wake me a few minutes earlier. The cats were still asleep on the beds, and no one had been in Amanda's room where some dried flowers were displayed on a high shelf out of the cats' reach. This flower was not dried, but it wasn't fresh either. My mom, dad, and I stood in the hallway and puzzled over the situation, finally deciding that the rose had to be a message of good luck from Amanda, since there seemed no earthly way for it to have found its way to my door.

Since then my parents and I have read that white roses are traditionally a token of love and good luck, so I guess Amanda was just letting me know she was with me that day. I was accepted and am currently a sophomore, continuing our family tradition of attending the High School for the Performing and Visual Arts. And the flower? It's in a small glass display case in my room to remind me that my sister isn't all that far away.

A transitional period can carry one overriding emotion, such as regret, sadness, excitement, or jubilation. It usually, however, presents a host of emotional flavors—boredom, anticipation, curiosity, and more, as Garry chronicled in his survey.

"She was preparing me."—Garry Roonan from Australia

My sweetheart died in 1993. I started to have spiritual communication with her six years later. I would think about her, and then notice coincidences happening around me. For example, I'd turn the radio on and her favorite song would be playing or I'd pick up a phone book, open it, and her name would appear in big letters. I always felt her love, getting goose bumps and tingling from head to toe, and incredible emotions hit me—nice feelings, not sad. Finally, I started hearing her in my thoughts and wondered if it was my imagination, until I got a very special sign, a confirmation that it was real. One night I was bored, so I went downstairs. I picked up a book, opened it at random, and directly before me in big letters were the words *Garry, I love you.* I looked at the title and discovered the book was about spiritual communication.

I began writing our encounters in a journal, because the information she gave me often came true later, especially in relation to her family. For example, she'd tell me they were at a particular place for a holiday, then I'd get a letter from her mum telling me exactly what my love had said. She has told me where things were around the house, in books and magazines. One time she said, "Garry, I can see a white dog in the book in the lounge room near the TV," so I went and had a look. It was there. She guided me to see the picture of a policeman in the newspaper that was rolled up on the kitchen sink, and then a ball in the passageway, and other specific items. I had never seen any of the things prior to her telling me, but they're always exactly where she said they were. As soon as I find them, I feel her energy straightaway.

I told my mum about my encounters, but I don't think she believed me. A short time later she had a stroke, and then I realized that was part of the reason I began to have the experiences. My sweetheart was preparing me for what was about to happen. Late one night she said, "Your grandmother is going to show your mother how beautiful this place is." Mum passed away shortly after on February 2, 2000 (my birthday).

Over the last three years, I have kept journals containing every spiritual sign and communication I have had. I believe they have helped sharpen my spiritual awareness. Doors continue to open for me, and I am blessed to experience the Otherside in so many ways. It's amazing—how aware we can become if we pay attention to what's happening around us. You start seeing your purpose unfold before you! It's nice to be able to inspire and bring comfort to others through my experiences. Life and love are eternal, as I have found out for myself in a very special way.

Garry's encounters occurred under many circumstances— when he was bored, curious, excited, sleeping, reflecting upon his love, lost in doing something, and so on. Regardless, each sighting helped him with a life-continuing transition, the loss of his beloved mother.

Whether encounters transpire to assist the dying or living, they occur during transitions. Akin to when they occur is why, which we will explore next.

The Purpose for Afterlife Encounters

At the heart of afterlife encounters lies one primary purpose—growth. As catalysts, apparitions manifest for the growth of everyone involved, as Jessica Wood's visual encounter with her brother, Justin, illustrated.

"He just stood there while she poured her heart out."—Mary Wood's Survey

My 13-year-old son left this earth on April 4, 2002. Jessica, my 18-year-old daughter, was very upset because she didn't tell Justin she loved him the last time she saw him. They said "I love you" all of the time. Those two really had some knockdown drag-outs when they were young, but they quickly grew out of it. Justin would do anything for Jessica. If she were lying in the sun, he would get the radio, plug it in for her, and ask if she wanted something to drink. I think our subconscious tells us to love and be close to certain people.

The second night after Justin was killed in an automobile accident, Jessica was lying in her bed. It was about two A.M. when he came to her, totally illuminated and completely dressed in green. He just stood there with a serene look on his face while she poured her heart out to him. She cried, and told him she loved him and how very special he was. He knew what great pain she was in and had come to her one last time.

Jessica and I talked about how Justin loved finding four-leaf clovers, which he did anytime he tried, right up until he left this world. I told her she should always remember that experience because they send us peace and love from up above. If we are believing, we will be lucky enough to have this peace. Maybe the verse "Seek and you shall find" from the Bible applies to these experiences.

Grief support requires a strong presence, which Justin provided. Jessica's encounter brings to light another point—the Otherworld is far more enlightened than ours. "I'm afraid I'll cry if I see him," and "I don't want to make her feel sad," people often say while thinking about possible encounters with their deceased loved ones. Apparitions welcome tears or anything that will serve our highest good. Their purpose is to help us grow, and externalizing our emotions fosters growth, as Jo Ann Thomas, former director for a grief center in New York, testified.

"And then I wept."—Story by Jo Ann Thomas

Shortly after my husband Bob died from cancer, I was advised that attending an Elisabeth Kübler-Ross workshop would help me understand and deal with my emotions. During the first three days, I learned many things about

myself and why I had a hard time expressing my feelings—
I was never allowed to during my childhood. Instead of
experiencing emotions, I stuffed them deep down inside.

Then, on the fourth day, Elisabeth came in to teach us.
I was mesmerized. What a fascinating woman. So simple,
yet so profound. The lessons she taught were pure—about
feelings, about losses that are like little deaths to us when
we are very young, and about unconditional love, the kind
that is giving, caring, and doesn't hurt.

It was late afternoon when Elisabeth asked, "How
many of you hate your mother-in-law?" I was the first one
with my hand up, and if I could have mustered the nerve,
I would have stood on my chair to make sure she saw me.
"I want you to go home and make amends with your
mother-in-law," Elisabeth said with her Swiss accent, pointing her finger at me. *Is she kidding or what?* I thought. "I
had the worst mother-in-law in the world," I shouted out.
But Elisabeth repeated, "You're to go home and make
amends with her."

"I can't. She's dead! And I'm glad, because she was a
mean woman," I exclaimed proudly, taking all the credit
for disliking her so much.

Elisabeth kept talking, "I don't care how bad she was,
you must make amends with her or you'll suffer for not
forgiving her when you die." I could tell that she meant
every word she was saying. Nevertheless, I asked sarcasti-
cally, "What do you mean, I'll suffer? How could she possibly make me suffer after I die?"

I was having my first confrontation with the great
Death and Dying Lady, as Elisabeth was known after her
book *On Death and Dying* became an international best-
seller. I didn't know that I had it in me to speak up that
way, but she made it so easy by talking about my mother-
in-law—a subject that I knew a lot about and felt very
strongly about.

"If you don't forgive her, you won't learn unconditional love, and that's one of your lessons here on earth.
We're all here to learn to love unconditionally. You need
to forgive those who hurt you before you die—that's your
unfinished business."

I still wasn't buying it. "How can I forgive my mother-in-law when she's dead?" I asked. "There's no way. And you just don't understand—she really was a mean person. Anyway, I can't forgive her because her children cremated her and I don't know where they scattered her ashes. Even if I did, who knows where she landed!"

Some of the participants were chuckling at my remarks, supporting me. But that made Elisabeth even stronger. "No, *you* don't understand!" she said sternly. "You need to forgive her! Listen to me, I just planted some mums outside the center this morning. Take some of them and go anywhere you like to forgive her. She'll hear you." I squinted my eyes, trying to think of an answer, but before I could speak she jumped in, saying, "Oh, are my mums too nice for her? Then go down to my farm and find some wildflowers. Just do it," she said, and waved me away. She was done with me. And I was glad too!

All night long, I thought about what Elisabeth had said. I had gotten the message—I needed to forgive my mother-in-law. I was determined that Bob's mother was not going to cause me more pain in this lifetime, and she was not going to disrupt my peace in the hereafter. According to Elisabeth, I could settle it right here, right now.

It was 5 A.M., the last day of the workshop, and I was off, walking down the road toward Elisabeth's farm. I looked at the wildflowers as she suggested, but nothing seemed right for my mother-in-law. Suddenly I spotted a bunch of black, thorny, dead flowers on the bank of Healing Waters stream. I slid down the hill, reached the bottom, and immediately knew they were it—those awful things were just what I needed. I pulled them out of the ground and held them up like a bright, shiny trophy. "This is definitely them," I said aloud and started back to the center.

While walking up the gravel road, I carefully studied the old, dried-up flowers in my hand. There were many thorns sticking out of the stems, and I felt each one represented how many times I had been hurt. *Yep, these have a lot of meaning to me*, I thought as I carefully put them in the trunk of my car for the trip home, never thinking about how I was going to use them to settle my unfinished business with my mother-in-law.

The day after I arrived home I took the ugly, dead clump of whatever-they-were to Bob's grave and told him, "I don't know how to get to your mother except through you." I apologized to him for the hurt she had brought him during his life. Because he remained the only link I had to her, I stuck the dead things into the ground next to his headstone. I then started repeating all of the awful things she said to me over the years and how much her words hurt. Pouring out my anger, resentment, frustration, and other emotions, I stayed there. Finally, when out of words, I finished with, "I don't know what happened to you in your life to make you so miserable, but all of a sudden I feel sorry for you. You lived such a sad life." And then I wept—for her.

As I drove out of the cemetery, I sensed her with me, in the back seat of my car. I slammed on the brakes and looked around but saw no one. I glanced up, thinking I might see her above me but nothing was there either. Then, I felt something being taken off my back, as if she was removing a very heavy coat. I know what I felt, but wondered, *Am I going crazy?* I didn't understand what happened, but I was sure something unique took place.

It wasn't until several weeks later that I realized—the feeling of the heavy overcoat being lifted off my back was my mother-in-law lifting the weight that I had been carrying toward her. For all those years, I had been holding onto negativity, hate, and resentment, carrying around all those feelings, that old unfinished business, without ever realizing it. And now I'm free.

While facilitating Elisabeth Kübler-Ross workshops, participants frequently disclosed their AEs to me. Deanna's was remarkable because it exemplified growth for everyone involved, including the discarnate. A decade later, she chronicled her episode for you, but changed several names for privacy.

"You must find them for me."—Story by Deanna Dubé

British actor Andrew Markham starred in a television series that aired in the 1960s. Although the show was very popular, it was yanked from the airwaves after two short seasons. Following the program's demise, Andrew returned to the stage, where he did his best work.

Good theater in Los Angeles is rare, so when Andrew brought his award-winning production to town during the late seventies, I just had to see it. I begged my mother for two tickets so my friend Susan and I could go as my sixteenth birthday present.

Our seats, third row center, were wonderful, and the play was exceptional. After the last curtain call, we hurried backstage to see if we could meet our hero and get his autograph, but we were stopped by the stage guard, "Are you with the show?" he asked. Susan and I thought he was asking if we had come from the show, so we nodded yes. He waved us on to the creaky old elevator that took us up to the stage level, where Andrew's dressing room was located.

When the elevator doors opened, there stood the handsome award-winning star, staring down at us. We were absolutely tongue-tied and said nothing as he excused himself to get on while we got off. I turned around as the doors were closing and put my hand on my chest, murmuring "Oh," in disappointment at a chance lost. Andrew was looking right at me, but Susan and I were just too shy and intimidated to speak. We turned to each other, wanting to kick ourselves for our severe lack of spines.

Just then, the director of the play saw us. He must have seen Andrew pass us and realized our disappointment; therefore, he arranged for us to meet his leading lady, another well-known stage actor. While we waited for her to emerge from her dressing room, the elevator "pinged" its arrival and out walked Andrew Markham. He smiled and walked directly toward us. "Hello," he said in his whisky-rich baritone voice. "Did you enjoy the show?" Neither of us could believe our good fortune—that he was there with us.

Afterward, with our programs signed and our heads filled with memories of a short but sweet conversation with someone we greatly admired, Susan and I wandered to the restaurant next door. The headwaiter doubted that he could find a table for us without reservations, but then he suddenly asked, "You're from the play?" We thought he was asking if we had come from the theater, so we nodded yes. He sat us at the show's table, along with the entire cast! They must have wondered what we were doing amongst them, but they couldn't have been nicer.

It was such a comedy of errors, but what struck me odd was that Andrew was sitting off to the other side of the room all alone. With a drink in hand and cigarette in the other, he stared off into space. I watched him for a moment or two and then his eyes met mine. I was absolutely struck by the loneliness I saw there. It was almost embarrassingly intimate. He held my gaze so long that it was as if he knew all my thoughts. Someone once said you can live a lifetime in a moment and that is exactly what it felt like—we shared a lifetime in that moment.

But fickle youth made me soon forget him, as I exchanged my affections for a series of rock stars as life went on. I didn't think about Andrew for years and, even when he came to town in other plays, I never saw him again.

It was the mid-90s, and I was in the breakroom with my coworkers reading the morning paper, trying to solve the problems of the world over coffee. I flipped over the page of the *Los Angeles Times* I was scanning and saw Andrew Markham's face starring back at me in the obituary section. Tears sprang to my eyes. I was amazed by the sudden and intense wave of grief I felt for his passing. I ripped the article out of the paper and excused myself to go to the restroom, where I bawled like a baby.

For a few days I felt as if I had lost a dear friend or family member. I couldn't understand the reaction as I had only met the man once, nearly 20 years ago. Why did his passing affect me so deeply? As a psychology hobbyist, I chalked it up as latent mourning for the death of my childhood dreams, and I felt better once I rationalized it as such. After putting Andrew in his place in my psyche, I moved on with my full and active life and didn't give it much more thought.

A year later, I was in the middle of a family medical crisis. It was also tax season. Since I was an accountant for a property management company, the first three months of every year were always a torturous blur of long hours, no days off, and gallons of coffee. So that, coupled with my mother's illness, made for a very stressful time—the worst time ever for a ghost to come and haunt me.

Similar to Haley Joel Osment's character in *The Sixth Sense*, I had childhood experiences with spooks (as I call them), and now I started feeling the presence of one again. I noticed lights flickering, cold and hot spots in my home, and a touch on my shoulder when no one was around. I was so busy with Mom and work that I tried my best to tune it out. It was just going to have to get an afterlife without me, because my energy was spent. My plate was just too full. But it had other ideas. A cup bounced off the counter, then my coffee pot overflowed for no reason. My cats stared off into space, then suddenly hissed and fluffed up their fur, running from the room.

Late one night, after a particularly exhausting day at work, I was home caring for Mother when my favorite framed photos fell off the wall. Exasperated, I demanded that the culprit show himself so I could have some peace and quiet. That was all it took. The apparition of a very tired and very old man formed in the corner. It took me a while to recognize that it was Andrew Markham.

"What do you want of me?" I asked.

"I need your help," he said. "You must find Jackie Sands and Emily Howe and tell them I'm all right. Please, please help me! It's imperative that they know I'm all right." I took a deep breath and agreed to do what I could. And so began a year I will never forget.

As the weeks went by, through dreams, I learned much about Andrew's life—things I had not previously known because he was a notoriously private man. Many gossip columnists tried to dig into his personal life, but came up empty because his friends were extremely protective of his privacy. Even the women he dated never offered kiss-and-tell stories after their relationships ended. But it was as if I suddenly had a window into his life, as he had lived it on earth. I saw moments of his impoverished childhood in Wales and his need to better himself. I heard him changing his speech patterns to appear highborn. As his fame grew, he easily moved within the circles of royal society.

Finally, Andrew's spirit announced that he would go, but he wanted me to keep looking for his friends and tell them his messages. He had been a devout Catholic, afraid of going to hell, and he wanted to make sure they knew he was fine. I promised to do that. He asked if there was something he could do for me. Jokingly, I said, "You can get me your old television series on videotape! I'd like to see it again." Just then, a beautiful shaft of light entered the room. Andrew walked into it, and then both disappeared. I was happy for his crossing over, but sad too. He had been my companion for weeks, and I enjoyed his presence in my life and had grown because of him.

Two months went by and I stumbled upon a group of people on the Internet devoted to Andrew's old television show. I started to correspond with them. Katie was particularly fun to talk with about Andrew as well as other subjects. About two weeks after I joined their group, she e-mailed me with delightfully shocking news. She wrote, "I dreamed that Andrew came and told me that I must make copies of his television show for you and to say it was a gift from him!" Katie had taped nearly all the rerun episodes from cable in the late 1980s before it was taken off the air.

Then other ladies in the group began to mention that they were suddenly contacted by Andrew in dreams and odd synchronicities. Even though Andrew would never come to me as strongly as he did in those first days, I occasionally heard his voice out of the blue urging me to find his friends. He was so insistent, always saying, "You must find them for me," almost nagging at times.

As more months went by, I tried to find Jackie and Emily on the Internet, but nothing came up. Andrew gave me the areas where they lived but no further information. Finally, one autumn day, I used a new search engine and typed in *Jackie Sands*. Up came an obscure post she had made on someone's web site and an e-mail address. I wrote her, explaining that I was curious to know if she was a friend of Andrew Markham and that I had some information about him that she might be interested in.

Five minutes later, she wrote back confirming that she had been his friend. I briefly and somewhat cryptically mentioned that I had something to tell her that was unusual—messages to deliver. Jackie asked me to call her, which led to our talking for three hours over the phone. She was excited by what I passed on to her from Andrew, saying she knew it was him without a doubt and confirmed every word he had told me. She even said, "He nags you now the way he used to nag everyone else when he wanted them to do something." Emily was scheduled to fly in from London in a few weeks, so Jackie invited me to meet them for lunch.

Emily was guarded when I arrived at the restaurant, but she warmed up when she realized I wasn't just another fan of Andrew Markham's. I told her what I had come to say, and she was at peace with it. She confirmed that Andrew was terrified of death and worried that he was going to hell. He had lived a full life and wasn't a saint. For him, the end was particularly traumatic because a priest visited him daily to administer confession for sins of the past and to ease his mind. But Andrew was so sure hell was coming that he couldn't find peace. I assured Emily that he was pleasantly surprised when he crossed over because he discovered hell didn't even exist! I also gave her some private messages, meant only for her and Jackie. They both laughed when I told them how I had gotten video copies of his old series. "Just like Andrew . . ." Jackie said, smiling, "always promoting his work!"

Before I left, Emily asked why Andrew didn't come to her since she was his best and dearest friend. I had asked Andrew that very question early on into his visitations. "Why me?" He said it was because I showed him compassion long ago. It was then that I remembered the moment in the restaurant when I felt his profound loneliness. I also explained to Emily that sometimes the dead choose people totally unrelated to their family to deliver messages because the family members might think they were just imagining the visits in their grief. "You know," she said, "just after Andrew died, I was walking out of church and begged him to give me a sign that he was all right. I suddenly heard the sound of something metallic hitting the ground behind me. I turned and saw a few pennies. No one was near me, but there were pennies! Andrew was a notorious penny-pincher during his life, so that had to be a sign from him raining down pennies from heaven for me!" I smiled, and on the long drive home I hummed the song, "There'll be pennies from Heaven for you and me."

Beyond illustrating that encounters foster growth for everyone involved, including the discarnate entities, Deanna's story demonstrated a number of other aspects. Apparitions carry their own agendas, offer something unique for each person affected, and are not necessarily created by longing or desire. It brings up the issue of pennies, common findings among the bereaved. Most find the coins face up, displaying the words IN GOD WE TRUST.

"Tell my parents Michael said pennies."
—A Message for the Zimmermans

"Wait . . . a young man just came in," said Theresa Marie, a medium I was interviewing for an upcoming research project. "He says 'Michael'. . . to tell you 'Michael . . . you don't know me . . . you talked to my parents a few days ago.' He says, 'Pennies . . . lots and lots of pennies. Tell my parents Michael said pennies . . . lots of them . . . everywhere . . . all the time . . . pennies.' Do you know who he's talking about?"

"No," I answered, "I don't think so. I spoke with two parents on Wednesday, and they mentioned their son. Actually, their exact words were, 'He brings us pennies . . . lots of them, everywhere, all the time.' But his name was not Michael."

"Can you check with them and call me back?" asked Theresa. "Michael said this is his way of proving that he contacted them through you."

Marilyn and Fred Zimmerman had introduced themselves to me over the telephone when they called from North Carolina. During our conversation, they mentioned, "We find pennies all the time, lots and lots of pennies, everywhere, and we know they're from our son Eric." Because their son's name was not Michael, I did not believe Theresa Marie's statements applied to them. Her specific words, however, were almost identical to theirs. After several days of thinking about it, I e-mailed Theresa's comments to the couple. Their reply: "That was our son—Eric *Michael* Zimmerman. See what we mean? He does that all the time."

Everyone involved received what they needed. Theresa Marie felt validated by hearing that she was correct, Fred and Marilyn were delighted to receive the message through a third party, especially since I did not know Eric's full name, and their response was fuel for me to continue in the field.

The need for an encounter can be far greater than life-enhancing, as Diane Botti pointed out. Diane and I met during a research project at the University of Nevada. Her humor, honesty, and sincerity were as refreshing as a blast of north wind in the Las Vegas desert, so I was thrilled when we continued working together at the National Institute for Discovery Science (NIDS). Cancer eventually stole Diane from the institute, but not from life. She chronicled her illness and encounter.

"You're going to be just fine."—Diane Botti's Story

From the time I was a small child, I spent most of my time with my grandmother. My parents divorced when I was four years old, so my mom and I moved in with my grandma. My mom had to work so Grandma was the person I was closest to. We had a very special bond. She would often hold me on her lap and sing hymns to me. Grandma would care for me when I would get sick, rubbing my chest with Mentholatum, fixing peppermint tea for my upset stomach, and boiling water with a drop of eucalyptus oil to make it easier for me to breathe. She had a nice home with a beautiful garden, where she taught me how to grow carrots from seed and care for flowers.

Grandma had a license to sell real estate and took me on her many journeys selling homes in the San Fernando Valley, California area—when it was mostly lemon trees, and orange, walnut, and avocado groves. I can still smell the fragrances as I recall the beauty of the Valley back then, before it was developed. I adored my grandma and was her shadow. She always called me her "little lady."

I must have been about seven or eight when a man came to our home and sold Grandma on some kind of aluminum siding job he said she needed. After thinking it over, Grandma changed her mind, so she called the man and told him she didn't want the work done. Apparently he must have argued with her, saying his men would be there in the morning to start the job, because she said, "If they show, I'll meet them at the gate with a gun!" I asked, "Grandma, do you have a gun?" She giggled and said, "No, but they don't know that!" I anxiously waited for the showdown the next morning wondering what my grandma would do if they came. No one ever showed up! What a fine lesson I learned from Grandma.

On February 22, 1997, I found a lump in my breast. It startled me. I made up my mind that it was coming out no matter what. I saw my family doctor, who didn't say much. He just sent me for a mammogram. I told him that I was frightened and he very calmly said, "Don't be." So, as usual, I carried on, had the mammogram, and didn't think much more of it. But then my doctor's office called at work and summoned me to come in immediately. Well, I knew when I got that call I was in trouble. And yes, I was very frightened.

My doctor gave me the bad news and introduced me to a general surgeon, whom I didn't like. So I went back to work and found a doctor that specialized in breast health. I'll never forget the calm voice on the other end of the phone: "We care about your breasts." That was it for me. I saw that doctor, a surgeon, who worked with a team that included an oncologist and a plastic surgeon. It turned out that the lump that I had found didn't show up on X rays, but a second lump was sitting against my chest wall. I was scheduled for a biopsy on March 27, 1997, and afterward, in the recovery room, the doctor told me that the lumps were malignant. Although he said I could spend the night in the hospital, I elected to go home to my own bed and my dog and cat. Guess I needed some very unconditional love at that moment in time.

Three days later I was back at the surgeon's office; he had by this time consulted with the oncologist. The oncologist told me that I needed to have chemotherapy as soon as possible. That was a blow. I was crying, but I had the presence of mind to review my pathology report and get a very detailed explanation of *why* it was absolutely necessary to undergo such a harsh form of chemotherapy. My oncologist literally drew me a chart, which left no room for doubt that the chemotherapy, followed by radiation, was necessary. He said that all of my hair would fall out, but that I would thank him in five years. Right then I didn't feel thankful for much of anything. I was bandaged, had tubes running out of my body, didn't know how much of my breast was left, and my almost waist-length blond hair was going to be falling out.

When I left the doctor's office with my first appointment for chemotherapy scheduled in three weeks, I knew I had to prepare for the journey I was about to embark on. I turned my attitude to one of "Don't count me out yet" and that became my mantra. I spoke it out loud as often as possible. Dianne asked me if she could assist with any type of visualization and I'd already chosen (but not shared with anyone) the cancer as sand being cleansed by water. So our visualization was one of the ocean washing the sand clean. I also decided to view the chemotherapy as the "golden elixir of life." I had my hair trimmed to just above my shoulders, then prepared myself for treatment.

All of my hair fell out three weeks after the first bout with chemo, so I bought wigs—a red one, long curly brown one, and the other was blond. I was having fun! My dearest friend, Vicky, came to take care of me. We had shared our most joyous and difficult life experiences together, and now she was putting her life on hold and helping pull me through. She drove me to my treatments, encouraged me, helped me put sod down in my back yard, and her daughter trimmed off the funny little hairs that were being pushed out of my head. I had chemotherapy treatments on Friday mornings, then couldn't choke any food down until about Monday evening.

I was fortunate enough to have a kind and generous employer who let me work in the library at NIDS between my treatments. I'm sure I got the better of the deal, because I found such peace being surrounded by the books Dianne had chosen for the library. It was indeed a very special time. I literally loved those books, and I loved that library, not to mention that I was lucky enough to be around some of the most kind and brilliant people I've ever met in my entire life, and perhaps in the entire universe!

My mother brought me a beautiful picture of Jesus knocking on a door, which I framed and hung on the wall opposite from my bed. I studied that picture and thought of all the Bible stories I had learned as a child. While I was enjoying the picture of Jesus, I spent a lot of time silently communicating with God between treatments, which were 21 days apart.

By the third treatment, I started to become very ill. The antinausea medication wasn't working, so I was throwing up the chemicals from my system. I was in the bathroom, choking, and couldn't breathe. Vicky came in and held me up, saying, "Breathe . . . breathe." She reassured me (again) that I'd be all right. After she put me back in bed and I was alone, it hit me that I just might not make it. In fact, I felt very weak and near death.

I looked at the picture of Jesus, feeling concerned for my son, Matt, whom I had been unable to be near. I didn't want to leave him. Then suddenly a wave of peace came over me, bringing me the knowledge and awareness that my loved ones would be okay without me. I completely surrendered to God and quietly communicated that whatever the outcome—to continue this life or pass on—I was at peace with whatever He had designed for me. I felt the truest sense of peace I have ever felt, like a baby in the hand of God. I drifted off to sleep.

Sometime during this nap, my grandmother very vividly came to me. She was holding me, stroking my arm as she did when I was a child and was comforting me, orally reassuring me, "You're going to be just fine." When I first awoke I knew this was not a dream. Grandma's presence was so strong I looked around the room for her. I could feel her. I closed my eyes again. I could still feel her! I *knew* then that I was going to make it. Grandma erased all doubt. It became an extremely peaceful time in my life because, with my grandmother's comfort, I had *no* question whatsoever that I was going to be just fine. After that, I had one chemotherapy and 33 radiation treatments, which I faced with less combativeness because I had inside knowledge that no doctor was privy to. It has been six years and I'm doing great.

Diane's visit with her grandmother brought physical, mental, emotional, and spiritual healing. Akin to most encounters, it arose when she needed it most. Rosa, an international business person, presents another example.

"Remember the book in my room."—Rosa from Puerto Rico

I hope you understand what I am trying to write. I speak good in English, but I must think in Spanish to write it. So remember that my English it's not so good.

My daughter was born Alexandra Sucre Mendez. She was beautiful. We moved from Venezuela to Ft. Lauderdale, Florida, in 1995, then transferred to Miami. Through the years my daughter remained very Latin. She liked dancing and her friends. Alexandra was a party girl in the good way. She was an A student, even in premed at the university, and was planning to be a doctor. She loved community work with the elderly.

My company transferred me to Puerto Rico for two years, and although Alexandra moved with me, she never liked it here. So every month she went back to Florida. She was only 18 on the day of the accident. She went out with new friends and the driver was drunk. Their car fell into a canal and my daughter drowned. She was the only one hurt, and she was a good girl—too good to die like this.

But I know Alexandra knew she was going to die, because a week before the accident she asked me, "Mami, would you like to know how much time we have left to live?" Then the day before she left for Florida, she told me about an accident she had a year before and said, "Mami, don't worry about me going to Miami—just remember the book in my room." I happened to find the book and wondered, *Why was she interested in this?* It was written by a medium, but at the time I didn't know who he was or anything about such things as mediumship.

After Alexandra was killed, I began to read it and felt comforted by what it said. Maybe she meant to leave it as a message for me. I don't know. But I would love to help people like me, to give them hope. Without hope I would be dead by now from the pain of losing my Alexandra.

So now I have to tell you that I saw my daughter one Sunday. I was slipping, falling down to the ground, when I felt her take my hand. I looked up to see her looking at me. Her hand kept holding mine until I was solid on my feet and then she disappeared. It was so beautiful. That is not enough for a mother to stop grieving, but it gives me hope that I will see her again someday.

As well as meaningful and growth-promoting, encounters are always spiritually correct, as Carol Poole points out in her book *Shared Blessings* (in progress).

"Mother, I Love you!"—by Carol Poole

Those on the other side are keenly attuned to our stages of the healing process. They seem to know what we need and just when we need to receive it. Guess you might call them "spiritually correct." It is not surprising that my experience should occur in a bookstore, since my first message from my son John occurred in another bookstore, just days after his passing in 1990. Back then I was shopping for a list of self-help books recommended by friends, when a book fell from the shelf across the aisle from me. It was *We Don't Die: George Anderson's Conversations with the Other Side* [Martin, 1988]. When I saw it, I experienced what I have come to identify as a "still moment"—a brief moment of knowing beyond any doubt that you have a soul connection to the experience. For a few seconds nothing else exists except the truth of that moment, and you know it was meant just for you. Although it was my first experience with the feeling that would become so familiar over the years, I knew instantly that it was a message from John. That "still moment" with George Anderson's book was the beginning of the profound healing blessings John continues to share from the other side. Following is the account of a message I received from John six years thereafter.

I was strolling along the metaphysical section of a used bookstore, which consisted of a three-sided alcove, barely large enough for two people. I scanned all the shelves and finally settled for a book on the bottom shelf. Nobody else was in that section, so I sat on the floor to read. After a few minutes, I decided the book wasn't interesting, so I replaced it and stood up to leave. As I arose, I saw a bright yellow Post-it note sticking out at my eye level. It was stuck on the edge of the shelf in front of the herb books. I knew it wasn't there before I sat down, because the bright, new yellow stood out in sharp contrast to the old used books. I also knew that no one else had been in that section. I felt a still moment emerging as I reached for it, and then I read the following message:

Mother,

I Love you!

I'm thinking of you!

Thanks for your (a drawing of a heart appeared here) *notes*

(Then the drawing of a butterfly concluded.)

There are many facets to this note. Although it was not in John's handwriting, it was printed by an adult, exactly as it appears above, including the exclamation points and the capital L in love. And herbs—the shelf where the Post-it was attached—was one of John's interests! Many times there is a touch of humor in his messages, and this one is no exception. I was working on my book, *Shared Blessings,* and wrote that I never received messages in the form of butterflies or rainbows because they were too subtle for me to recognize, but then I found this one signed with a butterfly.

John's messages have always been spiritually correct—arriving at just the right time and place to bring healing to my shattered heart. If I had found the Post-it back in 1990, when my wounds were so raw, it might have exacerbated my grief instead of having a healing effect. By 1996, however, I was far enough along in my grief process, and comfortable enough with receiving messages, that it was a meaningful and positive experience.

John dropped in to say he loved me, and I was elated. His messages always bring me great joy, peace, and healing, along with the feeling of being spiritually connected to him by a bond that can never be broken. Thank you, John.

Adam Wilk experienced an indirect encounter, which further verified that growth and spiritual appropriateness are aspects of AEs.

"He's always around you."
—Adam Wilk from New York

"Do you follow any particular religion?" asked Marcy, my newfound friend.

"Not really," I answered. "I was raised Jewish, but my parents were never super religious. My grandfather was more observant. He died last summer and I miss him. He gave me his car, but some thieves stole it about a month ago when I forgot to lock her up for the night. It was painful to lose Grandpa and his gift too."

"He's always around you," Marcy said. "You know that, right?"

"Oh man, Marcy," I said, leaning back in my chair. "You're not one of *those* people are you?"

"You mean one of those spiritual people?" she retorted. "Yes I am, as a matter of fact."

"So my grandfather is always around me, huh?" I mocked her, grinning.

"Don't do that, please," Marcy begged.

"I'm sorry. I didn't mean to be nasty. But look, you know there's really no scientific proof of all that stuff, right?"

"You'd be amazed at what you can see and feel if you raise your awareness and open your mind to it," she answered.

The whole notion of life after death was totally foreign to me and struck me as being extremely peculiar. It defied the common sense and logic laws that I lived by, but I was enjoying Marcy's company so I listened. She was born and raised a Catholic, but sought other means of spiritual enlightenment. She knew about other religions, including my own. "Jesus was Jewish, you know?" she asked, smiling.

"Yeah, I know, but I don't get any of that stuff anyway. I'm not supposed to believe in him, but no one ever told me why. It's crazy, the whole thing," I opined.

Marcy wanted to help me understand there was more to life than what our five senses take in daily. She seemed to know her way of believing could be comforting and soothing to someone in mourning—someone like me. But then she handed me a minuscule Bible. I looked at it for a couple of seconds, then became annoyed. "Just put it in your shirt pocket close to your heart and shut up," she advised. "What do you have to lose?"

"I must be out of my mind to listen to you," I countered. "I can't believe this. I'm going to hell—you know that, right? I'm going to Jew hell for this," I bellowed as I put her Bible in my pocket, the one that covered my nervous heart. "Do you think my grandpa would be pissed off at me for including Jesus in my prayers?" I asked.

"I don't know the answer to that, Adam," she said. "Why don't you ask him? Ask him all the questions you have. Ask him for help."

"What? I'm going to go to the cemetery and talk to a lifeless tombstone? I should go and get on my knees and pray and cry just like they do in the movies? No way, man. Uh-uh," I said, shaking my head back and forth.

"Maybe you'll get some answers," Marcy pressed.

"Marcy, I pray to God and Jesus, and I talk to my grandfather once in a while, but I can't ask him for favors. That's crazy. And isn't it disrespectful?"

"Why do you think they're there—to help us, to teach us, to love us, and to guide us," Marcy said.

"I know. I know," I answered. "But come on, there's really not that much proof that they hear us or that they can even do things for us Earthlings anyway. I mean, Marcy—fair's fair. Come on now."

"You have to believe," she said. "You have to try. Go talk to him. He'll hear you. I promise."

It was cloudy the morning I awoke with an undeniable heaviness in my heart. Ten years had passed since Grandpa had died. Marcy and I were still friends, and I had been thinking about her recommendations. I planned to visit my grandfather, but I knew it was going to be hard, just like all the times before. I took a long hot shower, got dressed, and headed out to Mt. Zion Cemetery.

My eyes, as usual, filled with tears as I passed through the gates—the gates to the final resting place of my dear grandfather. I hated the cemetery. It was so damn old and the roads leading in and out of the different sections were so narrow. Despite my dislike, I had managed to visit four or five times a year, telling him how much I missed him and how sorry I was that I lost his Malibu, but today I wanted to do something different. I wanted to see if asking Grandpa for help would prove useful. I planned to put forth some questions and ask his spirit for help and guidance. Marcy had told me that Grandpa was there to listen and help in his own way, and I wanted so badly to believe her, but I needed some proof—a shred of evidence.

I drove toward his final resting spot, parking my car on a small plot of land, unmarked and lifeless, eerily awaiting new arrivals. Silence hit me when I turned the engine off. As I walked toward my grandfather's plot, I realized how silly I was to have set the alarm in my car. Everybody around me was dead. Who was going to steal my car now? But I was still paranoid from ten years earlier, when I didn't lock Grandpa's Malibu.

I walked through rows of tombstones, staring at each name and wondered how that person had died. Some graves dated back to the 1920s and '30s; some were new. Some people had lived to a nice, ripe old age, but sadly, teenagers and babies were buried there as well.

I continued my journey to my Grandpa's tomb. A chill filled the air and the sky swelled with heavy rain clouds. An occasional speck of blue came through, giving the slightest bit of hint that the day could get better. Then there it was—part of Grandpa's name beckoning me from behind other headstones. Crying, I walked up to his space and squatted in front of his monument. I stared at the date of his death, chiseled into the marble, and remembered where I was and how I felt on that day so long ago. I still couldn't believe he had died, and I felt cheated all over again. So much time had passed, and so many things had happened to me that I never got to share with him. Balancing myself against his tombstone, I chuckled because this is just what I feared would happen—the scene seemed melodramatic, just like in the movies. I didn't want to be part of a ridiculous script, but here I was playing a role from my life's cinema.

I reached into my pocket and pulled out the little green Bible that Marcy had given me. Although I playfully waved it in front of my grandfather's stone, I hoped that if indeed he was there, he wasn't upset with me for having it. I began talking to him in my head, wishing he could hear. I was hoping that Marcy's beliefs about the afterlife held some meaning or truth.

"Hey Grandpa, it's me, Adam, your first grandchild. Well, actually, I'm not a child anymore. I hope you can see that I'm an adult now. I finally made it out of college. I hope you're proud of me. Grandma is still mad at me for losing your Malibu, no matter how many times I say I'm sorry. I wish I could communicate with you, Grandpa. I wish there was some way I could tell if you hear me or not. I miss you so much. I miss your kind words and your sense of humor, and most of all I really miss your advice. Marcy gave me this Bible and it has brought me lots of good luck when I carry it. Does that sound crazy or what?

I just feel comforted knowing that Jesus was very forgiving. Do you think Jesus would have forgiven me for losing your car? Or for not being a perfect person? Do you think God is angry with me because I'm a Jewish person and I talk to Jesus? I know I'm not supposed to, but I find Him comforting when I need help. Grandpa, I'm writing a book that I think is going to help so many people feel better inside and out. If I could just get someone to read what I've written. Can you help me, Grandpa? Can you help me get this book published? Can you tell me who I should pray to for help and guidance? Is it you? Is it God? Is it Jesus? I need you now more than ever to help me. I wish there was a way I could know if you're really here."

As I completed that last thought, a huge wave of emotion crashed on my shoulders and I began sobbing. I crawled on my knees, closer to his stone, and nestled the side of my face against the marble, crying aloud. I glanced out at the rows upon rows of tombstones and thought, *I'm sure many others have also longed to visit with their deceased loved ones just one last time.* I wiped my eyes and kissed my grandfather's headstone, then picked up a pebble nearby and put it on top—something my religion required me to do after visiting a deceased relative in a cemetery.

By the time I walked back to my car and sat down, I was drained. I tilted the seat back and closed my eyes, wanting to rest for a few minutes. But I underestimated how emotionally and physically exhausted I was, and the next thing I knew the sun's rays were dancing on my eyelids, waking me. A few minutes had turned into an hour or more. I felt refreshed from my nap, but more than that—I felt hopeful.

I sat up, turned the ignition on, and headed home. For the first time in a very long while, my mind was still. The quiet was nice, but then my cell phone rang,

"Hey Adam," Marcy began, "I have some real interesting news for you."

"I can't talk right now, Marcy. I'm driving."

"But I've got something good for you," she continued.

"Can't you wait ten minutes 'til I'm home?" I asked.

"This is very important," she insisted. "Pull over."

I relented and randomly turned onto a residential street and pulled my car in front of the first house.

"What is it?" I asked. "What's the matter?"

"Where were you, anyway?" Marcy inquired.

"I went to visit my grandfather and ask him for help, like you told me to. Now, what did you want to tell me?"

"Did you ask him for help with getting your book published?" she asked.

"Yes, Marcy. Now what do you want?" I asked.

"Guess who my mother just got off the phone with a second ago?" Marcy said. "Her friend from college decided out of the blue to call my mom. The friend's a published author, and she's looking for writers to submit stories for her next work."

I fell speechless.

"Adam? Are you still there?" Marcy asked.

"I don't believe what you're telling me, Marcy."

"My mom told her friend all about you and what you're doing. Her friend wants you to call her. I've got the number right here," she said.

"This is fantastic, Marcy. Tell your mother I said thank you so much."

"I'll give you a call later, okay?" she said.

"Okay," I answered as we broke connection.

I closed my eyes and put my head on the steering wheel, needing a minute to gather myself. I was thrilled that something wonderful had come my way, but I was also frightened, since I had just come from asking my deceased grandfather to help me. With my face still against the steering wheel, I turned toward the right side and opened my eyes. I couldn't believe it. A beautiful statue of Jesus Christ—I had pulled in front of a house with His image! His arms, outstretched to me, seemed to be beckoning me to take Him into my heart. Within milliseconds, I felt His love and His pain. I couldn't stop staring at Him. I continued until the setting sun cast a glow on His face, then shook my head in disbelief and wept.

I finally understood what this special man was about. I had always been curious about Him, and I felt a growing bond since Marcy's introduction, but now I was a true believer. And I had the answer to the final question I posed to Grandpa, "Who should I pray to for help and guidance?"

Clearly, the underlying purpose for afterlife encounters is growth. They offer enlightenment, wisdom, and trust that the universe is unfolding as it should. As a result, witnesses gather love, compassion, serenity, joy, and integrity.

Who is encountered depends on the circumstances, which we will explore next.

Who Appears?

Afterlife encounters fall into four categories according to who appears: (1) personal figures—deceased relatives, friends, pets, colleagues, neighbors, acquaintances, and so on; (2) historical or famous personalities—such as Alexander the Great, Winston Churchill, Mother Teresa, Marilyn Monroe, or Mickey Mantle; (3) spiritual figures—such as God, Jesus, Buddha, Mother Theresa, angels, or saints; (4) unknown—the entities are unfamiliar to the experiencers.

Let's consider the first category by turning to Ronald's encounter with a figure that was personal to him and his family.

"She forged my name."—Ronald's Personal Encounter

Ronald's family business, managed by his family for generations, was failing after his brother was killed in an automobile accident. "We've been in such grief that we let it get into disarray," Ronald told his sisters. They turned to their corporate bookkeeper for answers, and he found a number of checks, apparently written by his brother before the date of his fatal accident. As they began to investigate, more checks came through their commercial bank account. Upon close examination, all of the writing, including the signatures, was different from their brother's. "Who would do this to us?" they asked. It was some weeks later that Ronald stopped by to see me, asking for my opinion.

I was asleep last night when my brother came to me. He said, "Ronnie, it's Barbara. She's been postdating checks and forging my name. She's got my checkbook. Close the account or she'll keep on." Geesh. His wife? She'd never do that. Ridiculous.

Ronald did not want to believe his encounter because he loved and trusted his sister-in-law. His entire family did. Nevertheless, they probed and discovered that, indeed, Barbara was the guilty party.

Who appears depends on the circumstances. Certain situations are best accommodated by discarnate relatives, friends, coworkers, or other people we know personally. Sometimes, however, the famous provide what we need.

During my years at the hospice and Kübler-Ross Center, numerous mourners reported incidents with the illustrious. Afterlife encounters with famous figures are probably very different from what you would imagine, however, as Callie demonstrated.

"Because I've been there."—Callie's Encounter

Callie and her husband celebrated—their dream was coming to fruition. After trying to conceive for 12 years, she was finally pregnant. But then, shattered joy—a miscarriage. Remaining in bed for weeks, sobbing, Callie did not want to survive. I was thankful to hear her voice over the telephone.

"I think I'm losing my grip," she said. "I thought I saw something out of the corner of my eye. It was this smoky-looking form. The next thing I knew it started taking on colors, and then a woman was sitting there. Her skin and face were flawless, and she had this white coiffured-type hair. Then I almost fell out of my bed! It was Marilyn Monroe! I know it was her. I've seen enough photographs to know what she looked like. She was looking at me with such sad eyes. I looked down, hoping and wishing someone would come in and see her too, but when I looked up she was gone. Why was she here? Is that crazy or what?"

Callie waited for my response as I thought, *That's interest-ing. Two other bereaved mothers told me they encountered the movie star. All three of these women were born after Marilyn Monroe's death, were only vaguely familiar with her, and saw the apparition while fully awake and alone.* "No, it's not crazy," I finally answered. "And I wonder why she was there too, especially since other people have told me the same thing. One lady saw her two times, so if she appears again why don't you ask her, *Why are you here?*"

The next week arrived, along with Callie. Greeting me inside the door of my office, she said, "Well, Marilyn Monroe came again! This time I asked her, 'Why are you here?' and she said, 'Because I've been there myself. I'm just here to sympa-thize, to be by your side, to support you while you grieve.' But I still don't understand, why Marilyn Monroe of all people?"

"I was a teenager when she died, so I'm not that familiar with her life," I answered. "But if I remember correctly, she wanted a child very badly, especially with Joe DiMaggio, one of her husbands. I think she miscarried several times."

"It's strange . . . deep down I knew why she was there, but I just didn't know that I knew. This probably sounds odd, but I felt something when I saw her that I've not felt with anyone else. She seemed to actually hold my grief in her hands. It was bizarre, yet so comforting. Since seeing her, I've not fallen into that valley of despair. I mean I've been very down and out, but never as low as I was. I can't exactly explain it . . . I wish I could . . . but all I can say is that she lifted my spirits."

Famous posthumous personalities customarily bring some-thing unexpected and profound to their perceivers. Callie's account illustrates several other features surrounding afterlife encounters.

Apparitions do not always communicate, and in some cir-cumstances, the lack of dialogue is a matter of spiritual eti-quette. Discarnates do not want to intrude on our space, therefore remain silent. If witnesses initiate a conversation, the disembodied usually reciprocate.

Another common feature is ineffability. Profound spiritual experiences reach a depth that transcends language.

This brings us to our next category, encounters with spiritual figures. Let's begin with Patti DelSoldato's survey from New York.

"You were all alone, pulling him out."
—Patti DelSoldato's Story

One afternoon I was driving home when I noticed what looked like a movie scene—a car was lying on its roof and it was on fire, even the wheels. It evidently had just happened. There was car close by it, so I pulled over and stopped.

"Do you know if anyone's in that car?" I asked two men who were talking on cell phones.

They replied, "No, we don't."

I said, "Do you mean to tell me you're standing there with your cell phones plastered to your heads and don't know if anyone's in that car?"

"No one can go down there—the car's about to blow up," they said. I turned off my truck's engine, jumped over the railing, and ran down to the edge of the embankment. All the way, I screamed at the top of my lungs for Saint Michael to come and assist me. Forgetting that I was recovering from a hernia operation, when I got to the car I bent down and pounded the ground with my fists, yelling, "If anyone's in there, roll down the window." I didn't know if the widows could be rolled down, since most are electric these days. But the glass started going down and an elderly little forehead appeared, then some gray hair with blood on it. I begged, "St. Michael, come quickly . . . I need you." I screamed, "Please . . . Please come . . . Please . . . I need you." All of a sudden, from the Hutchinson River Parkway, I saw what appeared to be a black man. He looked more like a very large shadow running toward me at top speed, and his arms were high in the air. (Now that I think of it, he looked like he'd just landed from somewhere other than earth.) I reached into the window, grabbed the man's belt from behind, and pulled. He didn't budge, so I moved my left arm and hooked it under his armpit. I struggled and still couldn't drag him out. All of a sudden, I felt a rush of energy, then a swish, and he was somehow sucked out of the car. I held him on my side and looked up to see the two men rushing to help me. We carried him up the embankment and over the railing. After we laid him down, I covered him with a tablecloth from my truck and put a pillow under his head. He told us his name was Rudy and he was going to his son's house in Rye Brook for lunch. Paramedics arrived, and once he was in good hands I left.

I was notified a year later by the commissioner from Westchester's County Police Department, wanting to give me their Citizen Award of Merit for saving Rudy from certain death. "No, I can't accept it," I said. "I didn't save him. There was a black man who came off the Hutch and it was he who saved Rudy. I screamed for St. Michael to help, so he sent him. It wasn't me."

He said, "Okay, I'll look into it." After a month or so he called back and said, "I'm sorry, but no one saw a black man helping you. No one was down there until after you got him out. You were all alone, pulling him out of the burning car." I was shocked.

Later, when the commissioner gave me the award at a special ceremony, he said with a wink, "We tried to find your St. Michael but . . ." I started crying because all I saw was a shadow, and I know he was there. I really know he was.

My tears were from feeling confirmation. I was sure the commissioner winked because he tried to find the saint, but since no one else saw him, he (like me) definitely knew he was there to help get the old gentleman out safely. As I relive this experience over again now, the feeling—that I was given the strength through Divine intervention—is fantastic.

Patti provided four pages of documentation, including a copy of the Civilian Award of Merit certificate, signed by the commissioner and dated May 18, 2000. It reads as follows:

To Patricia DelSoldato, in recognition of her public spirit, bravery, and outstanding achievement on behalf of law enforcement, has been awarded a Civilian Award of Merit. In the early evening of May 14, 1999, Patricia DelSoldato was driving on the Hutchinson River Parkway in the town of Harrison. As she approached the I-287 exit ramp, she came upon a one-car accident in which a vehicle had rolled over, trapping its 78-year-old driver in the passenger compartment. The driver was not only incapacitated by his injuries, but was also in serious danger, as his vehicle had caught fire. Patricia DelSoldato courageously and selflessly rushed to the aid of the trapped driver and, with the aid of others, removed him from his overturned vehicle. Just moments after, the victim's car exploded and was completely destroyed. Accordingly, if not for the heroic actions of Patricia DelSoldato, a human life would have been lost.

Patti knew she could not complete the task alone—therefore, when no one came to her aid she called out for a saint. On that day, two saviors rescued one person.

It was another day in May when two persons found support in one small ethereal image. According to the AES, encounters with spiritual figures composed only 5 percent of the total. Simultaneous visitations accounted for 2 percent. Therefore, two people perceiving a spiritual figure together is rare. Angela submitted her survey, wherein she described her concurrent account, and then Carol vouched for their sojourn.

"Your mother told me."—Angela Dioca's Survey

I came home from work (about 5:45) and picked the phone up to call my mom, but it rang in my hand before I could dial out. My father was on the line, hysterical about my mother. I dropped everything and rushed over to their house. They live about five minutes away, but in rush hour traffic, it seemed like forever. I called my sister as I was driving, but I couldn't even talk—I could only scream for her to come over. When I arrived at my parents' house, I stopped my car in the middle of the street and ran past all of the emergency vehicles. On my way in, I noticed a little blonde-haired girl standing outside in front of the door, but I ran past her to my father, who was sitting, crying. The emergency medical team was in the bedroom trying to revive my mom and wouldn't let him in.

Then my attention was drawn to the little girl, who was motioning for me to come over to her. I walked outside the door and kneeled down to her level. She handed me flowers (which we saved) and said, "Your name is Angela. Your mother told me." She described my mother, then said, "Don't cry. Your mother wouldn't want you to." She was actually holding me up, physically and emotionally—a little seven- or eight-year-old child totally calming me down.

My sister Carol drove up and came running over to us. Again the little girl held on to her and told her to be strong. Then utter chaos broke out as we put Mom into an ambulance, locked up the house, and dashed to the hospital.

Several days later, my father saw the little girl in his front yard, praying in front of a statue of the Blessed Mother. He asked her, "What are you doing?" and she answered, "I'm praying for you." He asked, "Where do you live?" She stood up, smiled, and as she walked away she said, "Not here." To this day, we have not seen her again.

"Everything will be okay."—Carol Dioca-Bevis's Survey

My sister Angela wrote what happened in her survey, but I'd like to tell my side of the story. After work I stopped at Target to pick up a few things. I had my cell phone with me—I never carry it, but thank God I did that day. It rang and when I answered, Angela was screaming something about a heart attack and our mother. I will never forget the sound of horror in her voice as long as I live. I could not understand exactly what she was saying, so I ran out of the store and drove to my parents' house. I pulled up, jumped out of my car, and started running toward the front door. I saw Angela standing next to a little girl with very blonde hair that hung a little past her shoulders. She looked about eight years old and was very pretty. In one hand, the girl was holding a bunch of fresh picked roses, like a bouquet, and her other arm was around Angela's waist. I ran up screaming and crying, and the little girl looked directly into my eyes and said, "We were waiting for you . . . it's okay . . . everything will be okay."

As Angela and I jumped in my car to head for the emergency room, I asked, "Who *is* that little girl?" I know she was an angel sent to be with us.

Together, Angela and Carol saw, heard, touched, and engaged the image in conversation. Through her, the sisters found comfort, hope, and support. They remain convinced that the young girl, an apparition, was sent to them—not only because of her actions, but also because of her appearance. Discarnates exhibit a distinctive countenance, which is our focus next.

Their Appearance

Whole and functional, discarnate loved ones can romp with the deer, observe the lightning bug's glow, and hear butterflies passing by any time they choose. They manifest their best—physically, emotionally, intellectually, socially, and spiritually. Their energy is elevated, as Mary narrated.

"He was skipping."—Mary from Canada

Early in his life, my husband, Ed, was in an accident that cost him his legs. Throughout the years, we never heard him complain, but we (his children, grandchildren, and I) saw his daily struggle. He died after a long bout with lung cancer, which left me terrified of getting ill, and of dying.

Years later I started having problems with my heart. One morning I woke up and saw Ed standing in the doorway. He had this glow about him that I can't describe. He looked maybe 19—younger than when we met. He had so much energy that he was bubbly. It was amazing! And I couldn't help but look down because his legs were intact! Later that day, something caught my attention outside the window. It was Ed. He was spinning across the grass, frolicking like a little child. I sat up and watched him until he was down the hill and out of sight. I knew then that I had nothing to fear. I'd be okay, no matter what.

Widows and widowers avow that their spouses emerged youthful again. Offspring agree, adding that their parents were younger than before they were born. Similarly, bereaved parents and grandparents of adult children frequently say their beloved children appeared as they had during early childhood. Patty, from Washington D.C., questioned her nephew's encounter.

"She had the biggest smile on her face."—Patty's Survey

My nephew Kenny told me that he'd dreamed about my daughter, Jennifer Christine. It was as real as life, he insisted. Kenny went to bed at 3:30 A.M. and woke up during a dream, 30 minutes later. He couldn't go back to sleep because he felt like he'd really been with her. "The whole time I was talking to her, she had the biggest smile on her face," he said. "She was wearing a little white dress and white shoes, and she looked so sweet, running all around. But she was only about seven or eight years old."

We both thought it was strange that he would dream of her at that age. Kenny was older than Jennifer, so they didn't play together back then, and she was an adult when she died. Why would she appear as a young girl?

Kenny came over a few days ago and saw my collage of pictures. Jennifer was wearing her Communion dress in one. Her smile was sweet, her eyes so large and bright, and her hands were in prayer formation. Kenny stared at the picture and said, "She looked *just like that* in my dream." Jennifer was seven years old in the picture, the age when she was happy and full of fun. She was very sensitive, cute, innocent, and ran all around, just like in Kenny's dream. Can you tell us why she came to him like that?

I answered, "Discarnate loved ones appear as they did when they were at their best—physically, mentally, emotionally, spiritually, and socially. From their new world, they extend their most sacred selves, much as they did at times while in this one. Their afterlife personality, demeanor, and appearance mirror those they favored most during their lives. Bereaved parents often say their adult children's image was younger than at the time their bodies stopped functioning."

Patty confirmed, "That makes perfect sense. Jennifer Christine was happiest at age seven. It was her best year—physically, mentally, socially, emotionally, and spiritually. She was innocent, sweet, dramatic, and loved everyone. After that, she had one illness after another, so life was not easy for her."

Whereas adults often appear young again, infants and toddlers may seem aged, as Jenny's survey illustrates.

"He's almost as big as Tim."—Jenny Vanckhoven's Story

Tim was my first-born child. He was so special because he was a little bit of everything wrapped into one. He was an athlete—an all-star quarterback and pitcher by the time he reached the peewee leagues. He was a tough little boy, but also sensitive and compassionate. Tim fought for others who couldn't fight for themselves. He had a heart of gold, always seeing the good in people that no one else could see—a wise soul who often said and did what other children his age couldn't.

We celebrated Tim's tenth birthday on October 12, 1999. Three weeks later, we were laying his body to rest. I worried about Tim's spiritual beliefs because, although we talked about God, we were not regular churchgoers. I felt I had failed him in that respect, and I desperately wanted to learn if he had known who God was.

Tim had been an honor roll student and excelled on the TAAS (Texas Assessment of Academic Skills) test. The week after his funeral, I was looking through his papers from school and came across a math worksheet, still unfinished from the Friday before he died. I turned it over to the back and there amongst all his numbers he'd drawn a cross with "I love God" written over it. That was such a gift to me. I wondered, *How many ten-year-old boys, in the middle of doing a TAAS math worksheet, write this?*

With that, I thought back over the last two weeks of Tim's life. It seemed he had a deep sense that his time was drawing near. He was very emotional and teary about things that usually wouldn't have bothered him at all. One evening I left my children with Mother while I went to a Mary Kay party. When I called her to check in, she said, "The girls are fine, but Tim really wants you to come pick him up." So I did. Timmy and I went home alone, where we cuddled together on the couch, eating junk food and watching movies. I'm so glad I did that.

Tim was my shining star, my hero. My family and I were blessed to have been part of his life. Now we are blessed to share in his afterlife. Timmy verifies his presence through our surviving children, by telling them things they never knew.

He had been an only child for six years before his sister, Holly, was born. He was so proud of her that he carried her everywhere—even to show-and-tell at school. They were exceptionally close. Months after Tim's fatal accident, he came to play their usual game of hide-and-seek. Holly, four years old at the time, ran to me saying, "The other brother is here with Tim . . . I don't have another brother!" She was adamant, even saying she had seen her "other brother" sleeping between her father and me. What Holly couldn't have known was that I had another baby before her. Cody was born prematurely and lived only five days. Even though Holly didn't know about this child, she described Cody perfectly, saying, "He's almost as big as Tim." Indeed, Cody was a year and a half younger than Tim. Holly's afterlife encounter with Cody proved to me that our loved ones continue to grow in spirit. I reassured Holly that Tim would always be with us; then I remained open to anything else she might say.

Almost three years passed before Holly asked, "Mom, if Tim's always with me, why doesn't he let me see him anymore? It isn't fair that he can see me but I can't see him." We talked about it a little; then she went about her play. Days later, Holly was sick and sleeping on our living room couch when she awoke to a somewhat transparent figure sitting by her feet. She straightened out her legs trying to feel him, but he disappeared. I asked her, "What do you think that was?" Holly answered, "It was Tim letting me see him!" Holly said she never felt scared or frightened by her encounters.

My family and I longed to return to our vacation spot—a ranch with 3,000 acres of wide-open Texas spaces. We all loved it there, especially Timmy. Every time he went, he took his cousin Stormy so they could go hunting together. But now it was the site where he had died and I was nervous about going back. After we arrived, however, I sensed that Tim was enjoying all the old family traditions along with us.

One of my former rituals was to take pictures of Tim and Stormy after their hunt, so although she hunted alone this time, I snapped a few photos upon her return. Much to our surprise, when the roll of film was developed, on one of the pictures, beside Stormy, was a human form. Obviously, it was Tim—perfectly outlined in red—standing next to Stormy just as they had always posed. I showed it to the developers at the photo shop and asked if I could have exposed the film or if something could have happened during their developing process. They said, "If it had been exposed to light, the redness would be a straight streak or cover the whole picture. There's no explanation for it being in the form of a person."

Tim continues to prove he's with us and that he's a-okay. It's very important that I hold on to our afterlife encounters with him, so every time one happens I write it in a journal. It's easier to bear his death if I know there will be a tomorrow for him, and that there's a much bigger plan in this classroom called Earth for me. When the day comes that I've learned all I'm supposed to here and move on, the very first person I'll see will be Tim-man! Although I'm not planning to go there anytime soon, I no longer fear death, because when it's my time, it will be a great reunion and this whole thing will make sense to me.

Until then, I promise myself that I will feel all I need to feel and learn all I need to learn so this lesson will not be wasted on my family and me. I will leave this life with an understanding and appreciation for what I didn't possess before Tim's death. Plus, the idea of redoing all of this because I somehow copped out is totally unappealing to me!

I consulted with a professional about the photograph. Marsha Landers holds a master of liberal arts degree that includes 45 semester hours in photography. She is experienced in every type of film (slides, 35mm, movies, etc.) and has spent thousands of hours in darkrooms, developing prints. Marsha serves as a judge during photography competitions and has won many herself. Her e-mail response to Jenny's photograph is as follows:

The picture has the look of light getting into the camera and hitting the film before the shutter was actually clicked, but the shadow that overlaps the lighted area is *very strange.* I have never seen anything like it. If light gets into a camera, then it's going to expose the film in a certain area. But in this photograph, something kept the light off that one area. Similarly, when film is developed, light can get to the film. But again with this photograph, why isn't the whole area overexposed? There's still that shaded part within the overexposed area that I have to say is really strange. Light got to the film, but I can't explain the shadow. I suppose there is the possibility of a flaw in the emulsion on the film, but the other frames would also have a flaw. It could be a defect on the film, it could be contaminated chemicals, or it could be her loved one.

I understand what can cause flashes of light on photos, but in this particular case, there is that shaded area surrounded by the flash. There must be a logical explanation as to why it is that way, but the image is very strange to me. As a person who has faith in the afterlife, I like to think that our loved ones have ways of communicating with us. Maybe this is one such way.

Cody, in spirit, aged. Tim, however, remained ten years old. Why the differences? One theory is that apparitions reflect their self-concept. Accordingly, today Cody sees himself as older and projects that image, but Tim prefers his same age. A contrasting explanation is that discarnate figures appear in the form according to their purpose—that is, their appearance meets the need of their witnesses. Under that consideration, Cody appeared more mature for his family to indicate that he survives and continues to grow. Tim, however, manifested as his same age in order for Holly to recognize him.

Reflecting upon the survival issue, Holly's encounters were evidential. She identified a deceased brother whom she did not know existed, and received information unfamiliar to her that proved accurate thereafter. Whereas both brothers appeared to Holly in her environment, discarnate loved ones can be perceived in theirs, as Barbara described in her survey.

"We both saw him."—Barbara Green-Studer from Switzerland

When my father died after an illness, I spent the following night at my mother's house. I felt afraid and cold; then suddenly I heard his voice say, "What are you afraid of? I would never hurt you." Instantly the fear left me and I was at peace.

Exactly three months after his passing, he appeared to me in a very real dream and took me to his new job. In his lifetime, he had been a university professor and very well liked by his students. In the hereafter, he had two jobs, both of them involving teaching—one at a university of some kind and the other was a bit like the boy scouts. That same night, he also appeared to my mother. We both saw him as he had been in life before he got ill. I remember clearly how he looked firm again.

Another time, I had left an envelope containing a lot of money in a shopping cart. I was rushing around the huge supermarket, looking for that envelope. The security personnel gave me little hope, as there were over two thousand shopping carts. I asked my father for help, and a few moments later, the elevator door to the underground parking opened and a man was coming toward me, pushing my shopping cart with the envelope still in it.

Barbara's story emphasized a number of characteristics involving AEs. First, feeling cold is common for witnesses. Some researchers theorize that "supernormal perception brings about physiological changes that might lower the temperature of the body."[1] Many perceivers, however, reported an external coolness: "I felt a cool mass behind my right shoulder; then it moved across my body and out from my left side." I frequently asked, "Could it have been your environment—a breeze from an air conditioner duct or a draft from an open window?" Most inspected their surroundings and found nothing environmental that could have caused a temperature change.

Further common characteristics gathered from Barbara's account: apparitions can be perceived carrying on with their lives in the hereafter; they manifest in recognizable forms, according to our need; and last, they may appear tangible. Discarnate humans and animals can seem so tangible that after they disappear, witnesses search for living beings, as Noelle recounted.

"Hello dere."—Noelle's Survey

While backing out of my driveway about five summers ago, I noticed that our neighbor of many years had put her house up for sale. I thought back over the years.

The day they moved into their house, I met their daughter, Ann, who, like me, was seven years old. Her dad was the kindest person one could ever meet. He was so funny and attentive, always saying, "Hello dere," when he came home. Ann and I were in tenth grade when her father became gravely ill with hepatitis and died of kidney failure. It was a terribly sad time. He had always been so kind to Ann and she felt so alone without him. Shortly after he died, the phone rang and someone on the other end said, "Hello dere," and then hung up. She knew it had to be her dad.

Anyway, back to my backing down the hill and out of the driveway that summer day. As I got to the bottom, I stopped to let a man pass behind me. He was wearing a white fishing hat and white T-shirt, and was walking a small wiener dog. When I looked around to see if the man was clear, he was nowhere to be seen. I looked all through the cul-de-sac to see if he had walked between the houses, but there was no sign of him. It struck me as really odd. I was puzzled, but as I drove down the street I suddenly remembered that Ann's dad often wore a white T-shirt and a white fishing hat.

I shook it off and kept driving. But it bothered me so much that I actually took the risk of telling my sister, hoping she wouldn't think I was nuts. She reminded me that Ann had a wiener dog who died when she was in the second grade. It took me awhile, but I finally got up the nerve to tell Ann. She was so grateful. It seemed that her dad was telling her, through me, that he was visiting their home one last time before they moved. Ann also said, "My mom swore he appeared to her in their bedroom one night, and it was about that same time."

Ann told me a compelling incident she experienced last Christmas. She was talking to her father, telling him how much she wished he could see her children. Just then, she heard one of her little boy's trucks turn on in the basement. Her husband had taken the kids to the store, so she was home alone. A little rattled, she went downstairs to turn off the truck, making sure to precisely push the button to the "off" position. She said to herself, "Dad if that was you, let me know by the time I reach the top of the stairs." Just as she was putting her foot on the top rung, the truck turned on again. I very much want to believe in all this.

Noelle noted in an e-mail that toys driven by outdated batteries can operate seemingly on their own accord, but the truck's were fresh. Further, no incidents with the truck occurred thereafter. Indirect encounters, similar to direct, appear in forms we are most likely to notice. Another example transpired at the Elisabeth Kübler-Ross Center in Head Waters, Virginia.

"Did you hear?"—Phyllida's Guitar

My colleague Phyllida Templeton and I were attending the annual staff gathering in the upstairs meeting room. As the call to lunch rang out, Phyllida, who never left Ireland without her life partner—a crimson guitar—placed the instrument on her cushion.

As we waddled up the stairwell that afternoon, with our bellies overstuffed, Phyllida was discussing the schedule when we heard someone strumming an aria. "Oh, oh!" she said. "Ohhhh, ohhhh," I said, responding to her displeasure. We dashed inside the meeting room where the guitar was playing an unfamiliar but enchanting melody. Aglow in the spotlight furnished by the sunroof, midcenter in the octagon-shaped room, its strings strummed. Captivated by the surrealism of it all, we stood silent.

A friend peeked her head around the door, "Did you hear the awful news? Joan just got a call from California. Her nephew was killed in a motorcycle accident earlier today." Then, glancing toward the guitar, she, too, fell speechless. The bereaved aunt soon stepped inside. "My nephew was a musician," she said.

Did the young man manifest by that means in order to reach us? If so, why? To begin with, Elisabeth took great care while building the main room, making certain the acoustics were impeccable. To some, it left Carniage Hall lacking. Beyond the setting, were the people. Phyllida was a professional musician, songwriter, singer, and recording artist, whose musical instrument was more than sentimental to her. I was part of an orchestra for nine years. His aunt, furthermore, correlated her nephew with music. All of our attention was seized by hearing the guitar's strings sounding out such captivating notes. From the disembodied teenager's perspective, perhaps he preferred playing an original score to make his presence known, or manifesting in that manner was easy for him.

Afterlife encounters pull on our heart strings. They are gifts we could not receive any other way. Although we know and appreciate a great deal about them, the unknown stirs controversy.

SIX

Considering the Controversial

The reasonable man adapts himself to the world; the unrea-
sonable one persists in trying to adapt the world to himself.
Therefore, all progress depends on the unreasonable man.
———George Bernard Shaw

Controversy invites discovery. Many of my discoveries stemmed from conflicting information. Let's focus on two of the most controversial aspects surrounding afterlife encounters, beginning with how they are generated, and then spirit voices recorded with specialized equipment.

How Do Afterlife Encounters Occur?

What generates postmortem manifestations? Early researchers Gurney, Myers, and Podmore reported that posthumous contacts follow strong emotional ties.[1] Most contemporary survivalists believe love is the link—that loving energy serves as the medium between people here and in the hereafter. But what about visitations with former adversaries, or proxy encounters whereby the proxies did not have any connection to the deceased or survivors?

While attending psychology classes at the University of Houston, my professors asserted that physicists were conducting transpersonal experiments. Although his career was young, London biologist Rupert Sheldrake's work was among the required reading. According to Sheldrake, science must eventually recognize any phenomenon that continues to exist. I speculated that because afterlife encounters were prescience and remained prevalent, they were worthy of serious investigation. Surely, I thought, in due time his investigations would yield an answer for how apparitions manifest.

Rupert Sheldrake's original work focused on morphic resonance. His theory reminded me of the ancient American Native legend of the Silver Cord. According to the legend, when a mother gives birth to a daughter, the two women remain connected through an invisible, inaudible, intangible cord, that does not recognize time or space. No matter how far they are apart, even after death, their linkage continues via the cord. Indeed, Sheldrake proclaimed, people remain connected, biologically, through morphic fields—similar to an invisible, extendible rubber band.[2]

Sheldrake's explorations evolved with the new millennium. In his groundbreaking book *The Sense of Being Stared At* he illustrated that people being stared at from behind detected the stares. The phenomenon is possible through mental fields, which extend beyond our immediate reach.[3] Closely related is telephone telepathy. Have you thought about someone only to have the person call shortly thereafter? According to Sheldrake, that is the most common type of telepathy in the modern world.[4]

It seems logical that if personalities survive physical death, then we could connect with them through spiritual telepathy. Perhaps this is why they appear when we need them, spiritually. To date, however, there is no scientific explanation for exactly how either mental or spiritual connections occur.

I recently posed the question to Rupert, who responded, "Although telepathic encounters happen on the basis of social bonds, and above all on the basis of love, it's difficult to know if telepathy is the right model for communication with someone after they're dead. It's probably one of the best models we have, because this communication is more like telepathy than anything else. But it presupposes that the dead person is still surviving in some form capable of communicating with us. Although I think survival is possible, it goes way beyond any well-established facts in science at present. Even telepathy is controversial, although I think that recent research greatly strengthens the case for its reality."

One unfortunate reality remains—we do not understand the entire mechanisms of the brain, a physical organ within the body, much less the mind. Obtaining necessary funding to explore the consciousness of living beings is difficult. Can you imagine the struggle for funding afterlife projects? Lack of collateral forces many quality researchers to leave the field. Others turn to survival venues that require less financing, one of which brings further controversy—capturing posthumous utterances on audiotape.

Recording Spirit Voices

Many survival investigators have wanted to bridge heaven and earth through instruments of some sort. Thomas Edison died before his apparatus was complete. Dr. Wilson went to the Great Beyond before his attempts were successful, as well. Finally, claims of success brought literary publications, the most popular being Konstantin Raudive's book *Break Through*. First published in 1977, the book detailed how Raudive supposedly tape-recorded discarnate voices. A specialized field soon developed, along with a variety of titles—Spirit Voice Recording, Electronic Voice Phenomena, Instrumental Communication, Instrumental Trans-communication, and so on.

I investigated taping enthusiasts in Europe (where recording is more popular) and the United States. Let me preface my assessment by acknowledging that I investigate reported phenomena from a skeptical perspective, because my concern lies with the public, especially those in mourning. The professionals and hobbyists I met were genuinely kind and caring. Many, bereaved themselves, initially found comfort for their own grief, and thereafter offered help to others. Unfortunately, how-ever, no discarnate communication was evident during my investigations.

For example, Dr. William Roll, long-time researcher, and I arrived at a purportedly successful laboratory to observe the usual recording method among tapers. The principal taper and his assistant escorted us into a large room laden with reel-to-reel audio recorders, C-band radio systems, and windows that faced outside antennas. He then prepared one recorder and turned on a C-band radio. After the radio played for several minutes, he turned the recorder to *record* and taped three sentences. Next, he turned the radio off, rewound the tape, and then played it *in reverse* while we listened. Everyone in attendance reiterated what we thought was captured, but we each reported something very different. Therefore, we repeated the process.

This time, when he played the tape (again in reverse) we each transcribed the first sentence we heard. Then, one by one, we read the statement aloud. The principal taper was confident that the voice spoke to him: "The sun shines in your court today." His assistant claimed it spoke directly to her: "Take the day off this Thursday." To me, the comment was general, "The world is a wonderful place," but my colleague was certain that it wanted no part of the experiment, demanding, "Leave me out of this." For the second time, each person recounted some-thing very different from the other listeners.

We continued experimenting, but our results remained the same. Not once did any witnesses decipher identical utterances. The words, emotional tone, and intention behind the messages varied dramatically. As with a Rorschach ink blot test, we each projected our individual issues, personality, and essence onto the recordings.

The sessions reminded me of an extinct pastime among pop-music fans—playing phonograph records backward and lis-tening for hidden messages. From the Beatles' White Album, for example, some listeners heard "George is dead" but others insisted the voices were saying "Paul is dead."

Voice-taping enthusiasts continue to seek valid systematic

recording methods. With technology advancing as it is, perhaps a discovery is near. Meanwhile, let's consider spontaneous recordings.

Capturing utterances via answering machines, voice mail, audiovisual equipment, and other transmitting devices is becoming more common. Myriad audiotapes, along with descriptions of how they came to be, have been sent my way. Several were presented in previous chapters, and for those, my only explanation is metaphysical. Let's now turn to a 77-year-old grandmother in Australia who chronicled her experiences.

"Hello Grandma."—Survey from Phyllis Rose in Australia

About two years after my son Don died, I tried to telephone my daughter on her ordinary telephone, but there was no answer, so I called her mobile phone. It rang once, a queer-sounding voice said, "Hello Grandma," and then the line went dead. I rang her other telephone again and this time my daughter answered. She said that she was in her garden when her mobile rang once and went dead. Where did the voice come from? I didn't recognize it as Don's. Besides, he always called me "Philly" and my grandchildren are girls. But I wondered, *Could that have been Don?*

I asked a medium, and she said to set a tape recorder to *record* before going to sleep so I might hear his voice. I did this for weeks, but got nothing. Then one night I captured a little child's voice three times. It was giggling, and saying, "Hello," and then it said "Hello Grandma." I kept turning the tape back and listening. I played it a number of times to make sure I had really heard the child's voice, and then I set it to *record* again to try to get more. I thought of waking my husband, who was asleep in another room, but decided I would play it for him in the morning.

The next day, when I played it for my family, the tape was blank. They said I must have imagined it, but I did not! I was wide awake. And I had not expected to hear a child's voice—I was hoping for my son's.

I asked the medium for her opinion and she said, "You must've lost a child by miscarriage." I denied *any* miscarriages, but then later I remembered that both my daughter and daughter-in-law lost babies—my grandchildren. I did not imagine either of these occurrences. I believe they were from the other side.

My husband died last December, and I'm going to a medium this week. Good mediums are hard to find, but I need them to trigger these things for me.

Phyllis and I were discussing encounters when I said, "I wonder if we'll ever discover what induces them or a recording system."

"Look to mediums—they spawn the afterlife," she replied. What does mediumship offer? Let's take a look.

SEVEN

The World of Mediumship

Science, while perpetually denying an unseen world, is per-
petually revealing it.

—F. W. H. Myers

Uncle Harry's encounter at the Chicago's World Fair was
never far from my mind. I read sundry books and articles, and
searched the globe for an authentic medium. I quizzed psy-
chotherapists, parapsychologists, and thanatologists, "Do you
believe mediums really contact the dead?" "I don't know," was
their consensus. Three decades of exploring left me skeptical.
Then I happened upon a gentleman who challenged my perspective. This chapter is a synopsis of my journey through the
world of mediumship.

Although friends, colleagues, and clients described readings
that were as accurate as my Uncle Harry's, I had never witnessed one firsthand. By the time I arrived for classes at the
Institute for Psychotherapy in New York City I was jaded, and
their training added to my skepticism. The director, a behavioral psychologist, summarized the perils we were sure to face
as therapists and then chronicled one of his cases.

The director tested children with learning disabilities for
the public school system. One student, considered too illiterate
to continue in the first grade, was brought to his office. As he

began his routine relaxation technique, the six-year-old responded by speaking in fluent French. She named specific historical Parisians from a bygone era in France and then finished by belting out a perfect rendition of an opera solo. Stunned, he collaborated with professors in the language and history departments at a local university. From that point on, they assisted in further sessions, wherein the child provided accurate detailed information about Paris, along with names, addresses, and political climate for the dates she specified. The men visited the child's parents, who vouched that their daughter had never left Harlem or been exposed to the music, linguistics, or history she revealed.

The anecdote was such a break from the director's previous teaching that we all gasped, "Are you saying you believe in reincarnation?"

"No," he replied, "I'm simply saying that you will run into unexplainable cases, so be prepared by having qualified resources under your umbrella."

I pushed. "But there must be a reason for such things. How was she able to do that?"

"We have no explanation," he answered.

"What about mediums?" I asked. He rolled his eyes. "Wait. Let me tell you—" I attempted to narrate my Uncle Harry's encounter, but he interrupted.

"That woman simply dovetailed into your uncle's memory bank. One consciousness can dovetail into another and retrieve information. Mediums are dovetailing and observing. You see, they make some generalizations and then act on the subtle cues clients give them in response. Once they get a few things right, sitters jump in with information. People who see mediums are grieving—they need those guys to be right."

His conjecture made sense. I had left all of my sessions feeling disappointed that the mediums were so inaccurate and now I speculated why they were—I was careful not to impart any information.

My disappointment was soon overtaken by disgust. I was invited to appear as a panelist on a television talk show—the topic: life after bodily death. My fellow panelists, I was told, would also be professionals in the field of thanatology. I was greeted at the airport gate and whisked to an awaiting limousine, where a self-professed medium was nestled inside. She introduced herself, adding, "I'll be a guest along with you." Then, reaching for my hand, she pulled me inside and began, "I communicate with deceased loved ones by holding hands. I hate to be the bearer of bad news dear, but they say, 'She must prepare herself.' Your parents are getting older, and just like the rest of us baby boomers, you don't like to think about them dying. But the Otherside says you must, because they'll both die of cancer in the years ahead."

She continued during the long drive across town, until, finally, I sighed, thinking, *My parents died over ten years ago and neither ever had cancer.* "Oh . . . I know . . . I know," she whined. "You don't want to hear this, but you must prepare yourself for their deaths . . ." and she forged ahead. By the time our car approached the television station, I felt smothered by her barrage of inaccurate statements. I could not determine whether she was delusional (believing she was genuinely connecting with discarnates) or a charlatan. I wanted to give her an opportunity to utter something accurate—therefore, I said, "Thank you for the reading, but none of it made sense. Both of my parents are dead."

"Ab, ab, ab," she stammered and opened the door to the limousine, which was nearing the front of the studio.

Once inside, we were escorted to the green room, where I was relieved to see several colleagues—that is, until they clarified, "We are members of the audience . . . not panelists." We were volleying our concern about the guest when the door burst open, "Hey everybody! I'm Steve!" Much larger than his six-foot frame were his voice and mannerisms. Two leaps and he was hugging me. "I'm a medium," he bellowed in my ear, "a guest on today's show, and you're Dianne! Glad to finally meet you!" He leaned back, saying, "A female figure, an aunt or aunt-type person, with light brown hair is standing right there." He pointed behind me and continued, "She goes everywhere you go. She's handing you a bouquet of roses and that means she's saying, 'Take more time to smell the flowers.' Your work is heavy and you need to take time to do some lighter things. When you travel, she goes with you, and she also says you're a very spiritual person. . . ." The guy continued to yell out remarks about me, supposedly through my aunt, all of which were general or obvious. My hair color was light brown, so most likely I would have had a female in my family with the same. As for my work being heavy and my needing to take time for the lighter side of life, he was aware that I was employed as chaplain for a large nonprofit hospice. Traveling was a given as well—not only did I facilitate Elisabeth Kübler-Ross workshops and trainings throughout the United States, I had flown across the country that day to appear on the television show. My profession, furthermore, assured my strong spiritual beliefs. Regardless, I thought, *Wait! Hold off making assessments.* And then we emptied from the green room into the studio.

The two so-called mediums perched themselves on each side of me, and as soon as the cameras rolled they rolled as well. "Your mother is on the other side, isn't she?" Steve asked, pointing to an audience member who had to be in her 90s. "Oh, yes," she answered, wrestling back tears. "See?" he yelled, "I was right! I knew it!" Then Steve repeated a generality that he had delivered to me, "And she says you should take time to smell the flowers."

The other guest leaned forward, between Steve and the camera, motioned to a couple in their 40s, and yelled out, "A presence tells me you've thought about moving." Their eyebrows sprung high on their foreheads. "This presence . . . is . . . ?" "My dad!" the man blurted out, almost jumping from his seat. "He's so proud of you," she said, and continued to deliver vague declarations that most any son would appreciate hearing from his dad.

Rather than discerning the hereafter, the panelists were reading their clienteles' behaviors and applying their knowledge about the bereaved. Mourners hold certain commonalties—most think about moving or changing some part of their lives, dream about their discarnate loved ones, keep objects that belonged to their departed, feel strongly about something said or done, and so on.

Meanwhile, I sat stone-still, wishing I were someplace else. I was, finally, completely aligned with nonbelievers—convinced that mediumship was based on sensory cues, illusions, coincidences, delusions, fraud, and mourners' self-disclosures. As a result, I formed three categories for mediums.

Categories of Mediums

The three basic categories for people who list themselves as mediums are as follows: *sensitives, pseudomediums,* and *mediumship practitioners.*

The first category, sensitives, are, in reality, psychics. Whereas psychic consultants realize they discern information from their clients' psyches, sensitives believe they communicate with posthumous personas. Honest, but delusional, they can deceive themselves for a while. At some point, however, most become aware of their source, which forces them to make a choice—either retire from the field, shift their careers from mediumship to psychic counselors, or become pseudomediums.

Pseudomediums, the second category, consist of impostors. Many were gifted, well-meaning psychics whose egos fell prey to power, fortune, or notoriety. My associates fell victim to such circumstances. They happened upon an unknown but master psychic whose genuine desire, like theirs, was to help people. They brought him to the United States where their fame seeped over to him. His ego then emerged. It craved celebrity status and claimed mediumship as its vehicle. Deceit ushered the pseudomedium out of the country as quickly as my colleagues escorted him in. Charlatans can leave everyone involved feeling bruised.

Mediumship practitioners, the third category, legitimately practice the art of discerning. Experienced clinicians not only deliver specific and accurate statements, they issue information, unknown by the sitters, that is later verified. Because of my

Uncle Harry's encounter I included the third classification, but four decades of searching left me thinking that authentic practitioners did not exist. Then I happened upon George Anderson.

George Anderson—The Stradivarius of Mediums[1]

My flight from Houston was delayed due to badly needed thunderstorms, the summer of 1994. I was scheduled to meet with my staff at a luncheon before leading a bereavement training for health-care professionals, but by the time I arrived the food had been served and only one chair was available. As I took it, I wondered about the well-manicured stranger sitting across from me. *Who is he, and why is he with our group?* Just then, the host blurted out, "Dianne, this is George Anderson. George this is Dianne—give her a reading after she's finished eating." I was aghast, thinking, *If Elton John were here would she order him to perform too?*

George, an internationally recognized medium, was highly respected among my Elisabeth Kübler-Ross colleagues, who often discussed *We Are Not Forgotten* (Anderson) and *We Don't Die: George Anderson's Conversations with the Other Side* (Martin). Whether or not he really talked to the dead was of no interest to us. Instead, we were impressed by the therapeutic value of his work and his seemingly strong ethics. A number of workshop participants recounted remarkably accurate readings with George, but I remained convinced that mediumship was not possible, so his accuracy meant nothing to me.

But now, looking face to face with the famous medium, my mind raced back to Uncle Harry's encounter and traces of wonder washed over me. Lost in reflections of people describing their sessions with George, the host's voice jolted me. "Okay! Let's go! George, you go give Dianne a reading."

His discomfort was so obvious that I said, "Oh no, that's okay."

"Sure, he'll do it, won't you George?"

He nodded his head in the affirmative, but I nevertheless said, "Thank you George, but that's imposing on you."

"You don't want one?" he asked.

Forcing my curiosity back, my southern upbringing stepped forward to say, "You're not here to work—"

But the host interrupted, "Oh of course she does! Come on!"

Receiving a reading from George Anderson had never entered my mind before this day. Professionally, I contemplated, *Bereaved clients keep asking about him, so I'd like to have a session for future reference.* But personal thoughts—about Uncle Harry's encounter and my decades of searching—erupted. *What if this guy can actually contact the dead? I may never get this opportunity again.* Just then George bargained, "Let's trade. For once, I'd like to be on the receiving end. I'll give you a discernment, and in return I'll stay the weekend for your training." Under those conditions, I agreed and we hastened to his room.

My Private Session with George Anderson

The first thing that pleased me was our seating arrangement. George sat down on a sofa and motioned for me to sit beside him on his right. He then stacked two thick pillows behind his back, which placed him more than six inches forward in front of me. Next, he picked up a clipboard and placed it on his left thigh. As a result, I was almost directly behind his head. He could see me only if he turned around. The next thing I favored was his instructions.

> *I may ask you to validate some information by asking, "Is this correct?" or "Do you understand?" Answer yes, no, or that you understand only. Don't say anything more. If I ask about a name . . . let's say Mary, for example . . . just say "No," and not "No, it's Marilyn." If I say, "She died suddenly," don't say, "Yes, in a car wreck," or, "No, she had cancer." Don't try to help me. Let me do my job.*

George then whispered a quick blessing, dropped his head toward the clipboard in his left hand, and began swinging his right hand from side to side inches above the paper (his usual method for distracting internal chatter). Because his eyes were intently focused toward the clipboard and his body forward from mine, I was confident that he could not see my reactions to his comments. To avoid passing along auditory cues, I focused on my breathing. George began.

A male presence comes through . . . your father's father . . . your grandfather. He says, "George." Wait . . . your grandfather's name was George . . . is that right?

Yes.

I wanted to make sure someone wasn't coming through for me . . . calling out my name.

George paused, seemingly listening to someone or something.

He says that although you never met . . . I take it that he died before you were born . . . you still have a special connection. I don't understand what he means by that, but he says I don't need to understand because you do. It's only important that you understand. Do you?

"Yes," I answered, surprised that his initial statements were specific and correct. My paternal grandfather, George Davidson, and I both had near-death experiences wherein we rose into a tent of golden light sprinkled with particles that appeared to be glimmering diamond dust.

He says, "I've been with you from birth and will continue to be. Your sister could never adjust to your being born. She was always jealous of you and caused a lot of trouble in your family. You tried doing everything you could to make peace with her for the sake of everyone, but the situation was impossible. Forget her. She'll never change. You go your way and let her go hers. Don't fret about it or fool with her anymore."

George hesitated, seemingly to wait for more information to come his way. Meanwhile, I thought *He's nailed it so far, but he hasn't told me anything I don't know.* Although certain that he was reading my consciousness, I was impressed by his accuracy nevertheless and anxious to hear more. Since I was from Texas and accustomed to hearing slow southern drawls, George's New York City enunciation forced me to listen more intently.

Your dad is here and says thank you for all you did for him. You bought him everything he needed . . . from his eyeglasses to his shoes . . . but he most appreciates that you didn't just pay for everything . . . you were there and drove him. He teases about your being his chauffeur. You were very close, is that correct?

"Yes," I answered. From the time I could recall, Dad joked as he backed our car out of the driveway, "Some day, Honey, you'll be driving and then you'll be my chauffeur." When that time came, he took great joy in my escorting him around town; therefore, George's comment was touching and significant.

This can't be for you . . . a female presence comes through saying she's your mother, but you're too young to have both parents on the other side.

George paused, tilting his head far to the right, as though listening to someone.

Yes, she says she's your mother, but you're much too young to have lost both parents. That cannot be correct. Your mother isn't over there, is she?

"Yes," I answered. George instantly spun around and inspected my face, which in those days concealed my age. He then turned back and began swinging his right arm over the clipboard again.

I really thought I was off on that one. You look too young for both parents to be over there. But she insisted, and they're always right. I'm doubting myself now because you don't need this reading.

George paused again, sighing. Then began again.

No, you don't need this reading, but your mother says, "Continue." Like your dad, she appreciates everything you did for her. She says, "You were the one I could always depend on. I always knew I'd be okay as long as I had you. You were my rock . . . always there no matter what."

Those were the precise words my mother often said to me,
"You are the only one I can depend on. I know I'll always be
okay as long as I have you."

"Helen," your mother says, "I have an important message for Helen."
Will you take it to her?

"No," I answered.

No, you won't take it to her?

"No," I answered, keeping my answers as limited as possible.

What do you mean? I don't understand. You won't take the message?

"No. There is no Helen."

Well, she says, "Helen . . . Helen."

"That can't be. She didn't know any Helen."

Your mother says, "Oh, you know, Dianne, Helen! Helen!"

I was stunned. The inflection and pitch in George's voice
mirrored my mother's. When she thought I should understand
something she was talking about, she would say, "Oh, you
know, Dianne, Fifi! Fifi!" or "Oh, you know, Dianne, her dog,
Fifi! Fifi!" I could hardly believe what I was hearing. But still,
we didn't know anyone named Helen, so I repeated emphati-
cally, "There is no Helen."

Helen . . . Helen . . . Oh, you know, Dianne . . . Helen!

George insisted. Beyond mirroring Mother's southern
drawl, pitch, and common word phrase, he was perfectly dupli-
cating an uncommon gesture with his right hand—one that was
very common for my mother. I was overwhelmed. Mother's
accent, voice tones, language patterns, and mannerisms were
before me. It was as though George had become my mother.
Nevertheless, I was so sure there was no Helen that I refused
the message.

You won't take the message?

"No. There is no Helen."

I have to go with her. *They,* on the other side, are always right and she's saying there *is* a Helen, so I have to stick with what she says. But . . . if you won't take it . . . then I'll have to leave it with you.

Without skipping a beat, George continued.

Every time you travel out of state or to a foreign country, the first thing you do is go inside a church and light a candle for your parents. They thank you. You traveled a lot with them, but your dad wouldn't go to foreign countries, so now he's making up for it by going with you. They tell me that all your travels have a spiritual purpose and they like that.

You've been having spasms on your right side . . . here [he pointed to a specific location on his right side].

No.

Yes, you have.

Not exactly.

Anyway, don't worry about it. It will bother you from time to time, but it's nothing serious so don't be concerned. You really don't need this reading. . . .

George paused, which gave me time to think. I did not acknowledge the word *spasms.* I had been enduring discomfort on my right side, exactly where George pointed, but I described the sensations as "sharp pains" or "cramping." Medical tests indicated that adhesions, formed after my hysterectomy, were causing the pain, but were not a health risk. They worried me nevertheless, until now. *Spasms* was a more accurate description, and it put my mind at ease.

I was impressed with the accuracy of George's comments, as well as his conducting the session by looking down at his clipboard or toward the far left wall. *He cannot be reading my body language because I'm out of his periphery,* I thought. But then my mind tried to fit the experience into an old frame. *How can he be reviewing my life with precise names and details? Someone must have told him these things. But how can he be talking and acting exactly like my mother? There's got to be a logical explanation.*

Then, although George had no prior knowledge that I was a mother, he began speaking about my daughter in a matter-of-fact way.

Someone is extending white roses to your daughter, which means she'll be getting married probably within the year. Something about her wedding ring . . . it's rare or significant . . . an heirloom . . . passed from generation to generation. White . . . a lot of white and bright lights all around her . . . and you . . . at the wedding. Your family from the Otherside will attend, and you'll need their support in the coming years, because she'll get pregnant and it will be an extremely difficult pregnancy with serious complications. But she'll give birth to a healthy baby boy and both will be okay. He's going to be exceptionally bright, with a special purpose here, and that's why he'll survive. But it will be a very, very serious pregnancy . . . very serious.

I thought, *Whoa . . . he's way off on this one. She might eventually get married, but not any time soon, and I don't think she'll ever have children.* Then George continued with stunning predictions.

Joe . . . you have . . . em . . . Joe's are all around you . . .

He's got that one, I thought. My dad, husband, father-in-law, nephews, and nieces are named Joe or Jo.

But this Joe is your father-in-law . . . wait . . .

George, for the second time during the reading, swiveled his body around toward me, but on this occasion he looked directly into my eyes and spoke.

He's going to have trouble. It's his heart. It's serious. He won't leave the hospital. He'll die at the beginning of next year . . . February . . . mid-February.

My father-in-law was special to me, and the thought of him dying struck deep.

Now this is not definite. If he watches his diet, works closely with his doctor, and takes his medication as prescribed, he could overcome this.

George's eyes said more than his words. He turned around, and then, swinging his right hand over the tablet again, he continued.

But something goes wrong during surgery . . . very, very wrong. It's something about impurities or something in his blood and his heart gives out. It doesn't look good.

Your parents come through and thank you again. They congratulate you on your wealth. You and your husband will be very wealthy. In about ten years, something will bring you a lot of money . . . not one million . . . many millions. I don't know what it is . . . emm . . . no . . . it's not clear enough, but it comes to you by your labor. All your hard work will pay off in ways you never expected.

You have a lot of people over there. They all send their love and are proud of who you are and the work you are doing. They're helping you from the other side and will be. You'll be writing a lot . . . a whole lot. But you don't go after it—it comes to you. People will be coming to you asking you to write, so you'll be writing by invitation . . . books, articles . . . many things. You'll be offered a new career . . . writing.

Your grandfather George asks, "Do you know why good things come your way?" Do you?

No.

He says it's because you only think about how you can help other people. Everything good that has come to you has been the result of your trying to help others. Think back about your life and you'll see that everything special that's come to you, came from your helping someone else. And with that, they all send their love and there they go.

George looked at his watch. "Twenty minutes . . . that was short but you didn't need a discernment," he said, with his back still to me.

"Maybe not the way most people do," I answered. "But I've never received an accurate reading, and that was remarkable, so in that respect I did need it. Thank you."

"I'm only an instrument," replied George. Obviously shy and uncomfortable with praise, he stood and led me from the room.

Although his preciseness was impressive, I felt certain that George was mistaken about the name Helen and his predictions. I forced the session into a reality I could understand by speculating that George was the best sensitive I had ever met. But that was then. Let me recount the occurrences that followed.

The After Occurrences

After I settled into my normal routine in Houston, the discernment had all but faded from my mind when suddenly, seemingly out of the blue, a stranger called. "Hello, my name is Sheila Smith," she began. "I was driving down the street early this morning and passed by your mother's house. I don't know why, but I was drawn to it as if it was calling to me. I circled the block four or five times and just couldn't drive away. It looked vacant, so I stopped and got out. Just as I started knocking on the door and peeking through the glass, the man next door came over. He told me your mother died, so I'm wondering—are you going to rent it?"

"No, I'm not," I said with absolute resolve.

"My husband was hired as the new assistant minister at the Second Baptist Church around the corner from there," she explained. "We're moving from Dallas and need a place to rent for a while. Everything about the house . . . the location, size, large corner lot with plenty of parking . . . everything . . . it's just perfect for us."

"It sure would be," I replied. "My dad was the minister for Main Street Baptist, and he had the house built on that spot with his ministry in mind. The front room, the one facing the porch, was his library and meeting room."

We exchanged a few pleasantries, and then she said, "I feel even stronger now that we're supposed to live in that house. Can I leave my mother-in-law's name and phone number in case you change your mind? We'll be staying with her until we find a place."

"Sure," I said, scribbling her information on the morning newspaper. I thanked her for calling, and then telephoned my friend to relay the conversation.

"Maybe that's a sign," said Margie. "Maybe you're supposed to rent it. Why don't we investigate? It'll be easy since her in-laws are from here. They might be dependable people who'll take good care of the place and you won't have to sell it. Let me nose around for you." Within the hour, Margie called, saying, "My cousin knows the senior Smiths—his parents. They were members of your dad's church. Since your mother was the secretary and you still have the logbooks, why don't you see if you can find something about them in there?"

"Good idea," I replied. "Oh, and maybe they'll be in her diary. Every night, Mother wrote what happened that day and the people she talked to, so if she knew them at all they'll be in there."

With Margie's encouragement, I began scanning Mother's final five-year diary. While my index finger skimmed each page from top to bottom, my eyes searched for the name *Smith*. Then, even my breathing came to a halt.

> *Met Helen West at church today. She wants to come over for lunch tomorrow.*

There she was. Helen! Mother had mentioned Mrs. West's visit, but because the woman was my elder she never uttered her first name. *What would the message to Mrs. West have been?* I wondered. I then realized that George had delivered a statement that was beyond my consciousness. At that point, I no longer considered him a sensitive and telephoned my father-in-law in New Mexico.

Joe was serious about the afterlife, so while I recounted George's premonition regarding his health, he listened and then scheduled an appointment with his physician. The doctor, after administering a battery of tests, placed Joe on a highly restricted diet and heart medication. As the months passed, however, Joe became unconcerned and returned to his former regime. Then, in February, a sudden heart arrhythmia took him to an emergency room in Albuquerque. Heart surgery followed. During the operation, surgeons failed to remove all of the debris behind his heart valve, which caused a stroke and other serious complications. He died on the 19th—exactly as George foretold.

Some months later I heard George explain to a group, "I don't pass along information about upcoming tragic events. The only exception is if I think the person is strong enough to hear it and the tragedy or death could be prevented." I then understood why George had stopped and observed my reactions to his prediction about Joe's demise, and that his death might have been averted had he continued the prescribed medications.

I remained certain that George's forecasts for my daughter would never come to fruition. They too, however, proceeded exactly as he prophesied. She, indeed, was wed. I was the celebrant for her wedding—therefore, I stood with her and the groom. Throughout their candlelight ceremony, we were totally enveloped in white—the candles, walls, ceiling, carpet, room furnishings, and flowers. Because the jeweler did not have her specially designed wedding ring finished in time for the service, she was married in the same ring that my grandmother, mother, and I wore. Two years thereafter, following a horrendous pregnancy, which included hospitalizations, critical care, and blood transfusions, she gave birth to a son. Today he is in the gifted and talented program at his primary school.

George's accuracy was as hot as the summer's day almost a decade ago. The only exception is in regard to my finding wealth. Not only is that beyond my imagination, but I doubt that any medium's accuracy could reach one hundred percent. One thing is undoubtable, however—the future will tell.

Research with George

The weekend I met George, we discussed the storm of criticism he faced, mostly due to charlatans infiltrating his field. "That's where research is helpful," I said. "It exposes impostors. In my opinion, any medium who refuses to submit to any type of study or observation falls under suspicion."

"Well, I have," he informed me. "I've even let doctors stick me with needles for blood tests. But not one of them could tell me how I do what I do, and I'd like to know."

George's curiosity drove me. I consulted with colleagues from several universities about conducting research. Dean Radin and Jannine Rebman, two UNLV (University of Nevada, Las Vegas) parapsychologists, agreed to help orchestrate an initial study.[2] Our basic intention was to register possible anomalies with monitoring equipment while George sat inside a dimly lit enclosure, and he agreed to join us after the site was prepared.

First, Dean hired contractors who built a small, dark-walled room. Upon its completion, he installed standard video recorders inside and outside of the booth. He then rented a low-light fleer camera (which registered thermal images, similar to the military cameras used during the recent war in Iraq) and an infrared camera. Along with the two cameras, the rental companies, Stanford and Princeton Imaging, delivered a specialist to install, maintain, and protect their expensive equipment. After he placed both of their cameras inside the enclosure, Dean, Jannine, and I inserted an armchair with physiological monitoring instruments attached. Last, we connected all of the devices to a quad splitter box so that we, the camera technician, and invited observers could view, simultaneously, the different images produced by the cameras and biofeedback instrumentation.

The experiment was costly—therefore, we invited six individuals (university affiliates and students) to independently test the arrangement before George arrived. Over the course of three days, Jannine and I escorted each person inside the room, attached the biofeedback recording appliances, and then exited the booth. For the following 20 minutes, we focused on the monitors, which displayed the sitter's emotional and physiological responses (recorded by the biofeedback equipment), and bodily images (produced by the cameras). The fleer camera registered normally—that is, each participant's body reflected various shades of red, yellow, blue, orange, green, gray, and so on.

On the fourth day, George arrived. Upon his entering the booth, our cameras and biofeedback devices registered much as they had with the previous six sitters. The fleer camera was reflecting bright colorful patterns, but then, slowly, as he settled in the chair, the colors began to fade until George's image became totally white, except for two minute spots of black—his nostrils.[3]

The technician, standing by the back door with the stance of a bouncer in a bar, grunted, "Camera malfunction. I'll fix it." He stomped down the stairs, burst into the darkened room, knelt down before the camera lens, and then, much to everybody's surprise, George began discerning the man's deceased brother and cousin. Two images now appeared on the monitors—the technician's, which was colorful, and George's, which remained unchanged except for gray in the parting of his lips when he spoke. The consultant exited the booth visibly shaken.

Later compilation of the research data indicated that not only had the instruments registered something unusual with George's physiology, but anomalies appeared inside the booth as well. I hungered to know more and was soon given the opportunity. George and I were invited to facilitate a series of weekend bereavement retreats, with him working as the medium and me the grief therapist.

Working with George Anderson

Prior to the first retreat, I was concerned and telephoned George. "We have a predicament. The participants are scheduled to meet privately with me before their sessions with you. I'm afraid that during their readings, they'll think I passed along their information."

"They'll know something beyond ordinary explanation is going on," said George, "because I'll tell them much more than they told you. And I'll give some of them information that even they don't know."

Trusting that everyone involved would leave confident that the readings were spontaneous, we began our weekends.

Every evening, all of the attendees and staff gathered in the main room for a discernment. One particular Friday, midnight was approaching, George had been reading since early morning, and now a bothersome discarnate kept interrupting our group session.

"Wait your turn! Don't be so pushy!" George intermittently exclaimed. "Stronger personalities don't want to wait their turn and this guy's pushing right on through, in front of the others," he explained. "So okay, okay. All right all ready, Ben . . . back off a little! Go ahead . . . have your turn," he invited the invisible guest. "Who takes the name of Ben?" No one did. George looked to my side of the room, "It's over there." We all remained quiet. "Dianne, it's for you," said George.

Trying to be stoic, I murmured, "Maybe." Inside, however, I was joyfully thinking, *Ah, ha! I've got him on this one! Ben can't talk!*

But then George bolted to the edge of his chair, "Ohhhh, it's your *dog,* Ben, and he's still following you . . . in death . . . just as he did in life."

I could have thrown myself to the floor for a good cry. Our Benji-type mutt followed me everywhere—so closely that his nose hit my calf with every step I took. And Ben's personality was exceptionally strong. When another dog approached me, he always jumped between us. Small, medium, or large, the dog's size did not matter to little Ben. He fiercely snarled and stood his ground.

George discerning animal companions became a common feature for the retreats. Common as well were proxy readings—George delivering messages intended for third parties.

During another group session, George asked, "Who takes the name of Sonja?" No one spoke up. "A man comes through and says he's Sonja's father." George waited for someone to respond. "Who takes the name of Sonja?" he repeated. Again, no one spoke. "He says, 'I have a message I need taken to her,' so it's for somebody here." Silence still. Turning to me, George pointed and said, "You. You know his daughter, Sonja."

My supervisor's name was Sonja, but beyond our work at

the hospice I knew nothing more. A lesson I learned after my private discernment with George (wherein he asked me to deliver a message to Helen) was to not refuse anything—therefore, I said, "Maybe," and nodded my head for him continue.

George delivered a series of specific and personal declarations, supposedly from Sonja's father, and ended with, "He says the message is important, so be sure you take it to her."

As we parted company that weekend, George leaned over and reminded me, "Be sure to take that man's message to his daughter. He's persistent."

Throughout my flight home, I debated, *I can't tell her. The comments were so personal that repeating them feels like an invasion of her privacy. But he said it was important. But, still, Sonja isn't the type who'd be open to such things. She'll be offended. Her dad is probably alive anyway. But what if it is important, something she needs to hear?* Over the next two weeks, I approached Sonja in our private office, during leisure breaks, and at lunch, but my mind could not justify exposing her to George's words, so I decided to let it go.

It was a late Thursday night when my telephone rang. "Why haven't you given Sonja the message from her father?" asked George.

Impressed by his memory, I answered, "I don't know how."

"Listen, this guy keeps busting my chops! He told me, 'Dianne doesn't want to tell Sonja because she thinks it's too personal, but she has to tell her right away—it's timely and Sonja needs to hear it.' He's not going away until you tell her, so do it tomorrow. She needs it, he needs it, and I sure need it."

"Okay," I sighed.

"You have to. *They're* always right. Trust me."

"Okay," I muttered, "but how, where, and when . . . that's my problem."

"Don't make him wait over the weekend. Tell her tomorrow."

At the hospice, every Friday began with Sonja leading the staff in prayer and then leaving us with a lasting thought for the day. While she spoke on this particular morning, I requested in silence, "God, if you think she needs to hear about the discernment, give me a hand. Help me find a way. I'll do whatever you want me to do. Just give me a sign . . . anything to . . ." Just then, I heard Sonja concluding her invocation, "Won't you go about your day with a listening and receiving heart?" Perfect.

I pulled her into the counseling room. "I've been wanting to tell you something but didn't know how," I began.

"You can tell me anything," replied Sonja, backing up to sit on the sofa.

As I relayed George's statements—the message reportedly from her dad—tears filled her eyes. "Ohhhh, thank you. I needed to hear that. My family and I have been going through some . . . well . . . some things . . . and that's just what we needed to know. Thank you for telling me. What Daddy said"—Sonja paused to wipe a tear—"it's going to make a big difference in our family."

Proxy readings and discernments with pets were not the only common features that surfaced during the weekend retreats. Another typical occurrence was George stating specific information, unknown by attendees at the time, that proved true later. A number of participants confided in me after their sessions with George, "I'm sure he was mistaken about the accident. It didn't happen that way." Weeks thereafter, however, they contacted me saying, "He was right after all." They unearthed documents (police reports, autopsies, military records, and so on) that validated George's statements.

Meanwhile, news that I was working with George spread. A number of Houstonians asked that I invite him to our hometown where he could lecture before a large audience and then privately discern for their terminally ill or handicapped family members. George accepted the invitation, adding that he wanted to visit Houston the week prior to working.

Upon his arrival at the airport on Sunday, George looked exhausted.

"How are you?" I asked.

"Tired. I've not slept in days because a pilot by the name of Mark keeps talking to me. I thought I'd nap on the flight here, but he was on the plane chattering in my ear the whole way. He was telling me about his wife and how he's trying to get her to my lecture. She keeps changing her mind about it, so he's now going to her family to try to get them to bring her."

During the next four days George intermittently passed along the pilot's utterances regarding his life, death, family, and their misery surrounding his fatal accident. Other discarnates appeared as well, each placing explicit orders for gifts they wanted George to buy and bestow on their behalf. We frequented Christian bookstores where he filled most of their requests, but the pilot wanted a particular rose for his wife's upcoming birthday and they were nowhere to be found. It was late afternoon on Friday, hours before his presentation, when we drove to Flower Row, the largest wholesale/retail flower market in the county. We walked for blocks, searching every outlet. Then, across the aisles, George yelled, "Here! They're over here!" I rushed to see. The pail, holding a handful of solid white roses with a hint of pale pink on the petal tips, had just been delivered. "Mark says these're it. I'm to take these to her," he whispered. "Her family persuaded her at the last minute. They're on their way . . . she'll be there."

Within hours George was presenting the flowers to a tearful young widow who acknowledged, "My husband, Mark, always gave me roses exactly like these for my birthday."

"And it's only days away," her family confirmed, surrounding her in support. Giggling with delight while tears stroked their grief, they reenacted how she resisted the three-hour drive from Austin but finally surrendered to their pleas.

George described Mark, a pilot dressed in military uniform. He then relayed comments about the fatal accident and pinpointed the cause—a specific piece of the airplane that malfunctioned. George knew nothing about aircraft, yet he described the color and location of the broken rod, adding, "There's an ongoing investigation that claims copilot error. The family is spending a lot of time and energy on a pending lawsuit, but it wasn't the copilot's fault. If you'll check the airplane, you'll find the defect and other lives will be saved." George continued, addressing other issues until their discernment was complete.

The widow and family thanked him and agreed to inspect the aircraft. In parting, they vouched for the accuracy of George's statements—all of which he had been passing along to me since his arrival into Houston.

By this point I had no doubt that George was a mediumship practitioner, but several of my colleagues complained, "You're associating with a medium?" One offered her observations, "He came to our town after a tragedy and claimed he was discerning the dead, but everything he said was from our local newspaper. He researches beforehand and comes in knowing what to say. I can't believe you bought into that."

"I don't know what you experienced since I was not there," I replied. "But I've remained objective, overly skeptical at times, looking for fraud, sensory cues, illusions, coincidences, or any common means for his receiving the information. Although I, and my research colleagues, do not know how George received his information, we are certain about how he did not—and he did not rely on deceit. I'm sure of that. You just don't know him or understand how he works."

To George, discernments are much like solving a puzzle. If he fits all of the pieces together, then he believes the sitters got what they needed. If, however, he thinks the puzzle was incomplete, then he criticizes himself.

After one particular reading, for example, George and I drove to Saint Philomena's shrine in Dickinson, Texas. He obsessed all the way, "I didn't get all of it or I got something wrong. It doesn't make sense."

As we approached the church, I turned to him, "You got it, George. Can I tell you?"

"No! No!" he gasped. "Don't ever give me information."

"But you'll see . . . it makes sense," I persisted. "You got all of the pieces—you just don't know how they fit."

"Don't tell me anything," he said. "It has to come from the Otherside."

"But you keep beating up on yourself unnecessarily," I said.

"That's okay. I don't want anyone to tell me anything—ever."

"But George, you'll never see her again. She can't travel. The only way she got a discernment was by your flying into Houston."

"I still don't want you to tell me," he said without hesitation. "You don't know—I might run across her again somewhere and I must have peace of mind that everything I got was on my own. Besides, someone giving me information would ruin the challenge for me."

My respect for George's integrity swelled on that summer's night in 1995, and observing life's interconnectedness thereafter led me to understand his perspective.

Lives Intertwined

The Compassionate Friends Conference was held in Houston later that same year. During a luncheon, I mentioned the events that had occurred with George, the pilot, and our extended search to buy pink-tipped roses.

Eight years passed—September 2003. One of the conference attendees, Terri Huber, arrived from Oregon for a visit. "Do you remember the pilot you told us about at lunch—the one George bought those special roses for?" she asked. "I met his mother. Can I send her your e-mail address?"

"Please do," I replied. "I've often wondered about the investigation and how his family is doing, but I didn't know their names or anything." Within days, Neta Sharp, Mark's mother, e-mailed the following:

Mark was killed in July, 1994, and Gayle, his widow, moved to Austin months later. She attended George Anderson's lecture with her sister and friends. We knew little about him and were very skeptical, afraid she might be hurt more. After the reading, she called us in Portland, Oregon, where we live, and she sounded so happy and excited. Not only did she get roses, the kind Mark always gave her, but she was given permission to go on with her life. It made such a difference. And although I'm sure Mark is still in her heart, she is now happily married and has a daughter.

We would never have known about George wanting to buy the roses had it not been for Terri. During my first national Compassionate Friends Conference, she was talking about having seen you and you were relating about George being so focused on buying a certain kind of rose for a presentation. Terri couldn't understand why you were telling her, and since we barely knew her, it was amazing that she was repeating the story to a group of us. You didn't know any names, and Terri had no idea our daughter-in-law had attended the lecture, so we all just about fell over when I shouted, "That was Mark!" I was a believer after that.

The story about Mark bugging George for days was so, so like him. He was very persuasive and if he wanted something to happen, we usually ended up going along with him and enjoying it. He had such an infectious energy that people often told me, "Everyone always wants to be in the same room with Mark because that's where all the action is."

Mark was a Navy pilot and spent two six-month tours aboard aircraft carriers. When he was assigned to Meridian, Mississippi, to train students, we were relieved. But then the accident. Mark was training a student who had personal problems. We didn't know if he, as the copilot, caused the accident or if there was a mechanical failure, but something happened during takeoff. Mark ejected the student safely and then 1.8 seconds later ejected himself, but Mark's body hit a tree.

My husband Stan, Mark's father, graduated from the Naval Academy, did active duty for six years, and retired from the reserves as a captain. A lawyer by trade, Stan desperately wanted to find out what had happened and prevent it from happening again. For the first year and a half after Mark died, we were consumed by our pending lawsuit—concerning the part that caused the hydraulic failure, which resulted in the crash.

The military investigates their accidents, or mishaps as they call them, which means that any officer can be called to be on an investigative panel. Dr. Alan Diehl, a former Air Force officer, wrote a book about how incompetent their investigations are, and Mark's incident and photograph are in it. As Diehl pointed out, Mark's case was closed as inconclusive and the Navy continued to fly the airplanes. But then two similar accidents, one fatal, occurred at the same base with much the same facts. This time the investigative team found a mechanical flaw, so all of the remaining airplanes were fixed.

Our family and friends believed the cause of Mark's accident was also the defective mechanical part, just as George had described. And although we had a good case against the plane manufacturer, we settled out of court.

Shortly after, I, along with several others from Portland, went to see George for a group session. I transcribed our 20 minute discernment from my tape recording and have referred to it many times over the past seven years. It's amazing how accurate George was. He even said, "Mark says, jokingly, 'Your daughter will name her firstborn, a son, after me.'" Mark Schoen was born in January, 1998.

I could go on and on about Mark and our encounters with him. He was so dynamic and we still miss him intensely, but we have found a deeper meaning to life and are able to move forward.

Across the continent—from the Gulf of Mexico to the Pacific Northwest and back again—my mentioning the pilot and flower search had returned home.

Meanwhile, on the opposite coastline, another metaconnection was in the making. I flew to New York City to speak at a benefit for survivors of the World Trade Center attacks. As I stepped into the door of the ballroom, an attendee approached me, asking, "Do you by any chance know George Anderson?"

"Yes," I answered.

"I'd like to tell you . . ." she began.

I invited Jacki Mac to write the story she shared with me that evening.

"His kindness made such a difference."—Story by Jacki Mac

A number of years ago, my older brother, Cliff, had just started working as a chauffeur for a limousine company in New York. He was already very nervous about his new job, but then his boss told him he was to drive a medium to an event. Cliff didn't like that sort of thing, so now he was anxious! The medium turned out to be George Anderson. He was very kind to Cliff, so the drive went well.

Cliff was called to drive for George again. This time when he arrived, George asked, "Mind if I sit up front with you?" George began talking as if they were old friends, and Cliff was really liking his nonassuming way, but then George gave him an impromptu reading. He said specific things, including, "You've moved five times." Although most of the reading was true, Cliff still didn't like the subject, and he doubted George because he was sure he'd moved only four times. When Cliff went home and repeated the reading for his wife, she said, "Oh, but it was five! You forgot about the time we moved into the apartment while waiting for our house to be finished."

Cliff made an appointment for his wife to get a private reading. It was excellent, except George used a long Italian name for her deceased dad, and she was sure he was incorrect because she'd never heard that pronunciation. Her mother later confirmed, however, that George was right. Her father changed his name upon entering the United States.

Cliff no longer works as a chauffeur, but we will always remember George. His kindness to a young man just setting out in the world made such a difference for him, for me, and for our whole family.

Now I understand why George insisted, "Don't tell me anything—I might happen upon the person again." Our lives are so interwoven that we connect with one another by many different means.

The connection is not always positive, however. "What do

you think about mediums?" I'm often asked, and sometimes more specifically, "What about George Anderson?" In years gone by, my usual response was, "I know George to be ethical, honest, sensitive, and kind." A similar exchange prompted a grieving acquaintance to fly to New York for a discernment. She called thereafter, exploding, "I went all that way and paid all that money, but my brother didn't say our secret word. If that guy was real, my brother would've said the code we agreed on before he died. I expected to leave my grief behind, but instead . . ." She continued to rant uncontrollably, which serves as a warning for the bereaved and mediums.

Mediumship Practitioners and the Bereaved: Caution to Both

People in mourning often expect specific things from mediums—that they will connect with particular discarnates, divulge loved ones' names, reveal secret code words, cite specific dates, and so on. Mediumship practitioners, like the rest of us, have days that are better than others. Even on an exceptional day, however, they may not meet prodigious expectancies. Therefore, be forewarned, unmet expectations can leave sitters devastated.

Another caution surrounds self-expectations. Some mourners seek mediums as a means to end their grief. Mediumship sessions may temporarily relieve sorrow and longing, giving hope and comfort, but eliminate the grief process they won't.

The final caution: The bereaved are in emotional and cognitive duress. Under current federal guidelines, the newly bereaved must be placed in the Special Protection Group (along with young children, the elderly, mentally dependent, and terminally ill). In order to assure the highest ethical standards, safeguards are required for professionals. Uninformed clinicians lack awareness regarding their clients' vulnerability and special needs.

In my investigations, for example, numerous readers said, "Your mother misses you even more than you miss her."

Fortunately, I recognized the utterance as standard among the inexperienced. I knew, furthermore, that I had transcended all longing for Mother, and trusted that she was living in love, peace, joy—and not missing me. As a result, my psyche was not breached by their statements. Whereas I dismissed the declarations, the bereaved may not.

I received a long-distance telephone call from Pam, a former colleague. "I'm sorry to be calling you this late," she began, "especially on Thanksgiving, but I don't know what to do about my brother Karl. Last month, our mother had a sudden heart attack and died. It was totally unexpected, and Karl's really struggling with it." Pam and I discussed the approaching Christmas holidays, and how they can be especially burdensome for new mourners. She ended our conversation by saying, "My concern is that Karl told me, 'All I think about is Mother and that she hasn't found peace.' No matter how much our minister and I promise him that everyone over there is at peace, he keeps obsessing, fearful that she's missing him. He saw an ad in a magazine for a medium and he wants to go see her. Do you know . . ." Pam spelled the woman's unusual name, which was not familiar to me.

"Never heard of her, but that doesn't mean she isn't good," I replied. "In general, however, my advice to anyone considering a medium is to read everything you can on the subject. Be informed, first. Then, if you're determined to try it, choose one whom close friends and family have gone to and personally recommend. But then stay guarded. In Karl's state, I'd discourage him from going, especially to anyone inexperienced with grief-stricken clients."

I was baking Christmas cookies when Pam telephoned again. "My brother saw that damned woman yesterday! I can't believe she was so stupid! When Karl called her, he explained his situation—that he couldn't eat or sleep, worried about Mother missing him. After he flew all the way across the country to get some relief, you won't believe what she told him. 'I see your mother curled up in the fetal position, sobbing. She misses you so much. She's miserable without you.' He flew straight home, saying the only thing he can do is join her. He's now suicidal, so what am I to do?" Clearly, Karl's session was anything but therapeutic.

Grief is often exacerbated by unmet expectations, unrealistic self-expectancies, and inept clinicians. Whether mediumship is detrimental or therapeutic depends on the practitioners and patrons. Both require education, experience, and caution.

Exemplary Mediums Benefit

Qualified mediums can benefit the bereaved population. They provide evidence for survival of bodily death, which reduces death anxiety. They orchestrate the finishing of unfinished business between the living and departed. Practitioners facilitate the grief process by allowing mourners to externalize their emotions. Moreover, through mediums, continuing love and support are demonstrated—perhaps more than ever before. Further still, some clients reach a psychospiritual catharsis, which does not end with their sessions; it continues to evolve. Exemplary clinicians influence the bereft in another way, as Phyllis Rose, a 77-year-old grandmother in Australia, documented.

"He'll move it to show you when he's around."—Story by Phyllis Rose

Don, our youngest son, died of a brain tumor at the age of 35. We were utterly devastated. I felt that I couldn't go on living, remembering all that he went through. I tried mediums but they were useless, until I heard of an Italian woman. I went to her and she was amazing. She knew how my son died and gave me messages from him that nobody else could know. She said, "Put a tennis ball on a flat surface and he'll move it to show you when he's around." I did this for several days and nothing happened. Then I brought the ball into our bedroom and placed it on top of my bureau with a match on each side of it. The next morning I saw that the ball had moved—on an upward slope—to the edge of the bureau.

I was telling my daughter and granddaughter about this when I glanced toward the bedroom window and there he was, looking at me. The apparition only lasted for a few seconds, and I could scarcely believe that it had happened.

I'm going back to the medium this week because I need a trigger for these things. Good mediums are rare, and I know because I have tried quite a few.

A number of perceivers, similar to Phyllis, reported spontaneous encounters only after their discernments with practitioners. The most accelerated method for learning is vicariously. By simply being in the accompaniment of people who excel, we absorb some of their ability.

But are mediums capable of contacting the dead? How can they cite accurate, detailed, and even embarrassingly private information? We continue our search in the next chapter.

EIGHT

The Afterlife Watching Experiments

Science is not a dogmatic belief system or an ideology; it is a method of inquiry.

—Rupert Sheldrake

Many of the early systems for investigating mediums face scrutiny and debate. They nevertheless remain contributory to current investigations, which have evolved into the twenty-first century much to the effort of Professor Gary Schwartz.[1]

I first met Dr. Schwartz at a weekend survival meeting held by the National Institute for Discovery Science. It was five years thereafter, May 2002, when my colleagues from the University of Virginia and I flew to Arizona to canvass his latest research data. As we were parting, Gary mentioned an upcoming series of double-blind experiments that I found particularly interesting. On the eve of commencing the project, Saturday, the 13th of July, he telephoned.

We're ready to begin the Afterlife Watching experiments. I have four sitters and wonder if you'd like to be the fifth? It will involve three phases. Let me describe the first, Phase One.

Later tonight, I'll write the five sitters' names on separate sheets of paper and then place each in an individual unmarked envelope. Beginning tomorrow, Sunday, and every morning after for four days, I'll randomly choose one envelope, open it, and ask Susy to observe the chosen person during that particular day. [Author and survival investigator Susy Smith, deceased, was a mentor and friend to Gary.]

The next part is up to Susy, if she has survived and is able to communicate. Susy will follow the designated sitter on that person's given day and then report her observations to two different mediums.

The following morning, each medium will send all of the information he or she received, supposedly from Susy, to my research assistant, Christopher, at the University of Arizona.

Christopher will list each medium's statements separately, so he'll have two lists. He'll e-mail both lists to all five sitters. Chris will have only the first names and e-mail addresses of the sitters and mediums—nothing more.

Now for your part. First of all, everyone has a tendency to forget details, so you'll be taking notes. Periodically, write on paper, what you're doing and the time—even if it seems insignificant. Every morning, as soon as you receive the lists of statements from Chris, score each item by placing the letter that symbolized your answer—Y for yes, P for possible, and N for no—to the left of each item. Then, on the daily diary form provided, copy your notes. After you complete the lists and diary, e-mail them back to Christopher.

The study is double blind, so it's important that no one discusses it with anybody except their families—that way we'll prevent information leakage. And don't try to make anything fit. Be genuine. Score everything honestly. Let the data speak.

The project sounded inviting, especially with me not having the labor and responsibility of an investigator. I was delighted to participate, but I did not take my role lightly. My approach was to remain skeptical, methodical, and uncompromising throughout. I planned to mark a statement "Yes" only if I was one hundred percent certain that it was accurate and I could substantiate it in some way. Leniency, in other words, was not my strategy.

The Afterlife Watching Experiment, Phase 1

Armed with Gary's instructions, Day 1, Sunday, was uneventful for me. Most of my time was spent battling a computer, which eventually crashed. That night I reflected, *What if Susy Smith came by here today? Bored—that's what she would have been. What will a former survival investigator find interesting or enjoyable—if she survives, and visits with me?* I decided to fill the four remaining days with spiritual significance.

From that point on, I began every morning by lighting dozens of candles and saying a blessing for Susy. I then strolled into my office, turned on a 12-candlelight chandelier, responded to Afterlife Encounters surveys, and answered the forms from Chris. After lunch, I climbed the stairs to a room filled with my travel memorabilia and other keepsakes. All the while, I wore a flowered toga and sandals from Tahiti.

With each passing day, upon reading the mediums' comments and seeing how few applied to me, I grew more discouraged. By the final morning, Thursday, July 18, I was certain that my part in the experiment was not successful. I proceeded with my special morning candle-lighting ceremony and blessings for Susy, but my mind soon returned to normal responsibilities.

Before revealing my scores and notes for that day, let me present the list that Chris e-mailed to all five sitters. From the 53 remarks submitted by Medium 1, and 26 submitted by Medium 2, how many apply to you?

Day 5 Scoring for Thursday, July 18, 2002

Statements from Medium 1:

1. *Shows a birthday cake (medium believes this is coming up)*
2. *Sees the old TV show* The Wild Kingdom
3. *From this show are the names Dana or Brown, or a safari*
4. *Sees ironing*

5. *Person doesn't like to iron*

6. *Person doesn't iron much*

7. *Shows a woman named Laurie*

8. *Talks about a group of people around her*

9. *See a line running from the back, down her leg and to her foot*

10. *Something about the back to the right leg (sciatic nerve)*

11. *A big man who is on the other side around this woman*

12. *He wears a button-down shirt*

13. *He is a farmer*

14. *This woman has rings on almost all her fingers (medium refers to way gypsies have the same)*

15. *She drinks coffee*

16. *She drinks coffee in the afternoon at times*

17. *She has a journal or book she keeps notes in*

18. *She is a collector*

19. *She has a full house (lots of stuff in it)*

20. *She likes old stuff that holds energy*

21. *Something about her shoe (may have stepped in something, medium sees her lifting her shoe)*

22. *Sees angels*

23. *Sees jewelry again*

24. *Is showing the words gypsy jewelry repeatedly*

25. *This person is going out of town soon*

26. *She is going to be in a group of people*

27. *For some kind of convention*

28. *She is on the phone a lot*

29. *At one time she had a blue phone*

30. *Sees blue walls*

31. *Sees her feet with sandals on them*

32. *She is a pack rat*

33. *See lots of boxes with things stored in them*

34. *She also likes to display a lot of things as well*

35. *She was laughing yesterday*

36. *See her walking around her yard*

37. *She had the hose out*

38. *Has a hanging flag outside (not the American flag, but a flowery flag)*

39. See her in a car but going slow

40. See car troubles around her as well

41. The trouble's in the left front side

42. She has tarot cards (or something similar)

43. She reads people

44. She is a spiritual advisor, a healer

45. She has a sister who found out bad news

46. Something happened around a house and health

47. This woman is going to do or did some rearranging in her house

48. See something new like a bookshelf or table . . . only it's not new

49. Sees the grocery store

50. See sandwiches, seafood, and lettuce

51. Brings up her leg and foot again

52. Talks about the "magic man" and the skeptic

53. Sees a man playing cards

Statements from Medium 2:

1. Something was wrong with electrical appliances (anything electric)

2. Subject may have had a disagreement or misunderstanding with a coworker or associate

3. May have had his own personal problems on his mind

4. Legal advice or contract negotiations are around subject also

5. These are present more as business options

6. Feet pains (corns or other foot problems) seem to be bothering sitter

7. Subject's shoes seem too tight or uncomfortable

8. The shoes seem to be the problem

9. Subject seems to just love "bagels with a smear" (bagel with cream cheese)

10. Subject is from the East Coast

11. Subject is of ethnic decent

12. Subject has dark hair

13. Has blue or gray eyes

14. Subject has above average IQ

15. Is a little obsessive-compulsive

16. Their office or surroundings are usually very neat

17. Seems to be lots of delays around things yesterday

18. Subject waited for return phone calls

19. *Also waited for packages or people to arrive*
20. *Mail seems to be lost or misplaced*
21. *Some kind of mail sitter is waiting for what they won't receive until early next week*
22. *The mail's coming from California*
23. *Subject discussed family history yesterday (family trees, genealogy)*
24. *Something about creating or finding other family members*
25. *Something about a refrigerator not being cool enough*
26. *May have to buy a new fridge*

How many of the statements applied to you? For me, many were more than simply applicable, they held strong emotional significance. I was astounded that someone had, seemingly, been by my side on Thursday. I will present the two lists again. My scores (Y = Yes, P = Possible, N = No) appear to the left of each number and statements exactly as I e-mailed them to Christopher. Then I will bring you up to date.

Medium 1, Thursday, July 18, 2002:
P 1. Shows a birthday cake (medium believes this is coming up).
I scored the first sentence *Possible* because I could only think of my husband's September 13th birthday. Two months into the future did not seem "coming up" to me, but I thought, *Maybe, to the medium, the 13th is coming up. And I think another is closer, but I can't remember whose.* After e-mailing my scores to Chris, I remembered my birthday—August 2! Then, however, I was dumbfounded. While passing the cooking island where I burned candles for Susy, I noticed my personal event calendar. There, attached to Saturday, July 27, was a party invitation with a birthday cake depicted on the cover. Upon receiving it in the mail, I taped it to the bottom of the page and then forgot about it.
N 2. Sees the old TV show The Wild Kingdom
Although *The Wild Kingdom* had been one of my family's favorite television programs, especially my dad's, it did not seem specific enough to merit a Yes response.
N 3. From this show are the names Dana or Brown, or a safari

Most of the episodes we watched were in safari-type settings, but I could not recall the names Dana or Brown.

P 4. Sees ironing

Y 5. Person doesn't like to iron

Y 6. Person doesn't iron much

I now laugh at my denial in scoring the fourth statement—one bedroom in our home holds several piles of clothing that need to be ironed. I dislike ironing so much that they will probably remain there for some time.

Y 7. Shows a woman named Laurie

I had been speaking with Laurie, a bereaved mother.

Y 8. Talks about a group of people around her

During the experiment, I corresponded with many Afterlife Encounters Survey participants.

N 9. See a line running from the back, down her leg and to her foot

P 10. Something about the back to the right leg (sciatic nerve)

The right side of my back and hip had been painful for several weeks, but it did not extend to my foot. My dad and his side of our family suffered similar symptoms that led to their hospitalization and tests that revealed sciatic nerve problems.

Y 11. A big man who is on the other side around this woman

Y 12. He wears a button-down shirt

P 13. He is a farmer

My dad, muscularly built, measured six feet in height, and wore button-down shirts during their popularity. Although he was not a farmer by trade, Dad built a ranch-style home in Arkansas, covered several acres with vegetables and fruit trees, and then referred to it as "the farm" and himself as "the old farmer." He canned his harvests and gave them as gifts. Beyond my dad, a number of family patriarchs listed themselves as farmers on census reports, so there is a possibility that the man was a great-grandfather.

N 14. This woman has rings on almost all her fingers (medium refers to way gypsies have the same)

I do not wear jewelry.

Y 15. She drinks coffee

Y 16. She drinks coffee in the afternoon at times

The coffee comments were significant for me. I recently decided to try taking caffeine-free coffee breaks during the afternoons to see if I could free my mind as I replenished my body. I found them so delightful and revitalizing that I continued.

Y 17. She has a journal or book she keeps notes in

Y 18. She is a collector

Y 19. She has a full house (lots of stuff in it)

Y 20. She likes old stuff that holds energy

At this point I realized the comments were not reflecting my desire to bring joy to Susy. Instead, they revolved around emotionally charged areas of my life—my procrastinating about the stacks of clothes, friend's birthday party, newfound comfort in coffee breaks, and now this series of statements.

My mother, friends, and colleagues advised me over the years, "You should be keeping a journal or at least writing this down." For Christmas, 1999, my daughter gave me a ten-year logbook, saying, "I know you won't take time to journal, so this is just for jotting quick field notes." I used it on rare occasions, but during the experiments I found myself referring back to it and realized how beneficial my notes were. I then regretted not taking the advice so long ago.

As for the collector remark—I am. Big time. My passion is venturing into the backwoods of foreign lands and visiting with the people who live there. As I leave, I choose a keepsake, depending on its energy. To visitors, our house is a museum because it overflows with mementos from my travels. Adorning the walls and floor of one particular room are rocks, pebbles, shells, coins, charms, trade beads, photographs, paintings, drawings, and musical instruments. Thursday, I sat in the middle of that room, thinking, *Susy might enjoy the energy in here.*

Reviewing the statements thus far, I detected a pattern. Someone had progressively connected to many of my greatest joys.

Y 21. Something about her shoe (may have stepped in something, medium sees her lifting her shoe)

As I was preparing to walk outside, I reached for my shoes and found that one of my cats had used the left shoe for her litter box. "Now which of you did that?" I joked, looking around to see if the culprit exhibited any guilt. I then lifted the shoe by its heel and tossed it outside.

Y 22. Sees angels

Angels are among my mementos. With my last name being Arcangel, many angel cards and gifts are sent my way. Each is displayed in a special place. Beyond that, I make angels. Every person in my family, living and deceased, has a six-inch angel that honors him or her. Each angel, made from cloth, holds items (in miniature) that the person loved. My grandmother, for example, holds a baby (representing me), a cat, and an antique sewing machine. My mother embraces gardening tools, flowers, and a white poodle. My daughter holds a baby (represents her son), scrapbook, dog, and two cats. During the holiday season, I place the angels on our Christmas tree—thereafter, I hang them in different rooms of our home.

N 23. Sees jewelry again

N 24. Is showing the words gypsy jewelry repeatedly

I do not wear jewelry; therefore, scored both items *No*. Was I being too strict? My mind linked these statements with the earlier remark, *"This woman has rings on almost all her fingers."* However, if we consider *"Sees jewelry"* and *"showing the words gypsy jewelry"* anew, then the statements are plausible. One of the first things I do upon arriving in a foreign country is venture to the largest cathedral, light candles for my parents, and then purchase a medallion (charm) from their gift shop to commemorate the occasion. I collect ancient international trade beads as well. Whereas most people would bejewel their bodies with these items, I exhibit them throughout our home as special remembrances.

Y 25. This person is going out of town soon

Y 26. She is going to be in a group of people

Y 27. For some kind of convention

I was booking hotel and conference rooms for several upcoming grief conferences.

P 28. She is on the phone a lot

I marked this "Possible" because although I made an unusual number of calls about the conferences and was "on the phone a lot" for me, it nevertheless was not the largest portion of my day.

Y 29. At one time she had a blue phone

In chapter 1 of this book I chronicled a telephone incident that involved my deceased grandmother—the telephone was a blue Princess Thin-Line, the last gift she gave me.

P 30. Sees blue walls

I should have marked this *Yes*. Our bathroom is primarily windows and mirrors, but the partial walls are covered with pale blue wallpaper that reflects throughout the room.

Y 31. Sees her feet with sandals on them

I wore sandals—day and evening.

Y 32. She is a pack rat

Y 33. See lots of boxes with things stored in them

This was another emotional hit. I have single-handedly filled almost every room of our home with boxes. One room contains almost one hundred, each filled with books, toys, and games for my grandson. Another room is overtaken with travel paraphernalia—maps, notes, catalogues, electrical converters, water distillers, camera equipment, books, and clothes. My office cabinets are lined with boxes of letters, photographs, videotapes, audiotapes, manuscripts, dissertations, and other items that people have mailed to me. During the experiments, I walked into every room, pointed to the boxes, and jokingly asked, "So Susy . . . have you ever seen anything like this?"

Y 34. She also likes to display a lot of things as well

I do, all of which represent my favorite people and places.

Y 35. She was laughing yesterday

Y 36. See her walking around her yard

Y 37. She had the hose out

During the experiments, I periodically videorecorded my activities for documentation. On Thursday, I began taping my departure for the drive to dinner, and as I exited the front door and walked down the steps, our water hose was stretched across the porch steps. I filmed the obstruction, paused the camera, moved the hose, and then continued filming.

N 38. Has a hanging flag outside (not the American flag, but a flowery flag)

It was an American flag.

Y 39. See her in a car but going slow

P 40. See car troubles around her as well

P 41. The trouble's in the left front side

I now noticed that the statements ran parallel with my day. This series corresponded with my driving slowly. I was looking for the restaurant where I was to meet my colleague, Debbie Fancher, for dinner.

I scored "car troubles" as a possibility because, although my left front tire was leaking air, I did not consider it to be a real problem—after all, it transported me to and from my destination. The following morning, however, the left side rearview mirror fell off as I was backing out of our driveway. That was a problem—my car remained in the auto shop for two weeks, waiting for necessary parts.

Y 42. She has tarot cards (or something similar)

My grandson, Silas, had been displaying an ability to disclose what I was thinking. Therefore, while at the Rhine Research Center in June, I bought a deck of ESP cards identical to those used by J. B. Rhine for testing extrasensory perception. Since then, Silas and I had been experimenting and found that I have no ESP ability . . .

N 43. She reads people

. . . so, no, I cannot read people.

Y 44. She is a spiritual advisor, a healer

P 45. She has a sister who found out bad news

P 46. Something happened around a house and health

Y 47. This woman is going to do or did some rearranging in her house

Y 48. See something new like a bookshelf or table . . . only it's not new

P 49. Sees the grocery store

Y 50. See sandwiches, seafood, and lettuce

The first medium's list concluded with accuracy. I rearranged the bookshelves in my office and polished them to appear new. Thursday night ended with me slowing to pull into the grocery store, seeing the crowded parking lot, driving home, and making tuna fish sandwiches (in which I used plenty of lettuce).

I held no doubt that someone's consciousness was with me on Thursday. Considering my post-score discoveries, at least 75 percent of Medium One's statements were accurate. Now let's turn to Medium 2, for Day 5.

Medium 2, Thursday, July 18, 2002:

Y 1. Something was wrong with electrical appliances (anything electric)

I documented my appliance problems on several daily activity logs. The following is an excerpt from my e-mail to Christopher on Thursday.

Daily Diary
    Morning
    Watermelon for lunch, but garbage disposal stopped mid-cycle, as did the clothes dryer—booof—just like my computer on Sunday—no reason—but it reminded me about my new laptop computer. So I called the computer repairman who said there seems to be an electrical problem.

P 2. Subject may have had a disagreement or misunderstanding with a coworker or associate

P 3. May have had his own personal problems on his mind

Confidentiality kept me from scoring both of these Yes. I had just ended a professional relationship because his personal issues contaminated our work.

P 4. Legal advice or contract negotiations are around subject also

N 5. These are present more as business options

Both statements proved true. Upon receiving two bank contracts, due mid-July, I left them face up on a table and forgot about them. They did not catch my eye until one week after the experiment, which ended on the 19th.

P 6. Feet pains (corns or other foot problems) seem to be bothering sitter

Y 7. Subjects shoes seem too tight or uncomfortable

Y 8. The shoes seem to be the problem

I broke the bones in my right foot while water skiing and cannot find shoes to accommodate that foot. I wore sandals on Thursday, but hobbled from discomfort.

N 9. Subject seems to just love "bagels with a smear" (bagel with cream cheese)

I love heaps of cream cheese on bagels, but avoid them because of the cholesterol.

N 10. Subject is from the East Coast

N 11. Subject is of ethnic decent

N 12. Subject has dark hair

This string of statements did not apply to me.

Y 13. Has blue or gray eyes

Whether my eyes are blue or gray depends on the color of clothing.

N 14. Subject has above average IQ

I scored this No for two reasons. I think of myself as being average in every way, although I must admit that my IQ registers above. Furthermore, I speculated that the medium knew: Intelligence and interest in survival coincide.

P 15. Is a little obsessive-compulsive

N 16. Their office or surroundings are usually very neat

I can be a little obsessive if the problem is immediate and monumental, but my office is never neat.

Y 17. Seems to be lots of delays around things yesterday

Y 18. Subject waited for return phone calls

Y 19. Also waited for packages or people to arrive

Y 20. Mail seems to be lost or misplaced

P 21. Some kind of mail sitter is waiting for what they won't receive until early next week

N 22. The mail's coming from California

My colleague, Debbie, and I agreed to meet for supper and

that she would telephone as she neared the restaurant. She was delayed. I waited for her call, and again for her arrival at the restaurant. During dinner we discussed waiting for mail delivery—our contracts from Unity, and more. The following is an excerpt from the evening section of my daily log exactly as I e-mailed it to Chris.

Nice dinner. Fun. Always good laughs with Debbie, but she got very upset about her CD . . . that she mailed to me . . . was lost in the mail . . . not copyrighted yet.

Y 23. Subject discussed family history yesterday (family trees, genealogy)

P 24. Something about creating or finding other family members

One of my daily endeavors is helping my best friend search for her birth parents.

P 25. Something about a refrigerator not being cool enough

N 26. May have to buy a new fridge

Was I too guarded or in denial on this one? The refrigerator, not a full size but a mini, was not cooling properly. Although hopeful it would last, I nevertheless had just scanned sale brochures looking at replacement prices.

With the accuracy rate for Medium 2 being 69 percent, and 75 percent for Medium 1, my mind wondered, *Could Susy Smith have visited with me on July 18 and conveyed her observations to the mediums?* Neither I nor anyone else can say for certain. With certainty, however, I know that someone perceived many of my thoughts, emotions, and activities on that particular Thursday.

Phase 2

Much to my surprise, on the 7th of August, I received an e-mail from Christopher.

Hello again,

Phase 2 of our Afterlife Watching Experiment was conducted last week. The format was basically the same as

Phase 1; however, instead of being asked to follow the subject around for the day, our designated deceased individuals were asked to bring loved ones connected to our sitters to their readings with the mediums. For that reason, the readings did not need to be scored every day as in Phase 1. This has allowed us to include all of the readings in this e-mail.

I was not aware that discernments were being conducted, but after scoring the five readings given by each medium, I saw that Day 4 clearly applied to me. Before I explain, let's review the first "raw reading" verbatim. How many of the remarks apply to you?

Medium 1, Phase 2—The Transcribed Reading
Reading Day 4

I hear the name Betty that relates to this woman in some way. This is a mother-type energy and I feel she had a hard time seeing because she keeps pointing to her eyes and how she couldn't see!

Next, I am getting a pain in my knee and it makes me wonder who has the problem with the knee? Left knee. Who had work on their left knee?

Something here that is a little odd. I am seeing a man sitting cross-legged and he is playing the flute and a basket is in front of him. A snake rises out of the basket and moves to the motion of the flute. Hmm . . . hypnotizing . . . yes. OK, so since I don't feel like this sitter can hypnotize a snake while playing a flute, I do believe they can possibly hypnotize people? Something with being hypnotized relates here in some way. The only other thing this could mean is that the sitter saw something like this while on a trip.

OK, moving right along, I now see two men and one woman. I believe the one "set" is parents, a couple, for they stand together. This would be one mother and two fathers or a father and an uncle.

The one man, who is either the uncle or father, had

something wrong with his throat. Cancer? He holds his throat. Can't talk. He also stands separate from the "couple."

This woman, who seems to be a mother, is showing me she carried a silver-looking coin or medal in a black, small case or coin purse. She had arthritis in her hands. This metal disc seems like a token or something like that. She is holding it up to show me. So this silver/metal round thing is important. It is *not* a ring. It's flat.

The one man wore a sweater over his shirt often. It was a button-down sweater. It looks to be brown in color. He also is telling me he had something to do with maps—or blocking of something like homes or roads . . . I just see drawings flat on paper. Looks like a bunch of squares or designs. He used his hands, but not for hard labor, I see a pencil in it.

The month of September is important for this person.

He also tells me something about a promotion or, wait, is it a "promo" of some kind? Hmm . . . I hear pro-something.

The woman (mother or grandmother) was very religious. Feels more like the grandmother with this. She also has kind of funny hair. Pretty but a little wiry.

Now I am being shown a big fluffy. . . dog that looks like a *lion*. Unless it is a lion? *Very* furry . . . gold, orange, and brown colors . . . sitting next to the sitter. So it relates to the sitter in some way. However, I can't get lion out of my head, but I see what looks like a dog.

I see a woman who reminds me of Ruth Buzzi from *Laugh-In*. Remember that show? This has to be either the name or the looks. Hair is pulled back tight in a bun, parted in the middle. She seems to be wearing brown as well. Her energy seems more like great-aunt . . . could be friend of an aunt.

There is something really big here coming in . . . I keep seeing the word "slavery." There is something important in history in relation to the sitter's family or close friend. Whether this deals with the underground railroad, a safe-house connection, or records of some kind—I see a connection here. . . . They are taking me up the East Coast. And I feel I go all the way to Rochester, N.Y. There are many slaves here to represent themselves. They show this very clearly to me. I am being shown a house about 15 minutes from my house that was once used as part of the underground railroad. It was in an area called Lafayette. They connect me to that house *but* show me up East! I also see records of some kind . . . written records. This is really amazing. Now that I think about it, I think Rochester came up a couple days ago and here it is again! However, they show more of the East Coast . . . today. Not just the one area. *If* this sitter doesn't know about this, then someone around them does! It's just too strong to be off! I want to make sure I represent this because it's coming in very strong. There *has* to be a connection *and* proof in some way to this. Even if they don't think they know about this, they need to look into it.

Does this person also have memorabilia from the Civil War? I feel like I'm in the middle of a history book here or at least a history class!

They are *not* letting me out of the area from the west ends of Missouri to the East Coast. They take that and run from Florida to Missouri all the way up to the East Coast. OK, I'm going nowhere. Let me see what else I can get.

OK, there is a connection to Tennessee here. Also the Smoky Mountains.

I also hear the name Birch or Berch . . . a Bir or Ber and a Sch name . . . hmm.

This is really odd but I am *now* getting a completely different picture. As if everyone moved out of the way for this "new guy." He is showing me the state of Hawaii! I see the pineapples and sugarcane and the whole scene to get me there. There is a man here that claims he is the "dad or brother" to a man still here. He seems to think I can get this message to somebody there? He was showing me he was on a stretcher? Or something like that before he died? Something long and narrow that you lie on.

I hear this "hearty" laugh . . . receding hair line . . . tan head . . . I think . . . and I'm not sure, but it seems the color eyes didn't match . . . he shows me two colors. Unless he had two colors that were very pronounced in his eyes? Hmm . . . something about the two colors of eyes.

There is also something about a "baby" around this as well. A grandchild? They know about the grandchild. Are with the grandchild. Hmm . . . but it's only one specific baby . . . so if this has to do with more than one then it's the *one* that stands out. One was just born or is sick? Seems like maybe the body of this child. The neck or back area.

Hmm . . . I keep seeing the back of the body . . . I'm sorry I can't exactly place what they are saying about this baby . . . but there is some connection to this.

They are also talking about a big storm coming up in Hawaii . . . a hurricane . . . ugh. Hope I'm wrong. They show what looks like a hurricane . . . big buildings in pieces. Something about a hotel.

Now, how many statements applied to you? For me, the opening comments were accurate, but then they seemed to fade. Over time, however, the later became the most significant, as I will explain.

My Responses to Medium 1, Day 4

I hear the name Betty that relates to this woman in some way. This is a mother-type energy and I feel she had a hard time seeing because she keeps pointing to her eyes and how she couldn't see!

My mother, Betty, suffered with a degenerative eye disease. On her final day, she pointed to her eyes, complaining, "I can't see."

I am getting a pain in my knee and it makes me wonder who has the problem with the knee? Left knee. Who had work on their left knee?

My daughter and mother-in-law had knee surgery, and my husband has serious knee problems.

I am seeing a man sitting cross-legged and he is playing the flute and a basket is in front of him. A snake rises out of the basket and moves to the motion of the flute. Hmm . . . hypnotizing . . . yes. OK, so since I don't feel like this sitter can hypnotize a snake while playing a flute, I do believe they can possibly hypnotize people? Something with being hypnotized relates here in some way. The only other thing this could mean is that the sitter saw something like this while on a trip.

I recently bought my five-year-old grandson, Silas, a magic set that included a flute, pendulum, hat, cape, gloves, boxes, and other paraphernalia. After watching a movie, wherein snake charmers played flutes while cobras rose from baskets, I demonstrated the charmers' hypnotic procedure with similar parts from the magic set. Mimicking me, Silas pretended to hypnotize our cats, urging them to rise.

I now see two men and one woman. I believe the one "set" is parents, a couple, for they stand together. This would be one mother and two fathers or a father and an uncle.

My parents are deceased along with their brothers and uncles.

The one man, who is either the uncle or father, had something wrong with his throat. Cancer? He holds his throat. Can't talk. He also stands separate from the "couple."

My dad could not speak during the final three months of his life because of a tracheotomy (no cancer), but would he stand apart from my mother? Her favorite uncle, Tex, died from emphysema complications. He and my parents were close, so it is likely they would be together in the hereafter.

This woman, who seems to be a mother, is showing me she carried a silver-looking coin or medal in a black, small case or coin purse. She had arthritis in her hands. This metal disc seems like a token or something like that. She is holding it up to show me. So this silver/metal round thing is important. It is *not* a ring. It's flat.

Carrying a quarter was a major issue for my mother. She never left home without it. "*Always* carry at least one quarter to pay for phone calls in case of an emergency," she often said (public telephones operated for ten cents at the time). Her purse, with coins still inside, rests on my shelf—a reminder to always carry emergency cash.

As for the comment, *She had arthritis in her hands—*

Mother's knuckles became so enlarged and uncomfortable that she could no longer wear her rings.

The one man wore a sweater over his shirt often. It was a button-down sweater. It looks to be brown in color. He also is telling me he had something to do with maps—or blocking of something like homes or roads. I just see drawings flat on paper. Looks like a bunch of squares or designs. He used his hands, but not for hard labor, I see a pencil in it.

This string of comments described Mother's uncle, Tex. Cold by nature, he wore solid-color (brown, tan, or navy-blue) button-down sweaters over his shirts most of the time. He owned several businesses, but he most relished his sideline—designing commercial property and street layouts for Hot Springs, Arkansas.

The month of September is important for this person.

I was careful to schedule around September 13, my husband's birthday.

He also tells me something about a promotion or, wait, is it a "promo" of some kind? Hmm . . . I hear pro-something.

Two events applied. My colleague Debbie and I were discussing how to promote her CD, and I was conversing with colleagues about placing my Afterlife Encounters Survey on the Internet.

The woman (mother or grandmother) was very religious. Feels more like the grandmother with this. She also has kind of funny hair. Pretty but a little wiry.

My grandmother was very religious, and her hair became wiry in the months prior to her death.

Now I am being shown a big fluffy . . . dog that looks like a *lion*. Unless it is a lion? *Very* furry . . . gold, orange, and brown colors . . . sitting next to the sitter.

Chauncy, our gold, orange, brown, and white long-haired St. Bernard, was mammoth. Instead of barking, he roared like a lion—

loud and continuously. We speculated that he was bored with city life, and my parents wanted a guard dog for their home; therefore, we drove him to Arkansas to live with them. During the Afterlife Watching Experiments, I met with Debbie Fancher to discuss our PowerPoint presentation and gave her a photograph of Dad sitting with Chauncy on the back porch of his ranch-style home.

I see a woman who reminds me of Ruth Buzzi from *Laugh-In*. Remember that show? This has to be either the name or the looks. Hair is pulled back tight in a bun, parted in the middle. She seems to be wearing brown as well. Her energy seems more like great-aunt.

I remembered *Laugh-In*. I never thought about it prior to the medium's remarks but my grandmother's sisters (my great-aunts) favored the Ruth Buzzi character—with their buns, long chins, sweaters, and purses.

There is something really big here coming in . . . I keep seeing the word "slavery." There is something important in history to this with relation to the sitter's family or close friend. Whether this deals with the underground railroad, a safe house connection, or records of some kind, I see a connection here. . . . They are taking me up the East Coast. And I feel I go all the way to Rochester, New York. There are many slaves here to represent themselves. They show this very clearly to me. I am being shown a house about 15 minutes from my house that was once used as part of the underground railroad. It was in an area called Lafayette. They connect me to that house *but* show me up East! I also see records of some kind . . . written records. This is really amazing. Now that I think about it, I think Rochester came up a couple days ago and here it is again! However, they show more of the East Coast . . . today. Not just the one area. *If* this sitter doesn't know about this, then someone around them does! It's just too strong to be off! I want to make sure I represent this because it's coming in very strong. There *has* to be a connection *and* proof in some way to this. Even if they don't think they know about this, they need to look into it.

This began a string of comments that now seem evidential for life beyond bodily death. After my parents died, I flew to the East Coast to meet my dad's son for the first time. In the rock-walled basement of his home were etchings made by slaves who were hidden during the years it was used as a station on the underground railroad. Beyond that, I did not know more—therefore, to memory, I filed the medium's comment, "If they don't know about this they need to look into it."

Does this person also have memorabilia from the Civil War? I feel like I'm in the middle of a history book here or at least a history class!

I also hear the name Birch or Berch . . . a Bir or Ber.

This is really odd but I am *now* getting a completely different picture. As if everyone moved out of the way for this "new guy." He is showing me the state of Hawaii! I see the pineapples and sugarcane and the whole scene to get me there. There is a man here that claims he is the "dad or brother" to a man still here. He seems to think I can get this message to somebody there? He was showing me he was on a stretcher? Or something like that before he died? Something long and narrow that you lie on.

I hear this "hearty" laugh . . . receding hair line . . . tan head . . . I think . . . and I'm not sure, but it seems the color eyes didn't match . . . he shows me two colors. Unless he had two colors that were very pronounced in his eyes? Hmm . . . Something about the two colors of eyes.

There is also something about a "baby" around this as well. A grandchild? They know about the grandchild. Are with the grandchild. Hmm . . . but it's only one specific baby . . . so if this has to do with more than one then it's the *one* that stands out. One was just born or is sick? Seems like maybe the body of this child. The neck or back area.

Gary advised everyone involved not to discuss the experiments with anyone—family was the only exception. Therefore, I e-mailed the statements to a distant relative, asking if any applied to them. She delved into each comment, and then provided documentation, which I forwarded to Chris.

According to the deed from her county courthouse, the underground railroad home was previously owned by Henry and Floreene Brichard, and before them a religious group resided on the property and named it "The House of Mystics." She further disclosed, "The house is full of Civil War memorabilia," "my aunt had two distinctly different colored eyes" (she was Dad's daughter), and "my firstborn survived only a few days" (and the baby was Dad's first great-grandchild).

Further comments paralleled. *The state of Hawaii . . . a man here that claims he is the dad or brother to a man still here. He was showing me he was on a stretcher . . .* Dad's son owned a winter condominium in Hawaii. During the months before Dad died, he was transported from one critical care unit to another on a gurney. All the while, his physicians asked me to stay with him; otherwise he continuously called out for his son.

Dad wanted to make amends with his first family so badly that I wondered about the entire series of statements, especially, *"He seems to think I can get this message to somebody there . . . it seems the color eyes didn't match . . . he shows me two colors . . . two colors that were very pronounced . . . Hmm . . . Something about the two colors of eyes."* I had no idea that his daughter's eyes were two different hues—therefore, could Dad be offering physical evidence that his spirit exists and communicates? Because the comments were foreign to me, the medium could not have been dovetailing into my consciousness.

The format for this phase of the Afterlife Watching Experiments was for Susy Smith to connect with the sitters' discarnate relatives. What do you think? Was it successful with Medium 1?

Scoring Phase 2

I received a follow-up e-mail from Chris, wherein he passed along an explanatory letter and scoring form for Phase 2.

> After unanticipated delays, it is finally time to finish Phase 2 scoring with the two mediums. You will recall that this phase of the experiment involved two mediums attempting to obtain information about your deceased loved ones. It was double-blind—you did not hear the readings when they occurred, and you do not know which of the two readings (out of ten readings; two mediums times five days) were focused on your deceased loved ones and you.

Your scoring task is to read the actual transcripts for the five readings from each medium and rank each reading.

Chris has attached two files. Each file contains five readings—Day 1 through Day 5, for each of the two mediums. For each file, you are to read each of the readings, and then rank them from 1 (best applies to your deceased loved ones and you) to 5 (least applies to your deceased loved ones and you). Please record your rankings and answer some additional free-form questions.

If you have any questions, please e-mail Christopher and he will pass them on to me. As you know, until the three phases of the experiment are completed, I can't speak directly with you about the experiment. Thank you for your patience and devotion to this work. It is because of you (and hopefully your deceased loved ones) that this work is possible.

Blessings,

Gary E. Schwartz, Ph.D.

My scores for Medium 1, Day 4, edited for brevity, may provide more clarity regarding the experiments.

Scoring Medium 1, Phase 2

WHICH DAY BEST APPLIES TO YOU AND WHY?

I chose Day 4 because it held the greatest number of specific and accurate statements that related to me—my mother's name (Betty), the silver coin (a major issue for her), "Sch name" (I had just received a birthday card and letter from Jack Schwarz, a recently deceased mentor, who said we would always be together through the cosmos). The medium, furthermore, presented a significant amount of information regarding my dad's family—all of which I was oblivious to at the time of the reading.

PLEASE EXPLAIN YOUR PERSONAL SELECTION STRATEGIES.

My strategy was to be extremely conservative, making certain that my affirmative answers were documented or could be verified in some way. After the experiment, I sent Chris e-mails from distant family members, wherein they substantiated pertinent facts from county records and personal information.

**PLEASE RATE YOUR CONFIDENCE IN
YOUR CHOICE AND EXPLAIN WHY.**

I am very confident Day 4 was my reading for a number of reasons. First, the number of accurate comments—Mother's name came through, her eye problems, Dad's throat (he had a tracheotomy—the full story is documented in my book *Life After Loss*), Mother's issue about carrying a coin, and *"Dog who looks like a lion"* mirrored Chauncy, our long-haired St. Bernard.

Furthermore, on Day 4 the medium suggested, "If they don't know about this they need to look into it," which I did. My dad was estranged from his first family for decades. After his death, I briefly met his son, whose winter condominium was in Hawaii (the Hawaiian connection from the reading). His East Coast home, a farmhouse previously owned by "The Mystics," was used by the underground railroad. I knew about the etchings that remain in the rock-walled basement, but nothing more about his home or family.

**WHAT SUGGESTIONS WOULD YOU MAKE FOR IMPROVING
OUR METHODS OF RATING THE READINGS?**

My only suggestion is to add a post-scoring survey. After submitting my responses in Phase 1 and 2, I discovered information previously unknown by me—therefore, the mediums' statements proved more accurate over time.

The second medium's discernment on Day 4 applied to me as well. Let's review the "raw reading" exactly as Chris e-mailed it to all five sitters. How many of the remarks apply to you?

Medium 2, Phase 2—The Transcribed Reading

Reading Day 4

An older, male, father figure appears, acknowledging "West Point or the military." I'm seeing a figure of a man in an officer's uniform. Wants me to say the name "Max." Feels like a dog's name. Makes me think of a German Shepherd. I feel the male who has crossed wants to acknowledge the family dog that has passed and may have been buried in their backyard.

Father figure also acknowledges the sitter may be having some problems with their phone lines, either at home or at work. So much so, that they will most likely have a repair man out soon.

Now I'm hearing a child singing! I believe it is the energy of a young girl no more than five or six. I hear humming and a "La, La, La" sound as though she is trying to sing along to something. She wants me to say the name "Diedre." I feel this child passed many years ago. There's also a Charles connection to her. She makes me feel her passing was quite traumatic. A real struggle. It has an accidental feel to it. Very quick. I feel her lungs filling with fluid . . . most likely a drowning. May have something to do with a well. Could be connecting to yesterday's water pump.

Another energy enters—calls herself "Auntie." Shows me a lot of interest in the American Indian. I'm seeing handwoven rugs, tapestry, jewelry. She's connecting to a woman who is somehow connected to the university or a university. I do not feel she is blood related to the sitter. She feels much more like a guide. I do feel, though, that the person who she's connecting with has actually met her. She keeps repeating the numbers, 007, 007, 007. (I want to laugh to myself because I'm answering back—who are you, James Bond?) She is acknowledging a Suzie.

How many of the statements applied to you? Some were specific but others vaguely applied to me. I will pass along my responses.

My Responses to Medium 2, Day 4

An older, male, father figure who acknowledges "West Point or the military," a man in an officer's uniform, wants me to say the name "Max." Feels like a dog's name. Makes me think of a German Shepherd. I feel the male who is crossed wants to acknowledge the family dog that has passed and may have been buried in their backyard.

One of our favorite cats was named Max, but then the medium said, "Feels like a dog's name. Makes me think of a German Shepherd." My uncle, a retired officer from the military, owned many German Shepherds.

Father figure also acknowledges the sitter may be having some problems with their phone lines either at home or at work. So much so, that they will most likely have a repairman out soon.

I had been commenting to Chris that local telephone line difficulties were delaying my responses, but I had called for repairs.

Now I'm hearing a child singing! I believe it is the energy of a young girl no more than five or six. I feel this child passed many years ago. Her passing was quite traumatic. A real struggle. It has an accidental feel to it. Very quick. I feel her lungs filling with fluid . . . most likely a drowning.

I knew that on my paternal side of the family, several children died young; therefore, I called Dad's 98-year-old sister, Bertha. She confirmed some of the remarks. Her two sisters died around the ages of five, one after eating an apple at the county fair. Although she could not remember the exact cause of the second death, she recalled, "They both died a day or so after they got sick. The doctor came to our house but couldn't do anything for them. The girls' lungs filled up until they couldn't breathe any more."

Another energy enters—calls herself Auntie. Shows me a lot of interest in the American Indian. She's connecting to a woman who is somehow connected to the university or a university. I do not feel she is blood related to the sitter. I do feel, though, that the person who she's connecting with has actually met her.

Not Auntie, but Annie—Annie Snow. As one of the first-born Chickasaw, she is honored on a monument that stands in Oklahoma. We were not blood related—she was my husband's grandmother, who died several years ago. And I was working with several universities.

She is acknowledging a Suzie.

I ordered and read four books authored by Susy Smith during the experiments (as I documented in my daily logs). I kept singing "If you knew Susy . . ." and thinking she might not have liked that song, but read otherwise weeks thereafter.

Scoring Medium 2, Day 4

For brevity, I will combine the questions and my scoring. I selected Day 4, because most of the statements were accurate for me—our cat Max, my uncle who retired as an officer from the military, and then "the family dog that has passed and may have been buried in their backyard." I would normally consider comments about a dog's death and backyard burial vague, but the events just occurred and were very traumatic for all of our family. The remarks about problems with the telephone lines and repairs were specific and accurate as well. Moreover, my aunt confirmed that her sisters died in a way similar to the medium's description. The information regarding Annie—her being American Indian, our not being blood related, and my being connected to universities—was exact and meaningful.

Phase 3: The Telephone Readings

Until this point, neither the sitters nor the mediums had privy to names, but then we all received an e-mail dated February 17th.

> We are about to perform a most important part of our three-phase experiment—the actual phone readings. Each of you who are sitters will receive two phone readings, one with Janet and one with Mary.
> You will call Janet and Mary at your respective scheduled times, and they will audiotape the readings.
> After your readings are completed, Janet and Mary

will mail the tapes to Chris. We will have copies of the tapes made as well as transcripts. We will then e-mail you the transcripts to score.

Attached is a simple questionnaire that can be filled out by everyone—sitters and mediums—after each reading. As sitters, you will fill out the questionnaire twice—once for each of your two readings. As mediums you (Mary and Janet) will fill out the questionnaire five times, one for each of your five readings.

For the sitters, we would also like to ask you to take notes during the readings. This way you will have important information in writing for when you are reviewing the material later and filling out the questionnaire. Also this will allow you to follow up on any information about which you may not know or be aware.

Mary and Janet—feel free to conduct your readings as you normally would. Introduce yourselves, explain how you work, and do a normal reading. Sitters—feel free to ask questions and allow the process to flow.

Remember—*this is an experiment*—we must be open to what will happen, whatever it is. Don't worry if a given reading is a great success or not—just be genuine and let the data speak—whatever the findings are, our purpose is to allow the discovery process to occur.

I trust you will have a wonderful experience.

Warmly, Gary and Chris

Christopher's next e-mail contained the date (25th of February) and time (1 P.M. CST) for my appointed session with Medium 1 (Janet), along with her telephone number. The transcript of our session is as follows:

Telephone Reading with Janet Mayer, Medium 1
Hello, Janet. I'm Dianne, one of the research sitters.

Hi, Dianne. It's nice to hear from you. I'm going to explain how I do a reading, if that's okay, then we'll go ahead and just jump right in. First of all, I will focus on you, even though I didn't know your name. I try to see what I pick up around you and anybody who's crossed over, to see if they can come in and share something with me. If you hear me speak of a woman named Susy, it's because she's my mentor-guide, and whenever I do any readings she always shows up somewhere along the reading. She helps me focus or brings me to a picture that I need to see. Because I see a lot of pictures, and hear words or see words in my head, I'm not always correct on the exact interpretation, so keep that in mind. And I do interpret, so that is something that you'll have to say if it really fits with you. Also, some of the people I see may seem alive because to me they're all alive, and unless it comes out really, really strong, I don't usually know if they're passed or not. So if I mentioned somebody's name, and they're still here, don't get nervous and think that they're going to die soon—that's just how it comes through to me, okay? All right, we'll go ahead and start.

First, I have to mention that I do pre-readings. Yesterday I sat down to see what I could get for you, then this morning I meditated, and now I'll take if from there.

My first sense was a person, and I shouldn't say a woman, because a person named Pat keeps coming in and has come through during every reading. I don't know who Pat fits with, but I really believe the person is deceased and letting me know he or she is with us. So we'll leave it and go on. The next thing that I was getting around you was a lot of healing energy, a lot of medical energy, but it feels really healing. There's a lot of healing energy around you. I don't know if you're some form of healer, but that was the first thing that really came to me when I was doing this. Okay, the next thing that came through . . . I saw a foosball table, do you know what a foosball table is?

Yes, I do.

Okay. I guess it relates to soccer, so either there's something around you with a foosball table or somebody around you played soccer. I feel like you've been speaking because they show me your voice, and it seems like it's an important connection. So I don't know if you type or if you have something written, and then speak about it . . . I'm not sure how that connection fits . . . but that's how it comes through for me.

Okay, the next thing coming through . . . there's something about blindfolds over your eyes. And they're telling me . . . it's like I see you put on a little mask around your eyes at one time . . . I don't know . . . I'm not seeing it when you sleep, but there's something related to that with you. And at first I wasn't sure if they were trying to tell me that you have blinders on at times, if you were just looking too straight ahead and not looking out enough, or if you actually have something over your eyes. I wasn't sure how that fit for you. Do you understand . . . does it make sense to you?

Yes.

Okay because I was thinking: Boy, I'm not sure on that one. I also had something with Italian food. Now, I got this yesterday, so I'm not sure if that's your favorite food, if you're making it, or what's going on, but I had to throw that in. There's a woman here. She has dark hair and presents herself with an orchid in her hair. To me it seems like the hair is pulled back, at least on the one side where the orchid is. And it reminds me of an event like a wedding or something where . . . it had to be something fancy, but it reminds me of, you know, the tropical. So I'm not sure who she is, but that's how it comes through to me. There's also a man here, and he . . . ok, this is going to sound kind of odd, but he's showing me a ruby, it looks kind of like a ruby stick pin or a pin of some type. And he's wearing a suit and . . . let's see . . . yeah . . . that's what he's showing me. There's something about ruby, unless it's like an anniversary; I don't know what the ruby anniversary is, but I keep seeing ruby, and it looks like there's a pin on the lapel of his suit. It's actually pinstriped too by the way. He's telling me "pinstripes" so I'm going to write that down so I can remember what he's shown me. He backed away.

I'm seeing candles around you . . . and it seems like . . . it's kind of an odd way they show this . . . it's not as if it's a birthday. It seems like it's candles . . . big candles. Either you light a lot of candles or you do some kind of work where you have a lot of candles. I also see a second setting and this comes across as an office setting, and this is where I was thrown off, because I see bright ceiling lights, and it's what you would see in an office building or some kind of medical building or something like that, but it also seemed like the setting where I saw a lot of candles . . . it was like a working environment as well. So I'm kind of getting these two pictures at the same time, so I'm not sure if you're doing a of couple different things at once or not, but that's how it's coming to me.

The next thing is the name Sandy, or Sarah, because I see "Sa." And I don't know if there's a Sarah or Sandy around you. And this energy feels more motherly, grandmotherly type. And there's also like a Dorothy or

Doris that comes through with this, so I feel that they're in a circle with you. Let me see . . . the Sarah name sounds more like your mother's side, and the Doris or Dorothy energy comes more from your father's. For some reason that's the way they show it to me.

The next thing I get is a Chinese woman . . . well she's either Chinese or Japanese . . . and she's connected to you as well. She's around you and it's funny how they show it because they show it really close to you.

The next thing that they're showing me is diamonds in your throat. Okay . . . the odd thing is they're showing them actually *in* your throat. I've never seen anything like this before. To me, it has to be that you have a very important speaking voice or you know you need to treat it like diamonds because of how you use it. It's something about your throat . . . it's actually marquee diamonds . . . a bunch of marquee diamonds around your throat . . . it seems like your voice, the way you use it, or however you're using it, is really like a diamond. You know what I mean? Does that sound silly?

No, not at all.

It was just . . . I have never, ever, gotten something like that before. The next thing that comes around you is a woman behind you to the right, and I consider that your mother's side. And it feels kind of grandmothery, but the funny thing is, I get this bakery scent, and I see her doing something with some kind of flat bread or a pastry. Rolling it out because it's flat, and they're actually showing me the process. So I don't know if you have somebody on your mother's side who's in the bakery business or if she was a big baker, but it stands out really strong about this woman.

The next thing I'm seeing is a number of universities around you, and I feel like somehow you're connected or working with a number of them. It doesn't seem like it's one specific university, because I was trying to see if I could pinpoint it, and it doesn't come across as if it's just one. For some reason I want to say three or four . . . that's how they show it . . . that you're connected with three or four universities.

Now I'm seeing knives, and it looks like the kind of sharp knives you would use for cutting up food, but they say that it's not for food, that it's cutting up something with work. I mean they show me the food and knife, and then they take the food away, so to me that means the knives aren't used for that . . . that there's something else . . . hmm . . . does that make sense to you at all?

Hmmm.

The only other thing I can think of is an Exacto knife or something medical . . . I don't know . . . it's strange the way it doesn't relate to food but they're showing me these knives, so I don't know. The next I see are two boys . . . well it could be two men . . . but I have two boys in my head, but I'm thinking it could be two men, because I'm seeing something about them going in two directions. One is with finance or a CPA, and I feel like the other one went a whole different direction. And I can't tell if . . . hmm . . . yeah, I really only get the one that is working in some kind of finance, but they keep telling me that there's two brothers, that are connected, and they go in opposite-type directions. Where one is in finance and the other is in some kind of arts or something, you know, some other kind of media. But I'm trying to figure out if it's two brothers or if, because they're really close, it's two really, really good friends. But they seem like brothers to me, that's how it comes across.

One of the strongest things I've had so far today is a feeling of your father . . . this really strong, strong feeling. They're showing me a box with some files or papers in it that I feel are his. And, for some reason, I feel like they're yours, but they're his. So I don't know if you have them, or if you're in charge of . . . okay . . . I have to ask this because it's so strong . . . is your father passed?

Yes

Okay, that's what it is. If you have some of his things, it has to be his box with his papers and things. I feel a lot of illness throughout my body, so do you know what kind of illness he had or how he passed? I always ask the spirits if it was something like an impact, accident, or illness. And to me, it feels like it was something long and drawn out and . . . I don't know why, but I feel like I'm getting something about his clothes. Was he in a fire? I mean was there any kind of fire around him . . . I mean like when he was younger, because I keep getting something about a fire, and then I also feel like he had to get different clothes before he passed. I don't know if he had to get a smaller size or what exactly they're trying to tell me, because I feel his presence, but I don't feel like he's speaking to me. There's somebody else trying to show me what's going on, and they're telling me something about switching clothes around, and it happened one to two months before he passed.

That could have been.

I'm trying to get some details from him, and they're telling me about the box of items and clothes. I don't know if it was him, but who's the holy person? There's a real religious person, because they're showing me they have their hands together, like they're praying. Okay . . . something else . . . did somebody wear pearls, or some type of, um . . . I'm seeing beads around somebody's neck. At first I thought it was a pearl necklace but it's not. I believe it's some kind of prayer beads.

Not that I know of, but it could be.

That's really interesting to me . . . when I see something that I can't quite place. I mean, they're beads, but I think it relates somehow to the person who was praying. Okay, the next thing I get is some kind of celebration around you, and the way it's shown to me is that they are passing out cigars. And when I see that I think of a birth, so I don't know if there is somebody around you who just had a child. They're passing out cigars, so there's a birth, and that's exactly how it came out to me.

I keep getting a D name, and it's really funny because your name is Dianne, but I get Dana, or maybe Darlene, and there's something unusual that happened in a boat. It feels like some kind of boating accident, and I don't want to laugh, but I feel like it was something unusual and maybe funny.

Okay.

Just hold on to that one. When I got the picture, I saw somebody meaning to throw something in reverse but went forward, up into something. I saw it as a boat. So if you know of an incident like that, where they thought it was supposed to be put in reverse but went into drive instead and went through something, that's how I see it.

And I see bluebells around you . . . you know the flowers . . . bluebells. Don't know why . . . just came up. The next thing I get is something around you, expanding, and to me it looks like a slide show, or some kind of projector, or projection of something with slides, pictures, colors, and people. I'm not really sure what you do, but that's how it comes across to me.

There's an unusually tall man around you. This man seems to be, from what I'm thinking, at least 6'3". I mean he looks like a basketball player . . . really tall. I feel this connection to you, and I don't know if he's passed or if he's still here, but I just know he's a really tall guy and he showed up in the middle of my doing this. That's how it comes across, okay? I also hear the name Roger. Nothing came with it so I wanted to make sure I told you the name, so I at least have that out, so if something comes up with him I'll let you know. And I feel like there was somebody around you . . . how they show it is somebody drowning . . . and the way Suzie comes across with this, is the lungs were filling up with fluid, so I don't know if it was an actual drowning or if it was from like an illness . . . maybe the lungs were filling up with fluid from the illness. But that's how it came through to me, that basically a person drowned because of their lungs. I feel that is a really important part of the reading, and that the person is okay. It seemed like it was slow and drawn out, but I think it was really quick, and that is the only way I can describe it . . . just feels really fast. All right?

Okay.

I find this really interesting, because this is something else that never came to me before . . . I saw a little baby girl holding up her hand with her five fingers spread apart, so she was really showing me five. I don't know why. That's the only thing she showed me, and then she disappeared. But it was a baby girl, and she was holding her fingers out to make five.

I keep getting Patty or Patricia or Pat . . . for some reason every time I get her, I feel she's related to a sister's friend or the friend of a sister. And I don't know if you have a good friend and something happened to her sister, and her name was Pat, or if you have a sister and her friend's name is Pat. I don't have that information, so I just want to tell you that part. That name keeps coming up again, but I don't know who it's going to fit. It might not fit for you, but for her to keep coming in these readings, it's as if this woman is waiting around to be noticed. So I want to make sure to mention her, because I don't want to leave out anyone who comes through.

Now I'm getting the word gypsy and see rings on the fingers of somebody. I don't feel like it's you. I see a lot of rings on somebody's fingers, though, and I just get that kind of gypsy feeling with the colors and the whole energy. So I don't know if you had relatives in the past that were Bohemian or they had that kind of nature to them.

I'm still seeing blue around you . . . I keep seeing blue. To me that is a very healing color, and that's the healing field that I keep connecting you with. I could be totally off, but that's how it comes through to me. There's a man who was in an impact crash, and to me that makes me feel like a car accident. I feel like it was connected with work, either they were on their way to work, or on their way home from work, or doing something with work and they were in an impact crash. I don't actually have anything else attached to that. I'm trying to see if I can get anything else here for him . . . that's why I'm not saying anything. You know the strange thing is, I keep coming up against a wall, so it makes me feel like there has been something with a wall. I can't explain it any other way. That's all I'm seeing, but it just seems the impact. It was like coming up against a wall is the best way I can describe it, okay?

Okay.

I also see two little kiddies around you, and it's either a boy and a girl, or two girls and one of the girls is a tomboy. I don't know if they're related to you or if they're friends of your kids, but it's two of them and they have to be fairly close in age, because at first I thought they were twins. I felt like they were really close and I think it's a boy and a girl. Or else two boys, but the girl is going to be a tough girl . . . not little bows in the hair kind of thing. I'm getting Hawaii around you, and it was funny because as soon as Hawaii came in, they kept saying the big island, the big island, and then Australia. I kept hearing big island, big island, bigger, bigger, and I'm not sure if you've traveled to either of those places, but for some reason those two names both came in. But I feel like Hawaii actually stands out a little more, but the Australia one is still really strong. Did you lose a lot of loved ones in a very short period of time?

Yes.

Because they're telling me that it was bam, bam, bam. You lost them really quick. And um . . . your mother?

Yes.

Hers was fast because they're showing me quick, quick, quick, so I'm thinking that's how they're getting across to me. Your father stands out the most, right now. Almost like he's in charge, and that's the way it comes through. He may not be that type of man, but he comes through as if he . . . did he go first?

Yes.

That's why . . . he was probably there to greet the other ones who are coming through. And did you also lose someone young? Because they're telling me, they're showing me a family . . . almost like mother, father, and then a kid, but I'm . . . they were younger than you. The way it feels . . . it could be someone like your child or like a niece or nephew, because they're showing me like a younger person.

Yes.

Don't say it . . . I'm trying to figure out . . . I just keep getting quick. I also feel illness, so there's someone that went really quick and someone had an illness. Did somebody have something with their brain, because I see them showing me the head.

That makes sense.

So you understand . . . wait . . . okay it's starting again. I keep hearing a child, but can't place it. It's like they're showing me the mother, father, but then I see somebody else I cannot place. I cannot get it, but I know there's a lot of them . . . quick at one time. Do you have an aunt over there?

Yes.

Is she a little bit on the heavy side?

Yes.

Okay, and the funny thing is I see roses around her. I don't know if that's something she liked, or she wore the color, but they're showing me roses. Would she be the holy one, because they show me nuns around her. And I feel like when they show me nuns or priests, it's something of a religious manner. I don't feel like she had nuns around her . . . but that they were trying to get across that she was a spiritual person.

I don't necessarily relate religion and spirits in the same sense. When I say that, I mean you can be very spiritual, you can be very religious, or you can be both. When they show me people around her, I automatically picked up religion, but then they kind of pull them away. I don't know if that makes sense to you.

Yes.

I see angels hanging and it's not just one. But did you have an angel hanging for a woman, in honor of a woman, or one related to a woman? Because they keep showing me . . . something hanging and it seems to be like an angel or a fairy. And they're trying to associate that with a woman on the other side. For some reason I see angel wings, so I don't know if this was just a really good person, but there's something hanging. Did you have chimes or something that have like wings on them or something?

Yes.

Oh! I saw something like this, so you can tell me if you want.

I make an angel to represent each person in my family.

Okay! So you're the angel woman!

Angels everywhere.

The people who have crossed . . . they have angels.

Yes. Each angel represents someone who has died.

Okay then. That's it. I kept thinking, "Why do they keep talking about the angels hanging and wanting me to connect it to over there."

Yes, since we're further along in the reading, I can tell you that.

I keep hearing the words "light energy" around you as well, and, oh, once again, there's something you do that is healing. I keep getting that. I also see kids around you . . . I don't know why. I hear music and children laughing in the background. It's fun and uplifting, and it reminds me of different songs, where in the background I heard children laughing. That's what I associate with you, in some form, that's how it comes through. I don't know if that makes sense to you but that's how it came through for me.

Then a book. I saw cartoon characters, like a flash of cartoon characters. I don't know if there's some book you have with that. I also see something with your father and a hot air balloon or something that relates to him being in the air. But it seems kind of fluffy . . . and the other word that keeps coming up is zephyr. For that word to come up, there is something related to you and a zephyr. I know that sounds really odd, but I see it and don't know if it relates to your father because of the hot air balloon, or if it's something totally unrelated. I do see something around your father and hot air balloons.

I'm getting mathematical energy. I see numbers around somebody around you, so I don't know if you have somebody who is a mathematics whiz, or chemistry . . . I just see a lot of numbers and it reminds me of math courses.

They're jumping around a lot, so I'm going to ramble for one thing so it will stop. I hear jazzy blues music. And with this is, I feel the movement of swaying, so I don't know if it's a dance movement, if you like that kind of music and sway when you hear it, or if you dance. I feel like you're related to it . . . either you danced when you were smaller . . . did ballet . . . or you were in the arts, which means piano or something artsy . . . because they wrap a circle around it. When they do that, they want me to look at the whole picture. So to me it means that you did something creative like that.

I'm picking up somebody who had cancer, in their female organs I believe. I see the lower area . . . could be abdominal too . . . but I think it has to be a female because they're saying lower. There's either some kind of obstruction or there was something that had to be done in the . . . they're showing me ovaries. Actually they're showing me the left side area . . . a Tai Chi kind of movement, but I also feel like there's music involved, so I don't know if you're doing . . . are you doing some kind of dance . . . slow movement . . . but it's dance? I see it all around you. That's really interesting . . . it's a cross between doing some kind of movement and musical . . . like Tai Chi, which is a real slow body energy kind of thing.

I see leaky water around you. So I think there's going to be . . . either something happened with your pipes or faucet, or I think something is going to happen. Because they're showing me leaky water. And I feel like it's more in your kitchen area. Do you have a laundry room attached to your kitchen?

Yes.

It's somewhere in there, because that's how they're showing it. So just be aware of it. Don't go taking everything apart, but I see something with water around that, and it doesn't feel like a bathroom. It feels more kitchen . . . washer area. Actually, that's all I have. Wait a minute! Whoa . . . whoa . . . wait a minute! Did you . . . do you have . . . a brother?

Yes.

Did you lose a brother?

No.

They're showing me something about a brother, but they're showing me that you lost somebody and it seemed like a brother, but I could have my interpretation wrong. And your mom's passed so you couldn't ask her if she lost a child.

Actually, she did but it wasn't a boy.

I keep seeing a boy over there. I'm not sure how that fits in. I'm trying to figure out how, but I, obviously, was wrong. Is there anything you want to know, share, or add?

They're gone?

Yeah, it does that sometimes. I could be in the middle of something and they leave. But honestly, I see four people, and it looks like a father, a mother, an aunt, and it looks like a younger boy. That doesn't mean there aren't other people over there, but they showed up for me today . . . you know . . . came in differently. I wonder if the little baby girl holding up five fingers was your family?

I hadn't thought of that, but there were five of us.

I'm thinking that . . . because she died young?

She did.

I never saw that before, but if it related to you, that would make sense.

There were five of us . . . my mother gave birth to three girls.

They didn't say son. I was picking up something around your brother, but he's alive, so I have that wrong. I was thinking that there's a boy over there, related to the family. So I guess it could be that. I don't know, to be honest.

Did you by any chance get any names, maybe for my mother or dad?

No, I'm not very good with names. That's my weak point to work on. When I see names, I think, "That just popped in my head or is that really the name?" Now there's only one name that came up . . . I don't know if it's around you or not . . . it's Bill. I'm not sure where he relates, but that's the only person.

What I do is I sit here and I ask them to give me a name. But it's hard . . . it's like when you see a streak of lightning and then you remember the after-flash.

In case you're curious, you were right about a number of things. You said you were getting someone young, whose death was quick, and it had something to do with the brain . . . that had to be my sister-in-law who suicided. Before that, you were right . . . I lost a number of people in a short period of time, my mother's death was fast, my dad died first, and my aunt exactly as you described.

They're all together. It gives me comfort, even though I don't know you, to see that they are together, because when it's your time, you're going to have somebody there for you. They were kind of huddled . . . I mean really close . . . so I think they did that to tell me they were your family.

I'm glad you couldn't see me when you were talking about the candles because my face would have given you feedback. One of the first things I did during the experiments was go into my kitchen and light an array of candles . . . 25 or 30, maybe. Then, in my office, I have a huge overhead, candlelit chandelier that's very, very bright. I was amazed, because there was so much more. The blindfold over my eyes . . . about a week ago I had pink eye! I went to the doctor and got antibiotics, and then it went from one eye to the other eye. I was literally shut down and could not do anything because of pink eye, which I'd never had before. So I was literally wearing blinders over my eyes.

Well, like I said, I have to interpret the way I see it, and I don't know if it's the right interpretation or not. But it was funny when I saw that over your eyes because I was thinking, "Okay, what is he trying to tell me?"

Is there anything I can do for you? Do you have any questions about the reading?

No, I feel it was a good connection for me. It's funny, because I started the reading last night but it started off blank. It's interesting, the way that I see things, because I try to put it into perspective once I see it. The little girl showing me her five fingers stood out a lot. And the angels . . . I couldn't fig-ure out what they were trying to tell me . . . it didn't really connect. This helps me for next time, some things might click easier. I really appreciate you doing this and listening and taking the time because I know this is a lot of work for you too.

I wanted to give you the feedback. With the angels, for example, I could tell you were struggling, but the minute you told me what you were seeing, I knew exactly what you were talking about. And, by the way, my dad was a minister so his angel is holding a miniature Bible and other things that meant a lot to him. But, I knew those angels were never going to make sense to you.

It really didn't. I know sometimes I sound like I'm struggling and I am, because I'm thinking, "How do I explain what I'm seeing?" Well the other thing I would be interested in is the hot air balloon or zephyr. I mean if something like that comes to you, write it in the questionnaire so I can find out if it means something.

My dad feared flying. My mother and I would have traveled anywhere, but Dad refused to fly. As for the hot air balloon and zephyr, I have no idea.

Did something happen around him that he didn't like flying?

I don't know . . . maybe when he was a child. He was born in 1904, so something back . . .

Oh, the Hindenburg.

There you go.

That's it . . . the Hindenburg.

I don't know if that had any significance, but he would not get in an airplane or anything like that. Thank you so much for the reading. It was really good.

Well sure. Thank you. And I thank your family for coming. We had a nice little visit.

I completed the following questionnaire and then submitted it to Chris at the University of Arizona.

Questionnaire, Medium I

BEFORE THE READING BEGAN, HOW ACCURATE DID YOU ANTICIPATE OR EXPECT IT WOULD BE (FROM 0 TO 100 PERCENT)?

Five percent.

AFTER THE READING WAS COMPLETED, HOW ACCURATE DO YOU ESTIMATE IT WAS FOR YOU (NUMBER FROM 0 TO 100 PERCENT)?

Seventy-five percent.

WHAT SPECIFIC PIECES OF INFORMATION, IF ANY, WOULD YOU LIST AS INFORMATION DAZZLE SHOTS—ITEMS THAT WERE ESPECIALLY FACTUALLY ACCURATE AND NOT COMMONLY KNOWN?

I considered the following statements dazzle shots:

Lost a lot of loved ones in a short period of time, because all of my family of origin died within sixteen months.

Mother's was fast. Mother suffered a cardiac arrest and died within hours.

Someone young. Showing me family. Younger than you. Someone like your child, a younger person. Quick, illness, brain. My sister-in-law struggled with a chemical imbalance that ended in suicide, which I chronicled in *Life After Loss.*

Man. Impact crash. This is work related. Like hitting a wall. Gary's story is mentioned in my book as well. He was killed while on a delivery call for his workplace, and, indeed, it was exactly as if he hit a wall. His car, traveling fifty-five miles per hour, rammed head on into an eighteen-wheel trailer-truck that was stalled just over the arch of an interstate bridge.

Angels hanging . . . not just one . . . in honor of a woman. In honor of my grandmother, I made an angel for our Christmas tree and decorated it with miniature items that were meaningful to her. I continued making angels to represent every member of my family.

Drowning. Two of our dogs drowned in our backyard swimming pool.

Woman . . . Japanese. Judy's story is in *Life After Loss.*

Candles . . . office setting . . . being like an office environment with

bright lights and seems to be something similar or to do with the candles.
Ah! Finally! During the experiments, I lit candles and then turned
on the bright 12 candle-light chandelier in my home office.

Blindfold is over your eyes—a week ago. The week prior, I
dashed to my doctor with an eye infection. He diagnosed pink
eye and prescribed eye drops. I administered them every two
hours, and then covered my eyes with a cold rag. I thought I
would have to cancel my planned Friday trip but recovered on
Wednesday the 19th.

Slide show. Debbie Fancher, a professional singer, accompa-
nies my lectures by singing to our Memorial Wall, a Power
Point slide show.

WHAT SPECIFIC PIECES OF INFORMATION, IF ANY, WOULD YOU LIST AS EMOTIONAL DAZZLE SHOTS— ITEMS THAT WERE ESPECIALLY EMOTIONALLY SIGNIFICANT?

All those I listed above were emotionally significant. The
slide show comment, because our deceased relatives were among
those featured on the big screen. *Japanese woman* was meaningful because she had not been discerned before. *Dad . . . his
papers . . . in a box*—from his archive box, I pull out the sermons
Dad typed when I need them for reference. *Diamonds in your
throat* struck a timely chord. An internationally acclaimed psychic spoke those words to me some 15 years ago, adding, "If
you ever start talking about what you know, your life will take
off like a rocket to the moon, so be prepared because everything will totally change." Feeling comfortable with the familiar, I kept my mouth shut.

PLEASE LIST WHO YOU WERE EXPECTING OR HOPING WOULD COME THROUGH AND INDICATE WHETHER YOU BELIEVE THAT THEY DID OR DID NOT.

Mediums generally discern my mother; therefore, I
expected her. As usual, I cannot say whether Mother actually
"came through" or not, because all of the information Janet
provided during the telephone reading could have been
extracted from my psyche.

**WERE YOU SURPRISED BY ANY OF THE
INFORMATION RECEIVED IN THE READING?**

I was surprised by Janet's statements because she seemed to be highlighting stories from my book *Life After Loss,* beginning with *"Have you lost a lot of loved ones in a short period of time?"* She continued with the deaths of my parents, sister-in-law, Japanese friend, client who was killed, and so on.

"Candles . . . office setting" delighted me because lighting candles for Susy was a significant part of the project for me, yet neither medium mentioned them until now.

I did not want to cancel my trip to the conference, so strictly followed the treatments for pink eye as prescribed by my physician. Janet saying, *"Blindfold over your eyes . . . one week ago,"* was astonishing.

I was puzzled by Janet tying *"boat accident"* with *"funny."* Having been an avid water skier, I was in numerous boating catastrophes. I would not be surprised if one of the casualties appeared during a reading, but not something humorous.

Perhaps *"Diamonds in your throat"* was most startling. It reminded me of the psychic's forewarning, *"Your life will change if you reveal what you know."*

**HAD YOU MET THE MEDIUM BEFORE THE
BEGINNING OF THIS EXPERIMENT IN JULY 2002?**

No.

My final part in the series of experiments commenced when Christopher e-mailed Mary's telephone number along with the date (6th of March) and time (7:30 P.M.) of my reading with her. The transcript is as follows:

Telephone Reading with Medium 2, Mary Occhino

Hello, Mary. This is Dianne, one of the research sitters.

Hello. I'd like to explain a little about how I work. When I do a reading over the phone I use tarot cards. Not because I'm a tarot reader, because I'm not, and not that there's anything wrong with that, but that's not what I do. I use them to concentrate—I stare at them. Like some psychics will look at a pen and paper. When I do readings in person, I don't use anything.

What I'm going to do now is make you concentrate on me. Sometimes people are apprehensive before readings, so I'm going to shuffle the cards. As you hear them, tell me when I should stop.

Stop.

Now I'm going to cut them into three piles, and I want you to choose which pile I should work with—one, two, or three.

Two.

That's just for concentration. Now I'm immediately getting a woman who's crossed over, who comes in above you, which means older, and she's coming to you as a mother figure. A mother figure to me means mother, grandmother, aunt. Has your mother crossed, Dianne?

Yes.

Okay . . . she wants me to talk about the name Jean, Joan . . . a JN, GN name. When they give me a name it's either who they are, who they're with, or who they're trying to connect with here. Who's Joanne, Jean, Jane, Jeannine? It's a GN, JN name.

Yes.

Do you know?

I know one.

That's what you have to validate to me.

Okay.

How is that connected to your mom? Or how is that connected to you and I'll tell you if I think it's a valid connection.

She's a mother-in-law.

Oh, is she crossed over?

No.

There's something regarding her medical sign. That doesn't mean she's going to cross over, but there is a medical sign like tests, doctors' things around your mother-in-law. Do you know if she's been going for any X rays or any kinds of tests?

Yes, she has been.

That validates to me that your mom is trying to acknowledge your mother-in-law. There's something coming up with her, medically, and it doesn't have to be so bad. I don't know if you just had a conversation with her, or about her, recently.

Yes.

That's your mother acknowledging, "I hear you . . . I hear what you're talking about." It's like telling you that she knows current events. That's what Mom is doing. Mom is also acknowledging a problem with her back or spine. She's showing me what I would consider acupuncture . . . if it's not Mom, then she's talking about you.

Okay.

You have to validate. You have to give me something.

It's possible.

(Exemplary practitioners occasionally ask for validation; however, they rely on the information they are discerning and do not shift according to sitter's response. Mary, for instance, did not tell me that Mother had died or that my mother-in-law was alive, and then ask for validation—instead, she asked first and then responded. And now she needed specifics from me, rather than "It's possible." I wondered if she felt performance anxiety after reading Gary Schwartz's e-mail wherein he wrote, "We are about to perform a most important part of our three-phase experiment—the actual phone readings.")

Either your mom had a bad back or you have a bad back. Any kind of back surgeries, any kind of scars on the back?

No.

Okay . . . why is mom showing me the number ten or the month of October?

I don't know.

When I say the month of October, who do you think of? Anybody's birthday or anniversary then?

I think of Halloween.

How's that connected to Mom?

The only way I can think of is All Saints Day.

Did Mom love that holiday? Was there something special about it that she would bring me to October?

No. Not that I know of.

Is there somebody named Jack who she's trying to connect with here . . . or Jacky? My daughter's birthday is Halloween and her name is Jacqueline, so it's either that she's trying to acknowledge Jack, Jacky, or Jacqueline, and that's why she's bringing me here. Is there any connection to you with the name Jack?

No.

Do you have a white or light-colored car, Dianne?

No. (Red is the only car color I have ever owned.)

I don't know who I'm picking up then, because what I'm getting is a scenario of somebody who had a car accident. And somebody who has an injured back from a car accident. And this is not a premonition of what's to come . . . this makes me feel something that has happened in the past. Who's the J person in this family? Is there a J person? I should say.

There is.

Does this J person have any kind of problems with their spine or back?

Yes.

That's what I'm trying to connect with.

Okay, I've got it.

Now, there's also a lot of studies around this person, or learning. I feel like

I'm learning a lot of new information. Hold on . . . Dianne . . . your mother's making me feel there's something regarding cholesterol or heart problems.

Yes.

That's how she crossed?

Yes.

That's what she's showing me. When I stop talking, it's not because I'm doing nothing . . . I'm seeing a scenario and I have to put it in play. All of a sudden I'm seeing a woman and it feels like it's hard to breathe. I feel like I have to take deep breaths, or it's hard climbing stairs or walking. That's the feeling that I'm getting. And your mom's telling me . . . were you trying to connect with her . . . you were hoping to connect with her?

Not hoping, but expecting.

You were expecting, because she's the first one to open the door. She seems very open, and very open to this. And she's telling me that I'm not the first one to read her.

Right.

Other people have, and it's easy for her. She wants to talk about your dad. She's making me connect with your father . . . now your father . . . is he still here?

No. (Notice that Mary did not get the information on her own.)

Well there's something around you right now . . . are you holding anything of his right now . . . do you have something of his?

No, I'm not holding anything of his.

Was your father very musical?

Yes.

Your father seems to be right there with you . . . really very strong. I get him right there . . . not like a haunting . . . but a presence. Mom is coming through . . . I read her from you but still get the feeling of distance, like she is crossed. But your father is like . . . your mom passed before him . . . it's the feeling of a newness to him. Why is he bringing me to the month of December? I'm just going to tell you where he's bringing me. He's bringing me to the month of December, and he's showing me stomach problems or something regarding his aorta. But there's some connection between the stomach and the heart. But your father's saying . . . I'm going right up to my chest. He's also keeps making me hear music. It sounds like either harmonicas or that kind of a wind instrument . . . accordions . . . like polka music almost. He's also bringing me to the name of Richard . . . he wants me to say Richard.

There's something . . . hold on . . . I'm getting a younger person who crossed over, and younger means younger than you . . . who's trying to make their presence known. I'm getting a younger male. You don't have to tell me who it is . . . just tell me yes or no. But remember something, when I do a reading, sometimes it's not just for the person I'm doing the reading for. It could be for your neighbor or a very good friend . . . not to try and make it reach. But sometimes I get really strong information that comes in whole scenarios for other people that you're connected to somehow, and they're trying to find a way to come through, any way they can. I'm getting the image of a younger male, may have died in his late 20s, early 30s, in a car accident. Is that connected to you?

Yes.

He's coming through. He wants to say he's okay. He's telling me he's connected to Dianne or he knows Dianne.

Yes.

Have you been awaiting him? Have you been awaiting his coming through?

No.

You haven't? Because he seems like he's been trying to come through for you. Maybe somebody else didn't capture him or connect with him . . . say the other medium may not have connected with him. He's making me feel like this is his third try. Am I your third reading?

No.

How many?

Second.

Well he's been trying three times. I don't know if he came in other readings.

Yes.

Okay, so he's telling me it took him three tries before he came in, or he's been trying three different times and actually came in, but not every time. He's acknowledging he's okay and connected in some way. He's telling me to say "March." The month of March has either some connection to him, or to you, or to family around you . . . some kind of celebratory . . . some kind of anniversary in March. You understand that?

Yes.

Are you in boxes right now?

Yes.

I'm getting that. He's one of your guides and so are your mom and your dad. But this young man . . . you know it doesn't have to be our blood relatives for somebody to be guiding us, or guiding me to help you. He's showing me boxes around you like I'm packing or I'm moving things up and around. It's almost a feeling of moving. Were you thinking of moving at all? Or changing rooms around?

Yes.

Okay, because that to me is like a moving energy. You know feng shui?

Yes.

I'm moving energy. This is a good thing for you to be doing. You have to clear either an office space . . . an office . . . I don't know . . . is it the room you're in right now?

Yes.

That room is usually organized, but the boxes . . . gotta go. They are making energy go bing, bing, bing, off the walls. When that happens, things around our own lives will stay stagnant for a while. We'll be in a little bit of a limbo state. For instance, if I'm supposed to get a check from the bank, it will be a week late. Why do you have boxes in your room? It sounds silly, but the energy is getting mixed up around you . . . it doesn't know where to flow. So you have to clear up the flow by putting away mail. My own office right now is chaos, but I don't see yours as being really chaotic. This young man is making me feel cornered a little bit . . . like all of my room is not my own. And what happens is that that energy will float through our whole life, romantic, personal, as well as physical. And so as soon as you get that stuff out of the way, you will feel other things starting to open, other doors, other avenues starting to open in your life. It is, believe it or not, as simple as that sometimes.

I have to tell you—you're right on.

And I have to tell you it has nothing to do with me. It has to do with antennas, and my antenna's been hooked up for the last few days. I've been on overdrive. Now I'm getting the energy of a child who's crossed over and your mother's got the child.

Yes.

She's telling me she's got the child, and this child is connected to you. You understand that?

Yes.

Your mother received this child. Your mother's been rocking the child . . . it's the feeling of the rocking or being the grandma or that kind of maternal feeling from Mom. Who's John? She just all of a sudden says John.

The first thing that came to mind is my nephew.

Is that her grandson?

No. Oh, yes it is! I forgot about him! Yes, you're right!

Thank you . . . it's what we call psychic amnesia. Believe me, I've had people forget their own children's names and not because they're not bright people but because we get tunnel vision while thinking about the question. Grandma is actually talking about her grandson, and sending her love to him. There's something about a feeling of him, of trials and tribulations around John. I feel like I'm walking on unlevel or a balancing beam. How old is John?

He must be 40 something.

He's an adult.

Yes.

There's also legal things going on around him . . . proceedings . . . papers. But it doesn't really have to do with a lawsuit against him. She's just bringing it up. It doesn't mean you have to go searching for him or find out all this information. You'll hear about it, and Mom is telling me the outcome with him is good.

Now, I'm getting a man to your side—to your side means your contemporary, your peer—who's coming through as husband, brother, cousin, or friend to you. More than the person who was in the car accident, not like a dad, but more like a husband or a close friend or brother. And he wants the letter "H" . . . as in Harry, Henry. And what's the Chicago energy here . . . is there any?

Yes.

I don't have caller ID in my office, so I don't know where you're calling from. What I'm getting around you and around this gentleman . . . he's telling me he was from Chicago or that kind of Illinois feeling. Are you married, Dianne?

Yes.

Is your husband still here?

Yes.

He's appearing with you and your husband connected, like he's the common denominator between you and your husband, and it's the letter H connection. And, did you just get your taxes in the mail? There's something about taxes, he's talking about taxes. Okay. I'm going to tell you this . . . if you don't want to listen to the tape every two minutes to find the validations, I would say to write these things down for yourself. This connection to your husband . . . he's showing me medical and legal finds . . . like profession. Do you understand that?

No.

Like your own profession. There seems to be medical . . . doctors and lawyers around both of you. You and your husband, as well as this man. This man may have been an attorney. That's because he keeps showing me courts. Have you had any references to courts in your family . . . any kinds of lawsuits or courts?

Not currently.

I keep seeing this insurance check or insurance claim, and it's not a premonition. This is maybe something having to do with his past, or something having to do with the connection to your husband also. But I keep seeing somebody who made a lawyer . . . who was talking or made an insurance claim. I don't know why, but I keep getting this scenario. And again I don't, I don't censor anything I see, I just put it out there.

I'm also . . . your mother's making me feel . . . I'm hearing pigeons or doves. You know . . . hoo hoo . . . that kind of a feeling. And she's making me see what I would consider cages or somebody who . . . she wants to bring up the fact that somebody had pigeons or somebody collected birds. But not just one or two inside the house . . . outside birds.

I don't know.

Did you live on a farm or in the suburbs?

Suburbs.

Did your mother do lots of baking?

No.

The woman I'm getting makes me feel like that she either had a little farm . . . it doesn't have to be acres . . . it could be a backyard where she planted. I'm hearing the name Dolly or Doleane . . . it's a doll reference. If it's not for you, then I don't know who it's for. Is there another D other than you . . . female?

I don't think so.

I need you to ask any kind of question that's on your mind just to connect, I don't care what the question is. It could be about anybody or anything. I just need to connect, because there are other people trying to come through at the same time. In order for me to push them back and get the people you want, I need to hear your voice.

Okay. Great. The H person from Chicago, is he still there?

Yes, do you validate that?

Yes.

If I don't get a validation, a yes or no, then it feels like I'm flying a plane in the dark, don't know where I'm going, or if I'm even on the right track. He's making me see your husband . . . there's something regarding his leg.

Yes.

Now that I know I'm connected, I can go with it. He's acknowledging your husband's leg . . . there's pain in the leg or problems in the leg . . . and there's also something regarding your husband's head.

Yes.

And this is something that may have gotten acute in December because it gets more of a problem.

Yes.

This H person is very much connected to your husband, like a friend, and he seems to be very interested and concerned about him. But I think your husband really is going, again I'm not a doctor, but I think he's going to be okay. I just feel he's had a hard year.

Yes.

A really hard year and it's going to be a hard 16 months. It's nothing that goes away boom and it's gone. I feel there's recuperation . . . did he have any kind of surgery?

No.

What's the problem with his legs?

Shingles.

That is a problem. It's itchy and it hurts.

Yes.

But there's something else, having to do with your husband other than the legs, what's up with his head?

That's shingles.

That's shingles? There's something, again I'm not a doctor, but I play one on TV . . . no, I'm only kidding. I love it when I can use that line. With your husband, and I'm making light of it because there's nothing really drastic or bad going on with him, but there is a definite blood pressure connection with him. And what I mean is fluctuating blood pressure. And where he should be on medication, if he is he should stay on it, he's got to watch what he eats as far as sugar and salt intake.

You have borderline diabetes at all?

Not that I know of.

I'm getting the symbol of diabetes, either hyperglycemia or diabetes around you.

Yes.

To me, either way is in the diabetic family . . . either low or high sugar. And that was my symbol for you. You don't eat enough or you don't eat enough of the right foods. Do you have to eat small meals?

Yes.

Okay. Your mom and dad seem to be very strong around your energy, but what seems even stronger is the young child. Do you understand that?

Yes.

The young child seems to be directing me toward your health. Your parents are crazy about you, but I feel that maybe there's some distance regarding family. I don't know if it was a geographic distance or there was a feeling of not seeing them for a long time. Has it been many years since their passing?

Yes.

That's what I'm trying to say . . . a many-year kind of a feeling. And yet your father makes me feel that he could be still here—his energy is so acute.

Your father is showing me a fire. That doesn't mean he passed in a fire. But there's something having to do with either your life, or his and your mom's, and somebody had a fire. You understand that?

Yes.

Okay, because I'm not feeling there may have been fatalities, but there may have been injuries. I'm seeing smoke inhalation, things like that.

Yes.

That's what I'm seeing. And your mother wants you to know that, as well as the child, she has an animal with her. And this is something you cherished, this animal, because it's coming like a member of the family. And Mom is showing love to this animal. Is this animal buried in your backyard?

Yes.

Because I asked your mother where do I look, and she said in your backyard. That's the animal we're talking about. I'm trying to get his name. I'm asking them, but I keep seeing the letter B.

Yes.

I want to say Buddy or Buster or something like that, but it's the B. If it's not those names it's the B. And she's telling me it's buried in the backyard. And she says it's not easy, whatever that means. She's saying, "It ain't easy." But it's not like she's having a hard time, but it's like a joke. Like, "You think it's easy?" See in New York we have those kind of sayings. Like she's trying to say you think it's easy communicating like this? It ain't easy.

Right.

It's taking a lot of energy, that's what she's trying to say. Mom might have never spoken like that, but they'll come in my frame of reference, and I'm a Brooklyn girl and we always say, "It ain't." So Mom is making me feel this isn't easy. But she's pretty good . . . she's getting to like this, she says. She's getting used to the communication. It's like teaching somebody to ride a bike. In the beginning they're wobbling, but now she's riding and wanting everybody to let go and let her ride. She wants to keep doing this. She wants to keep getting read and keep the communication lines open. Before this research, you never got a reading?

I have had a reading.

She's making me feel that she's never come through so clear. She never felt so free, and it could be the exercise she's feeling. It's actually the energy we're exercising . . . the energy of your mother. They're always with you, always part of you, but we make them feel more than that when we are actually communicating with them. Do you understand that?

Yes.

You know you've got this energy around you, of someone who people come to for advice. I feel like I'm talking to a therapist.

Yes.

I do not read minds. That's not what I do. I read communications from your mom. Your mom is the whole show here . . . the whole show. She is very, very proud of you. And she's making me feel that she wants to talk about "the coincidence," and she has it in [quotation marks]. She's telling me there are none . . . no coincidences. There have been things happening around you that seem very coincidental lately and she wants to talk about the name Ray or Roy. Do you understand that?

Yes.

The coincidences that surround that person, there are none she's saying. So whatever that means, that's what she's trying to send. Your mom can probably communicate with you better now than when she was here, because she understands you on your level. My mother is still here, thank God. She is a very bright woman, but no matter what I discuss with her, I know she understands some of it . . . sometimes 85 percent and sometimes none of it at all. Your mother gets it now. No matter who we are, how many friends we have, how many colleagues we have, they can tell you they love you and understand, but until they cross over and highly evolve spiritually, they don't get it. Your mom gets it! She understands you. She really . . . hold on . . . I'm stopping because she's got me in front of a clinic. So I don't know if you . . . are you working with people with eating disorders?

No.

She's got me in front of a clinic, and she wants to talk about people with drug or food disorders. They're going to some kind of clinic. She wants to talk about this . . . it's really about young girls. There's something you're going to be doing in the near future. It doesn't mean you have to leave your job, but you may actually do this for a week or two, or maybe as a one-day volunteer. I don't know, but I'm seeing you in front of this redwood or cedar clinic. And it looks like it's very sunny, so to me it's not Chicago, or not midwest, because it looks warm. It looks like either California or Arizona. That's what I feel, like it's hot. And please don't think of it logically—logic has nothing to do with reading the other side. It's not logical, but it's real as far as I'm concerned. I see you in this clinic, and you're the person who helps decide who's able to be helped here and who's not.

Okay.

There is definitely a common denominator with your mother, who is again putting the [quotes] around "no coincidence."

Okay.

And I have to say Beth, Betty. Is that Mom?

Yes.

Thank you. I told you, she is the one who is controlling me. When they give me a premonition, Dianne, they'll give me a fact after it. She wants me to finally say her name, because I finally got it. When she was trying to talk about the clinicians, it may sound illogical to you, but to her it's not. She's seeing what's happening and what's going to be happening. This doesn't have to be so huge, but sometimes little moves we make in life, whether it be a phone call . . . maybe you as a therapist, you're going to have somebody call you and say, "Dianne, I need help with my daughter and I don't know where to go." I'm not saying that you'll be the one who has to help her, but where do I turn? And you'll say, "Let me do some research on it and I'll find something, I'll see what I can do." And as logic would have it, you start looking through brochures, calling other therapists, and they may direct you to someone who can help this person. That may be all of your job. It doesn't have to be extreme. You don't have to get on a plane, but there is a component here of a common denominator and that's you, the clinic, and the young girl. It's mainly the girl. Mom is making me feel that you may be able to help one person, and that may be the whole reason why you're in this world. Sometimes we think the reason we're here has to be extreme. Maybe we don't have to save the world . . . maybe it's just one life.

And I feel you've done a remarkable job already, but there's so much more to do. That's what I'm seeing. I'm glad she finally made it through. I'm glad Mom is doing this. Now she's making me see . . . she wants me to talk about Florida. There's some kind of Florida connection coming up with you, either you just came back or you're going to.

Yes. Going.

Oh you're going? Because she's actually showing me the map of Florida, but it's not a map like someday, it's either now or just been there. And that's her way of saying go, have a great time, have a great time, you're supposed to go around the 19th?

Saturday.

What's that date?

Actually, I'm not going. My family is.

That's okay. I saw the number 19 or the roman numerals XIX, and that's what she says. Do you have clocks in your house with roman numerals?

Yes.

Oh, she's funny! Because normally I get regular numbers, and she's making me see roman numerals and so she's in your home, not with me, and that's her way of showing it. And by showing little things that are abnormal to me . . . I normally don't get roman numerals . . . so that means there's something in their path of vision, around you, that they want to talk about. But they're telling me the trip is good. Go to Florida, it's healthy, and everything else. You'll be waiting, watching the time tick by while they're away. But you'll have your time for vacations or holidays. She's bringing up . . . the younger person who's crossed over is bringing up . . . image of horses. It doesn't have to be that they ride a live horse . . . it could be a rocking horse . . . but it's horses, horses, horses . . . I keep seeing horses.

I don't know.

That's okay. I still have the image in my head, of a young girl on a horse. And I don't know if they're trying to show me a picture of you.

Ah! That makes sense.

Okay. Thank you. You know the reason why I wasn't backing down is because they weren't. Sometimes if I'm off or connecting wrong, it'll just go away like an Etch A Sketch. But if they think they're right, like your mother thinks she's right, they'll keep it there and I can't erase it. I can't shake my head and make it go away, and that's what I'm getting regarding this younger child and your mom. They keep making me see a young person on a horse, a young girl on a horse, so they're either trying to get images of you, memories of you, or it was of them. Do you have any questions?

I can't think of any.

You can ask questions about anything. I'm conducting this the way I do a regular reading. I don't want you to feed me information . . . I want you to ask me a question.

What does my mother see, professionally, in the future for me?

Well, the first thing I get is pentacles all around, and that means money. Financially, extremely good. And she keeps showing me the number 77, or the number seven, and I'm seeing a redundancy of seven around you or Mom. What does the month of July, or the number seven have to do with either one?

An anniversary is in July.

Whose?

Mine.

So it has something to do with you. Your financial situation, not just yours or your professional, I would say it's got to be the two, you and your husband, the energy of both, because she's showing me the anniversary and the month of July. And you're still together with your husband right?

Right.

It's extremely good, especially in July, especially this July. Is your anniversary more at the end of July?

No. July 9th.

What's the 24th of any month?

I can't recall, but the 24th rings a bell.

Okay, just remember I said she's bringing up the 24th. And I'm going to tell you I feel there are a lot of changes going on in your own professional life . . . there are many. And I think you're going to be doing more than one thing in the future . . . diversifying from one thing to three. It's like an eclectic division in life, collecting different ideas to do things. And I don't think there should be just one thing that you should do, there are too many things that you're capable of. I would tell you to surrender, and that's what I'm getting around Mom. And this is the woman that told me your dog is buried in the backyard, and then told me her name, so I don't doubt it. I don't feel like you're going to stay where you're living. I don't see you staying in that state forever. I see you in a warmer climate. And I'm going to tell you . . . did you ever think about moving to California at all?

Yes.

Because that's where I'm getting you, in the southern California region. And it's not that far away, so it's not like you have to wait for another ten years. I'd say probably just three years . . . three years or 36 months. So maybe that thing with the West Coast is coming up for your job, and I think that you actually move to the West Coast. And again, this doesn't mean you have to start searching for places . . . it will come to you. The doors will open, if it's meant to be, and it's the right thing to do. You just stay on the course you're at right now, work as hard as you do normally, and the doors will open . . . the angels will appear. Not angels with wings, but earthbound angels will appear, and they'll open the doors for you. And you have a lot of doors to open, and a lot of changes are going on in your life. Do you have any other questions on your mind?

After we hang up, I'm going to think of 50. I have never had an extensive period for questions or dialogue with any other medium.

This is how I work. I like to hear Yes or No and ask questions. When the person asks me questions, it could be about anything. It could be, "Mary, is the sky blue?" The question has to make sense, but it doesn't have to be about the person who is crossed over. See, I'm not just a medium, I'm a medium-psychic, and all mediums are psychics. But we get stuck sometimes, working just with the other side. If we listen strong enough, they give us premonitions for the future, and that's where I work . . . with the other side. I say, "Okay, I know you're there. What do you want to tell me?" I don't want to just say hello and yeah there were fires in the house. That's great and terrific, but big deal. I want them to say what they can to help, what knowledge they have acquired that can help with life today. That's the big deal. So there's more to hear than just Uncle Harry saying how you're doing. There's more than, "When Grandma was around she loved tea." It's more than, "Grandma loved Shirley Temple." I've tried to take it to the next level and ask, "Stay with me now and tell me how I can help this person." Like your mother was saying, it ain't easy. We know it's not easy, because it takes an awful lot of energy . . . you included, because your mind is going back and forth with us. It's harder for Mom than for me. I'm drained afterwards, but she's got to stay. Think of an opera singer hitting a high C and holding it for an hour. If you think of the energy . . . that's the level your mother's got to hit for me to hear her. You understand?

I understand.

So I'm talking about a living energy. Your mother's still alive, trying to connect as energy, hitting that ahhh [Mary sings] so high, and actually making me see scenarios while she's doing it. And it ain't easy.

Can she tell me, or whomever you connect with, any names of people in my future . . . people I'm going to be working with?

Richard. Very strong. And somebody else . . . there's a Mark or Matthew, there's an MA person. But there are many more females. But who's the boss or the person who will be your director . . . Richard may be somebody who says, "This is what I have. Do you want to share it with me?" This Richard person is your peer. He's not your mentor, but you hold him in high regard. He's somebody you try to attain, not his success having to do with monetary, but his spiritual success. This Richard I feel is very unique as a human being. I actually see Gary's name. And not just Gary, but Gary Schwartz . . . his whole name. So you're going to be dealing with Gary, not just dealing with but working with. Whether it's research, volunteer, whatever it is, that's the working condition. I'm seeing three men, but lots of women. So your future career is very eclectic, and I'm seeing you writing. Have you published already?

Yes.

Okay, because your mother puts pen in hand . . . to me that's publication. I think your future, as well as present, is terrific. It's terrific, and I'm tired just thinking about it. I feel like you have a lot to do, and I think you really know to clear the boxes from the office, and then decide, even if it's in your subconscious, where your next move is. Not that you have to beg your husband and say "When are we moving?" but think about it. I feel like I'm cold where you are. I mean I'm freezing where I am. It's snowing. We got five inches today. I'm just so sick of it. But I'm cold where you are as far as . . . you know when you don't have contact with your surroundings you get cold. I have the feeling that the energy around your area, not your family, just in your area, feels cold. It means to me it's time to get moving. That doesn't mean you have to move now. It means to at least put the thought into motion. It could take three to five years, but the thoughts have to be put in motion. Okay?

Okay.

Dianne, it's been a pleasure.

Thank you so much, Mary.

Take care and God Bless. Bye bye.

Questionnaire, Medium 2, Mary
BEFORE THE READING BEGAN, HOW ACCURATE DID YOU ANTICIPATE OR EXPECT THE READING WOULD BE (FROM 0 TO 100 PERCENT)?

Five percent.

AFTER THE READING WAS COMPLETED, HOW ACCURATE DO YOU ESTIMATE THE READING WAS FOR YOU (NUMBER FROM 0 TO 100 PERCENT)?
Seventy-five percent.

WHAT SPECIFIC PIECES OF INFORMATION, IF ANY, WOULD YOU LIST AS INFORMATION DAZZLE SHOTS— ITEMS THAT WERE ESPECIALLY FACTUALLY ACCURATE AND NOT COMMONLY KNOWN IN THE READINGS?
Betty . . . your mother. My mother's name was Betty and she usually comes through during discernments.

Jean . . . on this side . . . medical sign coming . . . has health problems. You've been talking about this recently. My mother-in-law, Jean, underwent medical tests recently and we were reviewing her options at a family dinner.

October . . . car wreck . . . Jackie or Jack . . . wreck led to person having back problems. At this point in the reading, Mary said the name was "Jackie or Jack" but at the end of our session, she returned to the incident, saying, "It's a J name." My dad, Joe, was in an automobile accident in the fall of 1949. The car, which was totally demolished, was hit on the passenger side where Dad was sitting. Complications from his injuries brought him to the hospital twice and, even though he was under the care of specialists, Dad suffered spinal discomfort every day for the remainder of his life (40-plus years).

Mother died from heart or respiratory problems. Mother succumbed from a cardiac arrest.

Male . . . younger than you . . . he was in his 20s to 30s . . . died in a car crash . . . not related to you. Both Mary and Janet picked up on Gary, whose story is in my book *Life After Loss*.

Your mother is here . . . a grandmother figure to John. I said no at first, forgetting about my nephew (Mother's grandson). While estranging himself from our family, Johnny changed his name to John. Mary's passing comment, "Don't go searching for him or anything," was dazzling.

Your husband's health problems began in December. Joe had just traced his first symptoms of shingles back to mid-December.

Many years since your dad passed. Dad died on August 22, 1984.

They show me a fire . . . someone was harmed . . . smoke inhalation. A fire in my parents' home began in the back bedroom. While trying to extinguish it, Dad was overcome by smoke. He dropped to the floor, and then crawled out of the house on his stomach, elbows, and legs. Although firemen, paramedics, and neighbors encouraged him to go to the hospital, he refused.

WHAT SPECIFIC PIECES OF INFORMATION, IF ANY, WOULD YOU LIST AS EMOTIONAL DAZZLE SHOTS?

Your parents adored you—they did, and it felt good to hear that again.

Photograph of you on a horse when you were young—the mention of Mother's favorite photograph brought fond reflections.

Your mom is the whole show here—Mother is my strongest afterlife contact and the only persona I expect during readings. I would not say she is the whole show, but certainly a central figure.

It ain't easy—upon trying to master a new skill, Mother often said with a grin, "It ain't easy."

Mom is with an animal—holding it. It was a member of your family. See the letter B with the dog. Is he buried in your backyard? Ben, my favorite dog, is buried in our backyard.

Too many people are trying to come through, so focus on one person you'd like to visit—at this point, Mary stopped the discernment, which I had experienced with other clinicians. They too halted the readings, overwhelmed by the multitude of personalities fighting to get through the crowd. "We never know who needs the visit most," I explained, "and focusing on one specific individual might eliminate that persona. Tell them, 'One at a time, please.' Who appears first, and why, is amazing." Mary complied and then continued.

Boxes are all around you. You're in your office now. Get rid of those boxes. You recently moved rooms—Days prior, I moved my office upstairs, wanting to escape from the boxes and clutter. Regardless, plastic storage containers and several litter boxes were scattered throughout the room. Mary administered a mini-lecture about clutter, to which I acknowledged that my working area was in disarray. But then I referred to my former abnormal psychology and art history professors, who warned, "Creative people thrive on clutter. Never clean or organize their environment. The least you'll do is stifle their productivity, but most artists will not be able to create one thing."

PLEASE LIST WHO YOU WERE EXPECTING OR HOPING WOULD COME THROUGH AND INDICATE WHETHER YOU BELIEVE THEY DID OR DID NOT.

During my mediumship investigations, readers often supplied accurate remarks, supposedly from my mother. I expected Mary would do so as well, which she did. But was the information an extraction from my psyche? The reading, at certain points, illustrated a remarkable psychical meta-connection between the living, rather than a link with the afterlife.

WERE YOU SURPRISED BY ANY INFORMATION RECEIVED IN THE READING?

I was not particularly surprised by any of Mary's statements.

Update: While editing this material for publication, several previously irrelevant passages captured my attention. Mary mentioned October as being a significant month, which it had not been for me or my family. She further claimed seeing an insurance check or insurance claim, adding, *This may be . . . something having to do with the connection to your husband. But I keep seeing somebody who made a lawyer . . . who was talking or made an insurance claim. Again I don't censor anything I see . . . I just put it out there. There seems to be medical . . . doctors and lawyers around both of you. You and your husband, as well as this man. This man may have been an attorney. That's because he keeps showing me courts. Have you had any references to courts in your family . . . any kinds of law-suits or courts? This H person is very much connected to your husband, like a friend, and he seems to be very interested and concerned about him. But I think your husband really is going, again I'm not a doctor, but I think he's going to be okay.* Mary attached a disclaimer—*it's not a premonition . . . maybe something having to do with his past.*

Reconsidering Mary's comments, I saw that they were indeed relevant. My husband of 40 years, Joe, suddenly took ill on the 18th of October. He was rushed to the hospital and placed on life support. His lawyer and friend, Hickman, was a daily source of support. Joe died on the 6th of November, leaving me with many legal battles.

The experiments proved to be thought provoking in a number of ways, but did they offer evidence for life extending beyond bodily death? Did Susy Smith, in spirit, visit me during Phase 1 and report her observations to the mediums? Did she connect with my posthumous family during the second phase? Were the research mediums communicating with deceased personalities during the telephone readings? Whereas particular segments suggested disembodied existence, the concept may never be proven to disbelievers. To believers, however, the proof is in the experience.

NINE

Conclusion

Penetrating so many secrets, we cease to believe in the unknowable. But there it sits, nevertheless, calmly licking its chops.

—H. L. Mencken

Life's greatest mystery—is it unknowable? The discovery is ours to make, but according to Dionne, a senior health policy advisor for the Ministry of Health in her country, we keep overlooking it.

"De plank mis slaan."—From Dionne in Curaçao

Sometimes it is difficult for me to find the exact words in English to express myself. My mother tongue is Papiamentu, a mixture of Spanish, Portuguese, English, Dutch, and French. Most of us on Curaçao (an island in the Dutch Caribbean) communicate in more than one language, but I am more comfortable with Dutch since that is our official language. Some people actually believe that God has a special place in his heart for this island because nothing bad, like disasters or hurricanes, happens here. I know I felt blessed after my twin sons Jaden and Jared were born.

Both premature (32 weeks gestational age), Jared entered this world weighing 1,810 grams [3.99 pounds], and then Jaden at 2,095 [4.62 pounds]. They were initially placed in the neonatalogy intensive care unit (NIC) in iso-lettes. Jaden was moved to a "warmed bed" and then a normal bed in the medium care department before Jared.

When Jaden was three days old, a nurse rearranged him so he would be closer to my heart. I was a little afraid of holding him since he still had needles and tubes all over his body. But when I took him close to my heart and face, and looked at him, he opened his eyes. I held my breath and gasped. I could actually communicate with him. I felt so much love that I was afraid I would love him more than Jared. During the days that followed, for one reason or another, I spent more time with Jaden. Gladys, the nurse who took care of him from birth, asked if I would like to try breast feeding him, but I thought I would have enough time later. Later never came.

Early morning on the 30th of July, we were woken by a phone call from the hospital and told Jaden had died. It was so unexpected that the doctors and nurses were shocked too. They guessed that he was the victim of a hos-pital infection. We arrived to see him lying there only in his diapers. I wanted to hold him on my chest, skin to skin, but I was doubtful that it was appropriate. Then Gladys offered to help me. I felt such a relief that she asked, because it would have been terrible if I missed that chance. My baby Jaden looked so peaceful.

Afterward, I dressed him for our walk to the morgue. As we left the hospital for the other building, I cried, thinking, *It's so unfair that he was allowed to leave now when he was not able to see and feel the warmth of the sun.* We arrived and Gladys, who was still with us, said, "Take all of the time you want to say goodbye." It was cloudy and I wanted the sun to break through, but it wouldn't. Finally I told her, "We can't take more of your time. You can take him inside." Just as they were in the doorway of the morgue, one ray of sun burst through the clouds and shone right on Jaden. Gladys said, looking at me, "This ray is especially for him."

That night I was mourning and at the same time real-izing I had two sons who needed me to be there for them.

I was crying with my husband and mother at our kitchen table (which is under a window) when suddenly we saw something big fly by. Even in the dark, we saw it land on the garden wall. It then turned and looked directly at us. It was a large owl. I realized its presence had to do with the death of Jaden.

When confronted with the funeral, we did not know what to do. It never occurred to us that we would not be taking both of our little boys home, and after leaving Jaden's body at the morgue, we felt paralyzed. He was not baptized, so we were not allowed to have a religious ceremony. From everywhere, we started getting advice—the hospital, mortician, funeral agency, family, and friends. Everybody said in their own way, "You don't make a big deal over the funeral for a baby—just the father and mother bring him to his resting place." I feared the moment we would have to close the grave and leave his tiny body behind. I thought, *I'll never be able to do it.*

The sixth of August, one whole week after Jaden died, was the day of his funeral. I dressed him and arranged him in the white coffin that was made especially for him. We gathered with a small group of friends, hospital employees, our family, and Jaden's grandma, two aunts, and uncle who flew over from Holland. It was a small chapel in the garden of the cemetery, where the priest gave a simple service, saying the exact words I wanted to hear. It was peaceful, quiet, simple, and beautiful. And then, at the moment itself, as we closed the coffin, I felt such an incredible peace and tranquility of mind because I realized it was not *him* we were burying. I took distance from his body and took *him* into my heart. I knew he would be with me forever, no matter what I think or do. It was unbelievable. I thought, *Only God through Jaden could accomplish something this wonderful.* Thoughts about how beautiful the world is that He created filled me.

We planted a bougainvillea for Jaden and then headed for home in our car. My husband remarked, "It's sad to leave Jaden behind in that dark and cold place." Without even thinking, I said as a matter fact, "Oh no, we didn't leave him behind. He's right here in the car going home with us." My husband gave me a strange look, as if maybe he thought I'd gone mad.

From late night September eighth until early morning on the ninth, I was preparing Jeremy's (my older son) fifth birthday. All alone in the kitchen at 2 A.M., I was thinking, *Jaden and Jared were due on the ninth of September but were born premature.* As I filled party bags with treats for the children, the owl appeared again on the garden wall, close to the kitchen window. I could not miss it. It was looking straight at me.

A cat soon began appearing on the stone wall. One particular night I was in the kitchen and did not notice it perched in the dark. But as I was leaving the room, I heard a sound that made me turn and look out the window. There I saw it sitting in its usual place. I went to the bathroom (which is on the other side of our house) to prepare for bed, but heard meowing. The cat had followed me and was now sitting on the wall, bellowing. It moved closer, almost under the bathroom window. Its meowing became louder and louder. I stared at it for a while, making sure it saw me looking back at him, and then continued my chores.

This is what I didn't know—my husband had taken ill and was rushing home. By the time he got inside, he was so sick that we both thought he might die.

And the cat? It disappeared as soon as he arrived. I then realized it had come to warn me.

Since all of this happened, I've noticed that encounters have a special meaning. They always bring comfort and hope—but the comfort is not only for dealing with loss and the hope is not only for being together with our loved ones again one day. They comfort us as we deal with the less positive aspects of life. They bring us hope for a better tomorrow for this world.

While writing this, I keep asking myself, *Did that really happen, or was it just a product of vivid fantasy? Do those of us who have lost loved ones long to be with our deceased so much that we imagine afterlife encounters? Are they created by our minds?* But then, I know that is not true, because I experienced, lived it, myself.

There is Dutch saying, "De plank mis slaan." Translated, it means, in effect, "Missing the clue." That is exactly what we are doing. We keep looking for the answer to life's mystery and overlooking our greatest clue.

Why are afterlife encounters overlooked? Fear. Cultural and religious taboos teach us that the world of the living and dead must remain separate. Many perceivers deny their own visitations, excusing them as imagined. Of the perceivers who value their AEs, few disclose them—concerned that listeners will misunderstand, criticize, think them crazy, demean the event, use it against them, or mistreat the information in some way. Still other witnesses consider their accounts too personal to discuss, or that doing so will trivialize them or portray disrespect toward the departed. Regardless of the reason, when afterlife encounters are overlooked or undervalued, they become disenfranchised.

Disenfranchised encounters are either not revealed by perceivers, validated by listeners, or appreciated by both. They send the message: They don't matter. The fact is—they do. Encounters come from The Light.

"They can't get to me all."—Story from Phylida in Dublin

Late one evening, a young lad and lass were sitting on a street curb in Northern Ireland, outside of their children's home. Having already survived more death, abandonment, trauma, abuse, illness, and grief in their six years of life than most people experience in a lifetime, the boy turned to his frail little friend and asked, "My dear girl, how do ya' do it? How can ya' go on after all ya' been through?"

"Well, they didn't get me all!" she quipped. Lifting her eyes to gaze upon the distant stars, she said, "They can never, ever get to me all."

The young child understood. Deep inside each and every one of us is a sacred space where no insult, injury, illness, nor death, has ever or will ever reach. We all come from The Light and return at life's end. Meanwhile, for all of our days upon this earth we carry a portion of The Light within. The more we understand and become aware of that sacred space, the more we are able to connect with that which is far greater. Eternity, life's greatest mystery, is knowable. Afterlife encounters open the door.

Afterlife Encounter Survey—Phase 1[1]

ABSTRACT: The Afterlife Encounter Survey (AES) was a five-year international study designed to collect data pertaining to the effects, if any, afterlife encounters (AEs) have on recipients. Phase 1 measured respondents' levels of comfort during and after their encounters, then their levels of grief before, during, and after. Of the 827 individuals who submitted completed surveys, 596 had experienced AEs. From the affirmative responses, 582 respondents reported their encounters brought them comfort to some degree. Five hundred twenty-eight (528) respondents experienced AEs after the death of loved ones, of which 234 scored their grief at the highest level (10) prior to their encounters. At the one-year point, however, only 58 scored their grief at the highest level. My intention for the survey and this paper is to focus on the influence encounters pose on recipients—not to address the issue of survival. I will mention, however, that AES data suggested that the apparitional experiences were not created by longing or expectations. Of the 596 respondents who experienced afterlife encounters, 486 were not longing for anything of that nature, and of the 231 respondents who had never experienced afterlife encounters, 206 reported intense and extended longing.

Belief in the Hereafter reduces death anxiety among the general population (Arcangel, 1997; Moody and Arcangel, 2001;

Doka, 1993; Neimeyer, 1994; Osis, 1995). Whether real or imagined, paranormal beliefs can foster mental health (Taylor and Brown, 1988; Laski, 1961, 1968). Afterlife encounters (AEs), according to bereavement specialists, are considered normal (Arcangel, 1997; Datson and Marwit, 1997; Rosenblatt, 1983; Sanders, 1989; Stroebe, Stroebe, and Hansson, 1999; Rees, 1971; Shuchter and Zisook, 1999; Wolfelt, 1988). They are, in fact, an essential element for transcending loss (Arcangel, 1997; Bowlby, 1980; DeSpelder and Strickland, 1983; Gamino, Sewell, and Esterling, 2000; Glick, Weiss, and Parkes, 1974; Klass, 1993; Kübler-Ross, 1969, 1975; LaGrand, 1998, 1999; Neimeyer, 1994; Rando, Therese A., 1984, 1993; Taylor and Brown, 1988; Worden, 1991).

While working as a hospice chaplain, director of the Elisabeth Kübler-Ross Center of Houston, and the Gateway Center in New York, I noticed that afterlife encounters brought recipients comfort and hope. A number reported transcendence (rather than adjusting to, coping with, or finding resolution in the death, these survivors evolved mentally, emotionally, and spiritually). During my early research, however, I witnessed opposite ends of the spectrum. The phenomenon either lessened recipients' sorrow or caused an intense longing to have loved ones back, if only for a moment in time. The 1990s spiritual movement, with its focus on contacting the dead, brought a groundswell of attention surrounding the tremendous value of afterlife encounters, and I was concerned that many claims were exaggerated, therefore misleading. Although my main unrest centered on individuals in mourning, I wanted to know the effects encounters held on non-mourners as well.

Hoping to find data reflecting the influence encounters posed on recipients, I turned to psychical, bereavement, psychology, sociology, religious, and philosophy literature. Most books on the subject were published under the heading of parapsychology/new age/spirituality, and contained anecdotal information (Devers, 1997; Cohen, 1997; Guggenheim and Guggenheim, 1996; Kircher, 1995; Wiitala, 1996). Wright (2002) and LaGrand (1998, 1999) wrote outstanding books that included their interviews with AE recipients and presented brief synopses of classic research. Classic investigations resulted in significant data regarding afterlife phenomena (Barrett, 1926; Gurney and Myers, 1888–89; Myers, 1903; Podmore, 1897; Sidgwick, 1894, 1923). Jung (1965), Lodge (1916), and James (1958), furthermore, documented their personal accounts. Not any of these bodies of work, however, covered the levels of comfort or grief surrounding perceived discarnate visitations. At the onset of this study, Rhea White (long-time editor of this journal and authority in the field) searched through her files, then at the completion conducted a more extensive search for published and unpublished literature. Robert Neimeyer, researcher, professor, author, and longtime editor for *Death Studies* (the principal journal in the field of bereavement), loaned his expertise as well. With additional help from Andrew Greeley, my colleagues at the Association of Death Education and Counseling, and the staff at the Pasadena (Texas) Public Library, a limited amount of material was found.

Regarding comfort, Laski's (1961, 1968) Study of Ecstasy in Secular and Religious Experiences indicated that among her 63 participants, approximately 15% felt joy after their communion (direct communication) with "something else." Rees (1971), a practicing physician, surveyed 94.2% of the bereaved spouses from specified districts in Wales, 227 widows and 66 widowers. Two-thirds of his 293 respondents reported their encounters were comforting and helpful, 8 disliked them, and the remainder were neutral. According to Parkes (1972) "a comforting sense of persisting presence" was reported by 15 of the 22 London widows he interviewed (p. 58). Glick, Weiss, and Parkes (1974) reported that some widows from their study were so comforted by sensing the presence of their husbands that they deliberately evoked encounters. Bowlby (1980, 1982) and Greeley (1987, 1989) offered a treasure trove of valid and reliable data, including one common feature of perceived afterlife encounters: comfort. Osis (1961) and Osis and Haraldsson (1993) studied the emotional components of deathbed visions and found comfort an essential element as well as "the peace which passeth understanding" (p. 60). Datson and Marwit (1997) conducted research focused on personality constructs surrounding afterlife encounters and discovered that of the 87 bereaved participants who completed the Eysenck's Personality Questionnaire, 86% characterized their AEs as comforting.

Turning to grief, significant longitudinal research findings with the bereaved have been published over the years. Grief is an innate response to loss; mourning is the outward expression. Both are a process that is unique to each individual—not even identical twins grieve or mourn the death of their mother exactly the same. Although there is no template for bereavement, studies indicate the differences between normal and abnormal grief depends on intensity and duration. For example, Zisook, DeVaul, and Click (1982) reported that acute grief normally peaks between 1 and 2 years. Neimeyer's (2001) graph, based on research with 1,200 mourners over 10 years, demonstrates that most people do not return to the highest level of functioning within the first 25 months (p. 11). DeSpelder and Strickland (1983) reported that most widows actively grieve for 1 to 3 years, whereas Zisook and Shuchter (1986) concluded that most of the widows in their study had not adjusted after 4 years. Based on the Symptom Checklist-90-Revised (SCL-90R), an instrument that measures point-in-time psychological symptoms, parental and sibling grief usually continues for 2 to 7 years (Gilliss and Moore, 1997; Martinson, Davies, and McClowry, 1991; McClowry, Davies, May, Kulenkamp, and Martinson, 1987). These studies presented a common baseline for normal grief.

Our extensive search for data relating to grief and afterlife encounters eventually pointed to unpublished work. Devers (1987, unpublished master's thesis; 1994, unpublished doctoral dissertation) described encounters as grief resolving and personally transformative. Drewry (2002) investigated the role that after-death communication (spontaneous communication with deceased loved ones) played in the recovery of bereaved individuals. She chose 7 participants, and her criteria for choosing them were as follows: their experiences "spontaneously reduced their grief," "their grief was less intense because of the experience(s)" in the following hours or days thereafter, and the events "were life-changing in some way" (p. 46). From a total of 40 encounters reported to Drewry by her 7 participants, one "resulted in a complete release of grief . . ." (p. 4), and most of the other 39 resulted in "immediate relief, comfort, hope, love, emotional stabilization, encouragement, forgiveness, and the joy of a continuing relationship; however, after the initial relief the sense of loss returned along with its related grief" (p. 105). Furthermore, their afterlife contacts alone did not ". . . resolve all the grief they had surrounding the death of a loved one; completion of the grieving process is still required" (p. 105).

Although the effects of afterlife encounters has been explored, we could not find a large sample longitudinal study that measured the levels of comfort or grief.

Method

The Afterlife Encounter Survey was a five-year international survey designed to collect data pertaining to the effects encounters have, if any, on recipients. (I reiterate: whether the AEs were internal projections or external realities was never the focus during Phase 1 of the survey.) Phase 1 began on August 22, 1998, and ended on August 22, 2002. Respondents were asked to measure, on a scale from 10 (tremendous comfort) to 0 (no comfort), the levels of comfort they felt during, immediately after, one year after, and then the number of years it had been since their AEs and the level of comfort they felt "today." The section that followed focused on grief. Respondents were asked if their AEs occurred after the death of a loved one; if their answer was affirmative, they were asked to measure their levels of grief prior to, during, immediately after, days after, one year after, three years after, and then the number of years it had been since their AEs and the level of grief they felt "today."

Surveys were offered to grief workshop participants in New York and Texas. They were introduced during media events, such as my New York, California, Colorado, and Texas book tour, as well as national radio interviews. Surveys were available through the Rhine Research Center and the George Anderson web site. They were accessible to health-care professionals during meetings and seminars. Then, in order to reach an international audience and more participants who were not bereaved, webmaster Karl Fancher posted the survey on several Internet search engines. Initially, Internet participants were anonymous—upon submitting their questionnaires, they instantly received the automatic message, "Thank you for your survey." Many respondents submitted questions and comments that required further communication, however. We therefore made an addendum explaining, "Your survey will remain anonymous unless you provide your e-mail addresses or other contact information." To every individual who included a means for communication, I sent a personalized thank you, and in many cases correspondence between us commenced.

Most participants were from the United States (641), then Canada (43), the United Kingdom (25), Australia (26), New Zealand (19), Netherlands (3), Mexico (2),and then one from each of the countries as follows: Brazil, Germany, Hungary, Ireland, Lebanon, Morocco, Norway, Puerto Rico, Saudi Arabia, Sri Lanka, Sweden, and Switzerland. Of the 827 respondents, 575 were female and 191 were male. Their ages ranged from 3 to 81 at the time of their encounters.

The survey consisted of 22 questions, and began with a definition and explanatory introduction as follows:

> An afterlife encounter (AE) is any sense of being connected to, or in the presence of, a discarnate being (an apparition or ghost—spontaneous or facilitated by a medium). Most afterlife encounters are *visual*, wherein apparitions appear ethereal, surreal (more real than real), or as they did during their lives. Encounters can be *auditory* (hearing their voice, whistle, cough, or other familiar sounds). They may be *olfactory* (smelling a familiar aroma such as pipe smoke or perfume) or *tactile* (sense of touch-

ing or being touched). Qualifying as an afterlife encounter as well is the *sense of presence* (a definite, but unexplainable, impression of being in the company of a discarnate personality). Rupert Sheldrake (*Seven Experiments That Could Change the World*) conducted studies wherein experimenters stared at the back of subjects' heads without the subjects' knowledge. Most subjects sensed the stare and turned around to look at their experimenters. Recipients of AEs report that afterlife encounters involving the *sense of presence* have a similar quality. AEs can involve any combination of the senses.

Encounters fall into four categories: (1) Personal—deceased relative, friend, pet, colleague, neighbor, or anyone familiar to the experiencer; (2) Spiritual figure—God, Jesus, Buddha, angel, saint, etc.; (3) Historical or Famous figure—such as Alexander the Great, Winston Churchill, Mother Theresa, Marilyn Monroe, or Mickey Mantle; (4) Unknown—apparition is unfamiliar to the experiencer at the time of the encounter. AEs usually occur during dreams, reverie (between sleep and awake), or while preoccupied (lost in doing something).

Results and Discussion

The survey results were more favorable toward the positive affects of afterlife encounters than I had imagined, and they held other surprises as well. Because the survey focused on the levels of comfort and grief surrounding AEs, I speculated that few, if any, individuals who had not experienced the phenomenon would complete the survey. However, 231 (28%) of the surveys were submitted by respondents who had never experienced anything close to an afterlife visit. Most of those respondents reported strong and extended longings for encounters, and submitted questions as to why they had never experienced them.

The questions and results are presented in the appendix [to this article]. All percents are given based on the appropriate base number, specified in the appendix. For example, for questions about encounters, the 596 respondents who had at least one encounter are used as the sample size.

The results revealed that of the 596 respondents who had experienced encounters, 465 (78%) had experienced more than one (Question 2). A total of 950 people or pets were recorded in the nine different categories. Among the nine categories, *Parent* and *Other family member* accounted for the highest numbers, with 21% of the total each. The comment section of the survey revealed that from this latter category, grandparents were most often encountered, then siblings. Similar percentages reported encounters in the following four categories: *Not related* (13%), *Figure unknown to me at the time* (11%), *Child* (11%), and *Pets* (10%). From the *Figure unknown* category, many respondents revealed that the figures who were unknown to them at the time were family members from long ago—relatives the recipients had never seen or heard about (their identities were established later, often through photographs). Other respondents who reported encountering figures unknown to them at the time later discovered the figures were the relatives of acquaintances or friends. In more than one-half of the encounters with *Pets,* the animals were not alone; animal companions often appeared with deceased family members, even when the humans had died long before the pets were adopted. Encounters with *Spouses* accounted for 6% (unlike other investigators who focused on certain populations, such as widows, widowers, retirement communities, nursing home residents, or hospice patients—Rees, 1971; Parkes, 1972; Glick, Weiss, and Parkes, 1974; Bowlby, 1980, 1982; Osis, 1961; or Osis and Haraldsson, 1993; for example—I took my sample from a general pool). *Spiritual figures* 5%, and *Historical or famous figures* accounted for 2%.

Reviewing the modalities, 69% of respondents listed some form of visual encounter (Question 4): 19% were Visual only, 13% were a combination of Visual/Auditory, 8% Visual/Sense of Presence, and 8% Visual/Auditory/Sense of Presence. Other percentages are listed with Question 4 in the appendix. Single modalities accounted for 31% of the total: 19% Visual, 5% were the Sense of Presence, 3% Auditory, 2% Olfactory, and 2% Tactile. All other modalities, single and combinations, accounted for less than 5% of the total each.

Previous research exploring modalities produced mixed results. The AES findings were strikingly similar to Kalish and Reynolds's (1981), whereby 74% of their respondents reported some type of visual or visual/auditory experiences. In contrast, Rees's (1975) sample reported 14% visual encounters, 13% auditory, and 6% tactile. Contrasting further, 50% of the 87 participants in the Datson and Marwit (1997) study reported a sense of presence, 19% auditory experiences, 17% visual, 10% tactile, and 4% olfactory. The discrepancies were at least in part due to the manner in which the material was presented. Prior to the Afterlife Encounter Survey, distinctions between the modalities were pointed out to participants, then each modality was listed separately on the questionnaire and respondents were instructed to "check all that apply." Moreover, the AES was not presented as an after-death communication instrument; therefore, there was no presupposition that communication transpired.

Of the 596 respondents who experienced AEs, 582 (98%) reported their encounters were comforting (Question 5). However, 11 reported their comfort levels were low (4 to 0) during their encounters (Question 6), and 13 reported low comfort (4 to 0) immediately after their encounters (Question 7). Fourteen respondents found their encounters brought them no comfort or were frightening (Question 5). These results compare to the Datson and Marwit (1997) study wherein 8% of their respondents stated their AEs were frightening.

Based on written comments, AES participants declared two basic reasons for scoring AEs on the lower scales (4 to 0). Lack of understanding the phenomenon was most often associated with discomfort. At the time of their encounters, 10% of AES participants were between the ages of 3 and 17; among them were respondents who believed their deceased parents had returned to reprimand them. Silverman and Worden (1999) recorded similar findings. They interviewed 125 children between the ages of 6 and 17, at the fourth month and one-year anniversary of their parents' deaths. From their sample, 57% spoke to their departed parents, 43% believed their parents spoke in return, and 81% sensed their parents were watching them. Initially, 57% were frightened by their encounters; at the one year point, however, the children were "less scared by this" (p. 309). Both studies revealed that children who felt frightened by their AEs believed their deceased parents, as disciplinarians, were there to disapprove. Children who were not fearful believed their parents, as protectors or ambassadors, were there to help in some way. Adults reacted similarly in their encounters with disembodied superiors, according to the results of the AES. Most respondents who were initially uncomfortable or frightened stated they later wished or prayed for visitations; more than one-half succeeded, all of whom were tremendously comforted by their experiences. Upon final analysis, the encounters that were initially scored little or no comfort dropped from 5% to 1% over time.

The second reason respondents placed their encounters low (4 to 0) on the comfort scale was the issue of grief. For these recipients, perceiving their disembodied loved ones caused an intense longing to have them back again, either during their encounters or immediately thereafter.

The first portion of the AES documented 582 cases of perceived afterlife encounters wherein respondents reported considerable and persistent comfort. Individuals who were initially frightened, uncomfortable, or in acute grief, declared that their encounters became increasingly beneficial as they gained understanding about the phenomenon, shed their grief, or both.

The next portion of the questionnaire focused on grief. Of the 596 AEs reported, 89% occurred after the death of a loved one (Question 10). Because Questions 12 to 17 applied to different subsets of respondents based on the time since their experience, the percentages quoted here and in the appendix are based on the number of respondents to each question rather than on the total sample. Those who did not answer the question are omitted for that question.

Comparing the grief scales, 341 participants (66% of those who responded) scored their grief at the highest levels (10–8) prior to their encounters (Question 12); however, only 20 (5% of those who responded) scored their grief between 10 and 8 at the three-year mark (Question 17). On the lowest scales, 24 respondents (5%) scored their grief between 3 and 0 prior to their encounters (Question 12), but at the three-year point 208 (59% of respondents) scored their grief 3 to 0 (Question 17). Thus, there was a drop from 66% of respondents to 5% of respondents in the highest levels (10–8) of grief by the third year of bereavement and an increase from 4% of respondents to 59% of respondents in the lowest levels (0–3) of grief in that time. This is a relevant comparison, especially taking into consideration that 126 of the initial respondents (24%) were in their first year of bereavement (Question 18), thus could not score the third year.

Jessica Utts, the statistical editor for this paper, noticed a trend among the participants who marked their grief as extreme (8 to 10). Their scoring dropped substantially from "before" to "during," substantially again from "during" to "immediately after," and then remained that way for days thereafter. The scores were as follows (Questions 12–17): Before – 66%, During – 35%, Immediately after – 21%, Days after – 21%. Studies with the bereaved indicate that mourners need some kind of support. The stronger their support system, the better they fare. I have never witnessed any data that registered such a rapid decrease in the intensity of acute grief. I therefore surmise that no one could have been more supportive than the figures these individuals perceived, and suggest that afterlife encounters reduce the risk of abnormal bereavement for some people.

Whereas all respondents declared their AEs affected their grief, some scored their reactions unfavorably. These individuals reported their sorrow and longing actually intensified either during, immediately after, or days after their encounters. Upon close examination of the cases wherein grief was exacerbated, most participants experienced their encounters through mediums. The mediumship vs. spontaneous issue pointed to humankind's core psychological theme: fear of loss of control.

The recipients who experienced encounters through mediums felt they had lost their loved ones twice. Believing they must depend on mediums for future encounters, they felt helpless and hopeless. Four of these participators said they were almost as devastated after their discernments as they were at the moment of their loss. In contrast, perceivers of spontaneous (firsthand) encounters believed they could have another, and that future encounters would be more positive, because their previous experience taught them about the phenomenon and facilitated their grief process.

The outcome of this survey lends evidence that afterlife encounters affect bereavement. According to respondents, their grief and mourning were not extinguished, but the burden was lifted from time to time. Most recounted that just thinking about their AES gave them a reprieve, and the consolation they received extended beyond bereavement—they had transcended beyond the people they were at the time of their loss. As Childs (1997) discovered in her study, for some recipients the aftereffects of the phenomenon are similar to the aftereffects of near-death experiences—powerful and transformative.

Although the AES was intended to gather data regarding the benefits of afterlife encounters and not consider anything relating to the question of survival, readers of this journal may find support for the survival theory. As Emily Kelly (2001) surmised in her article, "Near-Death Experiences with Reports of Meeting Deceased People," ". . . several findings may weaken the primary nonsurvival hypothesis, that of expectation" (p. 229). Common lore among early psychical investigators remains to date: Encounters are the result of expectation or longing. Of the 596 AES respondents who reported afterlife encounters, 82% were not longing for anything of that nature, and of the respondents who were longing, most were with mediums. Of the 231 respondents who had never experienced afterlife encounters, 89% longed for them, many of whom declared holding an intense desire for decades. Clearly, expectation, desire, longing, or wishful thinking does not necessarily play a role in spontaneous accounts.

A final overview of the data collected during the Afterlife Encounter Survey points to the short- and long-term positive effects of the phenomenon. The effects proved so strong that 99% of respondents welcomed more encounters in the future (Question 20). Although I have long been an advocate for the benefit that encounters pose, the number of respondents who consistently scored their comfort at high levels surprised me. While reading more than 3,000 surveys (Phase 1 and 2), I often reflected upon Dennis Klass's statement (1993): "In the sorrow of grief humans need to be consoled" (p. 343).

Numerous flaws in the AES fall back to design. Future investigators may find the same problem: devising a relatively simple, concise study that provides ample data. My history taught me that public response to questionnaires, regardless how brief, is usually low. I therefore, in 1997, designed the survey as a pilot project and administered it to 78 colleagues. We omitted numerous questions, creating a questionnaire that could be filled out in minutes. Although participants could submit their surveys in person, over the telephone, through the mail, or via the Internet, more than 1,200 chose to expedite them over the Internet. Unfortunately, only one-half of those surveys were included because the respondents scored only the first items, then skipped down to the comment section and wrote brief remarks about their accounts. On one hand, the AES was too lengthy for many Internet participants to complete; on the other hand, we omitted items from the pilot that were needed in order to cover the full scope of the study.

One of the deleted items needed for a more thorough investigation was the issue of elapsed time (the amount of time that passed between the death and encounter). As the AES entered its third year, the findings were gaining in strength by collective numbers, but not gathering elapsed-time data. In order to acquire the needed information and resolve the problem of surveys being submitted incomplete, I designed a four-question survey. Phase 2 of the AES was introduced at the four-year mark, and within the first three months (without any promotion) we had collected 827 completed surveys—the same number of surveys collected during the four-year period of Phase 1. Clearly, for studies involving Internet participation, several brief questionnaires will yield the greatest number of returns.

Two additional items were deleted from the pilot—symbolic and electronic encounters. Participants, nevertheless, wrote about their AEs via symbols (feathers or pennies, for example) and electrical instruments (computer monitors, answering machines, etc.). Therefore, I suggest listing these categories in future investigations.

For researchers who want to avoid the problem of question-naires altogether, one solution is qualitative research. Qualitative research focuses on participants' stories and words (Carverhill, 2002). Both participants and researchers benefit from this method. Reminiscing fosters grief, and listening to reminiscences leaves researchers with a vast repository of infor-mation. Bennett and Bennett (2000), one a folklorist, the other a psychologist, collected data through anecdotes wherein respondents controlled the agenda, reminisced, and told stories "on themes of their own choice" (p. 142). As a result, Bennett and Bennett established an innovative database.

Future research could focus on spontaneous versus facilitated encounters, or bereaved individuals compared to nonbereaved (individuals who have not experienced any significant losses). One suggestion to investigators: Proceed with caution. The AES revealed circumstances that caused intense grief for those in mourning. Whereas afterlife encounters were comforting to the point of bringing ecstasy to the major portion of perceivers, a small percentage was negatively affected. Those individuals ini-tially felt a strong desire to connect with their dearly departed, but thereafter found their grief was exacerbated by the event. Under current federal guidelines for healthcare professionals, mourners are part of the "special protection groups" (along with children, mentally dependent, elderly, and the dying). Individuals in acute grief are more vulnerable than the general population because their mental capacity is under duress. In order to ensure their well-being, it is imperative to employ extra safeguards.

Note: One referee of this paper was concerned about the lack of discussion regarding veridicality, asking, "Are they real or are they products of the ordinary mind alone?" My focus for the AES was to gather data pertaining to comfort and grief. Gathering, or presenting, evidence for survival never entered the equation. While posting the results, however, I thought about popular lore. According to popular lore, the majority of AEs occur within 24 hours of the death; thus, they must be hallucinations caused by longing. The data from this study suggested otherwise. With the help of Erlendur Haraldsson, I designed Phase 2 of the AES, which focused on the elapsed time between death and AEs (to be presented in a later paper).

Appendix

1. Have you ever experienced an apparitional encounter?
   Total surveys completed   827
   Numbers and percentages of respondents
   Yes 596 (72%)   No 231 (28%)

2. Have you experienced more than one encounter? (n = 596)
   Yes 465 (78%)   No 129 (22%)   N/A 2 (0%)

3. I have encountered (check all that apply)
   Different types of encounters totaled 950
   Parent 195 (21%)   Spouse 59 (6%)   Child 100 (11%)
   Other family member 199 (21%)   Not related 121 (13%)
   Pet 98 (10%)   Spiritual figure 50 (5%)
   Historical or famous figure 21 (2%)
   Figure unknown to me at the time 107 (11%)

4. My encounter/encounters were (n = 596)
   Single modalities: Visual 114 (19%)   Auditory 16 (3%)
   Olfactory 12 (2%)   Tactile 10 (2%)   Sense of Presence 31 (5%)

   Two modalities (combined modalities represented by first initial)
   VA 76 (13%)   VO 10 (2%)   VT 2 (0.3%)   VS 48 (8%)

AT 2 (0.5%)   AS 21 (4%)   OT 3 (0.5%)   OS 10 (2%)
TS 15 (3%)

Three modalities:
VAO 4 (0.7%) VAT 21 (4%) VAS 52 (8%)
VOS13 (2%)   VTS 15 (3%) VOT 8 (1%)   OTS 6 (1%)
AOT 1 (-%)   AOS 5 (1%)   ATS 6 (1%)

Four modalities:
VATS 21 (4%) VAOS 12 (2%)
VOTS 7 (1%)   VAOT 7 (1%) AOTS 4 (0.7%)

All modalities: VAOTS 26 (4%)

5. Did your apparitional encounter bring you comfort in some way? (n = 596)
   Yes 582 (98%)   No 10 (2%)   N/A 4 (0.7%)
   If yes, please answer questions 6 to 9 as they apply to your most comforting encounter. Rate the level of comfort it brought you on a scale from 10 to 0 (10 being a tremendous amount, 5 some, 0 none). (582 answered in the affirmative but for Questions 6 to 9, the percentages are based only on those who responded for each question.)

6. The comfort I felt at the time of my encounter was (n = 578)
   10: 376 (65%)   9: 43 (7%)   8: 58 (10%)   7: 25 (4%)
   6: 17 (3%)   5: 48 (8%)   4: 4 (1%)   3: 4 (1%)
   2: 1 (0%)   1: 2 (0%)   0: 0

7. The comfort I felt immediately after the encounter was (n = 578)
   10: 368 (63%)   9: 53 (9%)   8: 54 (9%)   7: 35 (6%)
   6: 11 (2%)   5: 44 (8%)   4: 4 (1%)   3: 3 (.5%)
   2: 5 (1%)   1: 1 (0%)   0: 0

8. The comfort my encounter brought me one year after the experience (n = 553)

10: 367 (66%)   9: 47 (8%)   8: 55 (10%)   7: 27 (5%)
6: 12 (2%)   5: 35 (6%)   4: 1 (0%)   3: 5 (1%)
2: 2 (0%)   1: 2 (0%)   0: 0

9. Today, the number of years after the experience is (n = 427)
   2–5: 148 (35%) 6–9: 40 (9%)   10–19: 119 (28%) 20+: 120 (28%)
   The comfort it brings me is (n = 427)
   10: 285 (67%)   9: 18 (4%)   8: 40 (9%)   7: 23 (5%)
   6: 14 (3%)   5: 35 (8%)   4: 7 (2%)   3: 1 (0%)
   2: 1 (0%)   1: 3 (1%)

10. Have you experienced an encounter after the death of a
    loved one? (n = 596)
    Yes 528 (89%)   No 48 (8%)   N/A 20 (2%)

11. If yes, was your first apparitional encounter after the death
    of a loved one? (n = 528)
    Yes 488 (92%)   No 32 (6%)   N/A 8 (2%)
    **Did your afterlife encounter affect the level of
    your grief? If yes, please answer questions 12–18 as
    they apply to the loss that caused you the most grief
    prior to the encounter. Rate the level of your grief on
    a scale from 10 to 0 (10 means you were consumed by
    grief, 5 you felt some grief but it did not interfere
    with your daily life, 0 you felt no grief).** (528 answered
    in the affirmative but for Questions 12 to 17 percents are
    based only on those who responded for each question.)

12. Before my afterlife encounter my grief felt closest to level
    (n = 518)
    10: 234 (45%)   9: 45 (9%)   8: 62 (12%)   7: 51 (10%)
    6: 48 (9%)   5: 46 (9%)   4: 8 (2%)   3: 6 (1%)
    2: 6 (1%)   1: 7 (1%)   0: 5 (1%)

13. During my afterlife encounter my grief felt closest to level
    (n = 497)

10: 85 (17%)   9: 35 (7%)   8: 56 (11%)   7: 49 (10%)
6: 33 (7%)   5: 80 (16%) 4: 29 (6%)   3: 37 (7%)
2: 26 (5%)   1: 38 (8%)   0: 29 (6%)

14. Immediately after the encounter my grief felt closest to level
    (n = 503)
    10: 37 (7%)   9: 30 (6%)   8: 47 (9%)   7: 39 (8%)
    6: 29 (6%)   5: 118 (23%)   4: 36 (7%)   3: 45 (9%)
    2: 38 (8%)   1: 48 (10%) 0: 36 (7%)

15. Days after the encounter my grief felt closest to level
    (n = 495)
    10: 25 (5%)   9: 30 (6%)   8: 50 (10%)   7: 49 (10%)
    6: 34 (7%)   5: 102 (21%) 4: 30 (6%)   3: 55 (11%)
    2: 52 (11%)   1: 54 (11%) 0: 14 (3%)

16. One year after the encounter my grief felt closest to level
    (n = 489)
    10: 58 (12%)   9: 58 (12%) 8: 26 (5%)   7: 26 (5%)
    6: 21 (4%)   5: 76 (16%) 4: 37 (8%)   3: 44 (9%)
    2: 52 (11%)   1: 50 (10%) 0: 41 (8%)

17. Three years after the experience my grief felt closest to level
    (n = 354)
    10: 5 (1%)   9: 2 (0.5%) 8: 13 (4%)   7: 14 (4%)
    6: 19 (5%)   5: 49 (14%) 4: 44 (12%)   3: 33 (9%)
    2: 56 (16%)   1: 70 (20%) 0: 49 (14%)

18. Today, the number of years after the experience is (n = 354)
    3–5: 104 (29%) 6–9: 11 (3%)
    10–19: 119 (34%)   20+: 120 (34%)
        My level of grief is (n = 363)
    10: 2 (0%)   9: 2 (0%)   8: 11 (3%)   7: 15 (4%)
    6: 7 (2%)   5: 34 (9%)   4: 28 (8%)   3: 37 (10%)
    2: 41 (11%) 1: 98 (27%)   0: 88 (24%)

19. Were you longing for anything of this nature? (n = 596)
    Yes 88 (15%)   No 486 (82%)   N/A 22(37%)

20. Would you want an afterlife encounter in the future?
    Yes Respondents on Question 1
    Yes 589 (99%)   No 5 (1%)   N/A 2 (0.3%)
    No respondents on Question 1
    Yes 206 (89%)   No 4 (2%)   N/A 21 (9%)
    Total (n = 827)   Yes 795 (96%) No 9 (1%)   N/A 23 (3%)

21. If you desire another, how often would you want an encounter?
    Yes responses on Question 1
    Daily 187 (31%) Weekly 94 (16%) Monthly 98 17(%)
    Yearly 44 (8%)   Less 13 (2%)   Don't know 146 (24%)
    N/A 142(%)
    No responses on Question 1
    Daily 74 (32%)   Weekly 72 (31%)   Monthly 9 (4%)
    Yearly 5 (2%)   Less 5 (2%)   Don't know 60 (26%)   N/A 6 (3%)
    Total responses
    Daily 261 (32%)   Weekly 166 (20%)   Monthly 107 (13%)
    Yearly 49 (6%) Less 18 (%) Don't know 206 (25%) N/A 20 (2%)

22. Age and country at time of encounter, and gender
    Age:
    20 or less 73 (12%) 20–29 100 (17%) 30–39 146 (24%)
    40–49 143 (24%)   50–59 90 (15%)   60–69 30 (5%)
    70+ 4 (0%)   N/A 10 (2%)
    Country:
    No respondents
    United States 148 (64%)   Canada 21 (9%)   Australia 18 (8%)
    New Zealand 12 (5%) United Kingdom 7 (3%) N/A 25 (11%)
    Yes respondents
    United States 516 (87%)   Canada 22 (4%)
    United Kingdom 20 (3%)
    New Zealand 8 (1%) N/A 10 (2%)   Others 19 (3%)
    (Australia 3, Netherlands 3, Mexico 2, Brazil 1, Germany 1,

Hungary 1, Ireland 1, Lebanon 1, Morocco 1, Norway 1, Puerto
Rico 1, Saudi Arabia 1, Sri Lanka 1, Sweden 1, Switzerland 1)
Total respondents
United States 664 (80%)   Canada 43 (5%)
United Kingdom 27(3%)
Australia 21 (3%)   New Zealand 20 (3%)
N/A 35 (4%)   Other 17 (2%)
Gender:
Yes respondents (596)
    Female 435 (73%)   Male 135 (23%)   N/A 26 (4%)
No respondents (231)
    Female 140 (61%)   Male 56 (24%)   N/A 35 (15%)
Total respondents (827)
    Female 575 (70%)   Male 191 (23%)   N/A 61(7%)

Dianne Arcangel
University of Virginia
Division of Personality Studies
P.O. Box 800152
Charlottesville, VA 22908-0152

References

Arcangel, D. (1997). Investigating the relationship between the Myers-Briggs Type Indicator and facilitated reunion experiences. *Journal of the American Society for Psychical Research*, 91, 81–95.

Barrett, W. F. (1926). *Death-bed Visions*. London: Methuen.

Bennett, G., & Bennett, K. (2000). The presence of the dead: An empirical study. *Mortality*, 5, 139–157.

Bowlby, J. (1980). *Loss: Sadness and Depression, vol. 3*. New York: HarperCollins.

———. (1982). *Loss: Attachment and Loss, vol. 1*. New York: Harper Collins.

Carverhill, P. (2002). Qualitative research in thanatology. *Death Studies*, 26 (3), 195–207.

Childs, A. (1997). Positive emotional effects of the near death experience and facilitated altered states of consciousness. Unpublished doctoral dissertation, California Coast University.

Cohen, S. S. (1997). *Looking for the Other Side*. New York: Clarkson Potter.

Datson, S. L., & Marwit, S. J. (1997). Personality constructs and perceived presence of deceased loved ones. *Death Studies*, 21 (2), 131–147.

DeSpelder, L. A., & Strickland, A. L. (1983). *The Last Dance: Encountering Death and Dying.* Palo Alto, Calif: Mayfield Publishing Company.

Devers, E (1997). *Goodbye Again: Experiences with Departed Loved Ones.* Kansas City, Mo.: Andrews and McMeel.

——. (1987). Experiencing an encounter with the deceased. Unpublished master's thesis, University of Florida, Gainesville.

——. (1994). Experiencing the deceased: Reconciling the extraordinary. Unpublished doctoral dissertation, University of Florida.

Devers, E., & Robinson, K. M. (2002). The making of a grounded theory: After-death communication. *Death Studies, 26,* 241–254.

Drewry, D. J. (2002). Purported after-death communication and its role in the recovery of bereaved individuals: A phenomenological study. Unpublished doctoral dissertation, California Institute for Human Science.

Doka, K., with Morgan, J. (eds.) (1993). *Death and Spirituality.* New York: Baywood.

Gamino, L. A., Sewell, K. W., & Esterling, L. W. (2000). Scott and White Study – Phase 2: Toward an adaptive model of grief. *Death Studies, 24* (7), 633–661.

Gilliss, C. L., Moore ,I, & Marie, I. (1997). Measuring parental grief after childhood cancer: Potential use of the SCL-90R. *Death Studies, 21* (3), 277–288.

Glick, I. O., Weiss, R. S., & Parkes, C. M. (1974). *The First Year of Bereavement.* New York: John Wiley, Interscience.

Gorer, G. (1973). Death, grief and mourning in Britain. In Anthony, E. J., & Koupernik, C. (eds.) , *The Child in His Family: The Impact of Disease and Death.* New York: John Wiley.

Greeley, A. M. (1987). Hallucinations among the widowed. *Sociology and Social Research, 71* (4), 258–265.

——. (1989). *Religious Change in America.* Cambridge, Mass.: Harvard University Press.

Guggenheim, B., & Guggenheim, J. (1996). *Hello from Heaven.* New York: Bantam Books.

Gurney, E., & Myers, F. W. H.(1888–89). On apparitions occurring soon after death. *Proceedings of the Society for Psychical Research, 5,* 403–485.

Irwin, H. J. (2002). Proneness to self-deception and the two-factor model of paranormal belief. *Journal of the Society for Psychical Research, 66.2,* 80–87.

James, W. (1958). *The Varieties of Religious Experience.* New York: New American Library.

Jung, C. G. (1965). *Memories, Dreams, Reflections.* New York: Vintage Books.

Kalish, R. A., & Reynolds, D. K. (1976). *Death and Ethnicity: A Psychocultural Study.*

Los Angeles: Ethel Percy Andrus Gerontology Center, University of Southern California.

Kastenbaum, R. (1992). *Psychology of Death.* New York: Springer.

Kelly, E. W. (2001). Near-death experiences with reports of meeting deceased people. *Death Studies,* 25 (3), 229-249.

Kircher, P. (1995). *Love Is the Link: A Hospice Doctor Shares Her Experience of Near-death and Dying.* Burdett, N.Y.: Larson Publications.

Klass, D. (1993). Solace and immortality: Bereaved parents continuing bond with their children. *Death Studies,* 17, 343-368.

Kübler-Ross E. (1969). *On Death and Dying.* New York: Macmillan.

—— (ed.). (1975). *Death: The Final Stage of Growth.* Englewood Cliffs, N.J.: Prentice-Hall.

LaGrand, L. E. (1998). *After Death Communication: Final Farewells.* St. Paul, Minn.: Llewellyn Publications.

——. (1999). *Messages and Miracles: Extraordinary Experiences of the Bereaved.* St. Paul, Minn.: Llewellyn Publications.

Laski, M. (1961). *Ecstasy in Secular and Religious Experiences.* Los Angeles: J. P. Tarcher.

——. (1968). *Ecstasy: A Study of Some Secular and Religious Experiences.* New York, Greenwood Press.

Lodge, S. O. J. (1916). *Raymond or Life and Death.* New York: G. H. Doran.

Martinson, I., Davies, E., & McClowry, S. (1991). Parental depression following the death of a child. *Death Studies,* 15, 259-267.

McClowry, S., Davies, E., May, K., Kulenkamp, E., & Martinson, I. (1987). The empty space phenomenon: The process of grief in the bereaved family. *Death Studies,* 11, 361-374.

Moody, R., & Arcangel, D. (2001). *Life after Loss: Conquering Grief and Finding Hope.* San Francisco: HarperSanFrancisco.

Myers, F. W. H. (1903). *Human Personality and Its Survival of Bodily Death.* (2 vols.). London: Longmans, Green.

Neimeyer, R. A. (ed.) (1994). *Death Anxiety Handbook: Research, Instrumentation, and Application.* Washington, D. C.: Taylor & Frances.

Neimeyer, R. A. (2001). *Lessons of Loss: A Guide to Coping.* Philadelphia: Brunner Routledge.

Olson, P. R., Suddeth, J. A., Peterson, P. J., & Egelhoff, C. (1985). Hallucinations of widowhood. *Journal of the American Geriatric Society,* 33, 543-547.

Osis, K. (1961). *Deathbed Observations by Physicians and Nurses.* New York: Parapsychology Foundation.

——. (1995). In search of life after death: Science, experience or both? *Academy of Religion and Psychical Research Annual Conference Proceedings,* 24.

Osis, K., & Haraldsson, E. (1993). *At the Hour of Death.* New York: Hastings House.

Parkes, C. (1972). *Bereavement: Studies of Grief in Adult Life.* New York: International Universities Press.

Podmore, F. (1897). *Studies in Psychical Research.* New York: G. P. Putnam's Sons.

Rando, T. A. (1984). *Grief, Dying, and Death: Clinical Interventions for Caregivers.* Champaign, Ill.: Research Press Company.

——. (1993). *Treatment of Complicated Mourning.* Champaign, Ill.: Research Press Company.

Rees, W. D. (1971). The hallucinations of widowhood. *British Medical Journal,* 4, 37–41.

——. (1975). The bereaved and their hallucination, in Schoenberg, B. et al. (eds.), *Bereavement: Its Psychosocial Aspects.* New York: Columbia University Press.

Rosenblatt, P. C. (1983). *Bitter, Bitter Tears: Nineteenth Century Diarists and Twentieth Century Grief Theories.* Minneapolis: University of Minnesota Press.

Sanders, C. M. (1989). *Grief: The Mourning After, Dealing with Adult Bereavement.* New York: Wiley.

Shuchter, S. R., & Zisook, S. (1993). The course of normal grief, in Stroebe, M. S., Stroebe, W., & Hansson, R. O., (eds.), *Handbook of Bereavement: Theory, Research, and Intervention.* New York: Cambridge University Press.

Sidgwick, H. (1923). Phantasms of the living. *Proceedings of the Society for Psychical Research,* 33, 23–29.

Sidgwick, H., & Committee (1894). Report on the census of hallucinations. *Proceedings of the Society for Psychical Research,* 10, 25–422.

Silverman, P. R., & Worden, J.W. (1993). Children's reactions to the death of a parent, in Stroebe, M. S., Stroebe, W., & Hansson, R. O., (eds.) *Handbook of Bereavement: Theory, Research, and Intervention.* New York: Cambridge University Press.

Stroebe, M. S., Stroebe, W., & Hansson, R. O. (eds.) (1993). *Handbook of Bereavement: Theory, Research, and Intervention.* New York: Cambridge University Press.

Taylor, S. E., & Brown, J. D. (1988). Illusion and well-being: a social psychological perspective on mental health. *Psychological Bulletin* 103 (2), 193–210.

Wiitala, G. C. (1996). *Heather's Return: The Amazing Story of a Child's Communications from Beyond the Grave.* Virginia Beach, Va.: A.R.E. Press.

Wolfelt, A. D. (1988). *Death and Grief: A Guide for Clergy and Others Involved in Care of the Bereaved.* Muncie, Ind.: Accelerated Development.

Worden, W. J. (1991). *Grief Counseling & Grief Therapy: A Handbook for the Mental Health Practitioner.* New York: Springer.

Wright, S. (2002). *When Spirits Come Calling: The Open-minded Skeptic's Guide to After-death Contacts.* Nevada City, Calif.: Blue Dolphin.

Zisook, S., & Shuchter, S. R. (1986). The first four years of widowhood. *Psychiatric Annals,* 15, 288–294.

Zisook, S., DeVaul, R., & Click, M. (1982). Measuring symptoms of grief and bereavement. *American Journal of Psychiatry,* 139, 1590–1593.

Endnotes

Chapter 2

1. Rupert Sheldrake, *Seven Experiments That Could Change the World: A Do-It-Yourself Guide to Revolutionary Science.* Rochester, Vt.: Park Street Press, 2002.

2. Rupert Sheldrake, *The Sense of Being Stared At: and Other Unexplained Powers of the Human Mind.* New York: Crown, 2003; The sense of being stared at: Experiments in schools. Journal of the Society of Psychical Research 62: 311–23, 1998.

3. Phyllis Silverman and William Worden reported similar findings, in Children's Reactions to the Death of a Parent in *Handbook of Bereavement: Theory, Research, and Intervention,* edited by Margaret Stroebe, Wolfgang Stroebe, and Robert Hansson, New York: Cambridge University Press (pp. 300–316), 1993.

4. Adapted from Annette Childs's unpublished doctoral dissertation, "Positive Emotional Effects of the Near Death Experience and Facilitated Altered States of Consciousness," California Coast University, 1997.

Chapter 3

1. Andrew M. Greeley presented data from the American Institute of Public Opinion (AIPO) Survey, the General Social Survey (GSS), and the Survey Research Center (SRC) in his book *Religious Change in America,* published by Harvard University Press in 1989.

2. "On Apparitions Occurring Soon After Death," written by the late Edmund Gurney and completed by F. W. H. Myers, was first presented to the Society of Psychical Research on January 28, 1888, and published in the Proceedings of the General Meeting on March 25, 1889. Their three criteria for evidence of survival remain standard today.

3. Apparitions manipulating physical objects was one of Andrew Lang's (1898) main considerations. Gurney and Myers, however, did not include the phenomenon among their criteria. The controversy lingers. Some parapsychologists speculate that the perceivers, not the apparitions, moved the objects by psychokinesis (PK—mind over matter).

4. From Rupert Sheldrake's (2003) *The Sense of Being Stared At.* New York: Crown, p. 9.

5. G. N. M. Tyrrell (1962) *Apparitions.* N.Y.: Macmillan, p. 98.

6. Andrew M. Greeley (1989). *Religious Change in America.* Harvard University Press. Father Greeley compiled the American Institute of Public Opinion (AIPO) Survey data and the General Social Survey (GSS) and Survey Research Center (SRC) data.

7. Gurney and Myers (March 25, 1889), "On Apparitions Occurring Soon After Death," *Proceedings of the General Meeting,* SPR (p. 426). Although the paper, written by the late Edmund Gurney and completed by F. W. H. Myers, was presented at the Society for Psychical Research on January 28, 1888, the findings are the most circulated to date. Gurney determined two reasons why mourners experienced more AES—they were excited about their experiences, so remembered them; and they were more open or receptive.

8. Within hours accounted for 12 percent, weeks totaled 14 percent, months 17 percent, and one year 10 percent. Then 2–9 years accounted for 17 percent, 10–19 registered 11 percent, 20–29 totaled 9 percent, and 30 years or longer 10 percent.

9. Report on the Census of Hallucinations presented in G. N. M. Tyrrell's *Apparitions* (1962).

Chapter 4

1. G. N. M. Tyrrell (1962) *Apparitions.*

2. Andrew M. Greeley compiled data from the American Institute of Public Opinion Survey (AIPO), General Social Survey (GSS), and Survey Research Center (SRC). He presented the findings in *Religious Change in America* (1996) published by Harvard University Press.

3. Roper Organization Inc. (1991) conducted the Unusual Events Survey for the Bigelow Holding Company.

4. Roper Organization Inc. (1991), Unusual Events Survey; Bob Bigelow (1995) personal communication.

5. Andrew M. Greeley compiled data from the American Institute of Public Opinion Survey (AIPO), General Social Survey (GSS), and Survey Research Center (SRC). He presented the findings in *Religious Change in America* (1996) published by Harvard University Press.

6. Adapted from Investigating the relationship between the Myers-Briggs Type Indicator and facilitated reunion experiences by Dianne Arcangel, *Journal of the American Society for Psychical Research,* 91, 82–95, 1997.

7. Looking at the individual groups, the Extroverts reported slightly more encounters (95 percent) compared to Introverts (84 percent), but 95 percent of Intuitives contrasted with 41 percent of Sensors, and 93 percent of Feeling types over 33 percent of Thinking. Then the Perceivers (86 percent) and Judgers (85 percent) were almost identical.

8. From the General Social Survey (GSS), presented by Andrew M. Greeley (1996) in his book, *Religious Change in America.*

9. Greeley, Andrew M. (1996) in *Religious Change in America,* published by Harvard University Press. Olson P. Richard, Joe A. Suddeth, P. J. Peterson, and Claudia Egelhoff, Hallucinations of widowhood in the *Journal of the American Geriatric Society,* 33, 543–47, 1985.

Chapter 5
1. G. N. M. Tyrrell (1962) *Apparitions,* N.Y.: Macmillan, p. 81.

Chapter 6
1. *Phantasms of the Living* by Gurney, Myers, and Podmore, 1886.

2. Rupert Sheldrake, *A New Science of Life: The Hypothesis of Formative Causation,* London: Blond and Briggs, 1981; *The Presence of the Past: Morphic Resonance and the Habits of Nature,* New York: Times Books, 1988; *Seven Experiments That Could Change the World: A Do-It-Yourself Guide to Revolutionary Science,* Rochester, Vt.: Park Street Press, 2002; *Dogs That Know When Their Owners Are Coming Home: And Other Unexplained Powers of Animals,* New York: Crown, 1999; "The Sense of Being Stared At: Experiments in School," *Journal of the Society of Psychical Research* 62: 311–23, 1998.

3. *The Sense of Being Stared At,* New York: Crown (p. 279), 2003.

4. Rupert Sheldrake investigated the phenomena and then reported his findings in numerous journal articles, including "Experimental Tests for Telephone Telepathy," *Journal of the Society of Psychical Research* 67, 3:184–199, 2003.

Chapter 7
1. As a result of studies conducted with a variety of mediums at the University of Arizona, Dr. Gary Schwartz considered George the Stradivarius. More information can be found in his book (with W. L. Simon) *The Afterlife Experiments: Breakthrough Scientific Evidence of Life After Death,* New York: Pocket Books, 2002.

2. For further reading, see Dean Radin and Jannine Rebman's 1996 article, "Are Phantasms Fact or Fantasy?: A preliminary investigation of apparitions evoked in the laboratory," published in the *Journal of the Society for Psychical Research,* pp. 65–87.

3. On the infrared scale, white is the greatest measure of heat. Whereas a running or recently run automobile engine will register white, one that has been off for some time will appear black.

Chapter 8
1. Gary Schwartz, Ph.D., received his doctorate from Harvard University, served as a professor of psychology and psychiatry at Yale University, director of the Yale Psychophysiology Center, and co-director of the Yale Behavioral Medicine Clinic. He is currently a professor of psychology, medicine, neurology, psychiatry, and surgery at the University of Arizona, and director of the Human Energy Systems Laboratory, located at the university. He has authored more than

four hundred scientific papers, edited eleven academic books, co-authored *The Living Energy Universe* with Linda Russek, Charlottesville, Va.: Hampton Roads, 1999; and authored *The Afterlife Experiments* with William L. Simon, New York: Pocket Books, 2002.

Appendix

1. This appendix is an early version of the paper submitted and accepted for publication by *The Journal of the American Society for Psychical Research,* in press. Dedicated to Robert Morris, a continuous champion for the AES and my work in his field. Thank you to the following people who helped design or circulate the Afterlife Encounters Survey: Andrew Barone, Andrew Greeley, Bob Bigelow, Bruce Greyson, Debbie Fancher, Diane Bigelow, Emily Williams Kelly, George Anderson, John Palmer, Rupert Sheldrake, and Sally Feather. For help with literature searches, my gratitude to Robert Neimeyer, the staff at the Rhine Research Center, Pasadena (Texas) Public Library, and Association for Death Education and Counseling. Appreciation to my assistant and statistician Silas Thompson. Special acknowledgment to Rhea White for her extraordinary support throughout the project, and to Karl Fancher of Kaf Designs for posting, maintaining, and hosting the survey on the Internet. Appreciation to Jessica Utts, JASPR's Statistical Editor, for her clarifications and editorial suggestions. Thank you, Suzanne Brown, for accepting, editing, and preparing this paper for publication. Most of all, my heartfelt respect and gratefulness to every person who participated in the study.

Glossary

afterlife encounter (AE): any sense of being connected to or in the presence of a discarnate entity.

Afterlife Encounter Survey (AES): a five-year international study that collected data pertaining to the effects, if any, afterlife encounters have on recipients over time.

anomaly: unexplainable phenomenon.

apparition: postmortem entity; discarnate person, animal, or being. Associates with a person rather than a place.

discarnate: afterlife persona (see apparition).

discernment: a reading given by a medium; a session wherein the medium supposedly contacts discarnate beings.

disenfranchise: to discount, disregard, dismiss; to consider something as insignificant.

eighth sense: the invisible, inaudible, intangible connection between the living and discarnate.

ghost: a visual representation of a discarnate entity; associates with a place rather than a person.

hallucinating: perceiving something for which there is no eternal cause.

illusion: an external event that is misperceived or misinterpreted.

mediumship practitioner: consistently delivers specific, accurate statements, and provides information (unknown by the sitter) that is later verified.

perceiver: person who experiences the encounter; percipient, witness, receiver, recipient, observer.

pseudomedium: impersonates a mediumship practitioner; charlatan; is aware of his/her inability to discern discarnate personas.

psychokinesis (PK): mind over matter; ability to mentally manipulate objects.

recipient: (see perceiver).

sensitive: person who is able to discern information though clients' psyches.

survival: specialized field wherein researchers investigate the possibility that something exists beyond bodily demise.

survivalist: person who investigates the possibility that consciousness, spirit, personality, or some aspect of the living survives after the body ceases to function.

thanatology: the study of death and dying.

thanatologist: professional in the field of thanatology.

Supportive Resources

Bereavement Literature
Adult Bereavement—Books and Articles

Bowlby, J. *The Making and Breaking of Affectional Bonds*. London: Tavistock, 1979.

——. *Loss, Sadness and Depression*. New York: Basic Books, 1980.

——. *Attachment*. New York: Basic Books, 1982.

Doka, K. (ed.). *Disenfranchised Grief: Recognizing Hidden Sorrow*. Lexington, Mass.: Lexington Books, 1989.

Gorer, G. *Death, Grief and Mourning in Contemporary Britain*. London: Cresset Press, 1965.

Glick, I., R. Weiss, and C. Parkes. *The First Year of Bereavement*. New York: John Wiley Interscience, 1974.

Jacobs, S. *Pathologic Grief: Maladaptation to Loss*. Washington, D.C.: American Psychiatric Press, 1993.

——. *Traumatic Grief: Diagnosis, Treatment, and Prevention*. Philadelphia: Brunner/Mazel, 1999.

Kübler-Ross, E. *On Death and Dying*. New York: Macmillan, 1969.

Moody R., and D. Arcangel. *Life After Loss: Conquering Grief and Finding Hope*. San Francisco: HarperSanFrancisco, 2001.

Neimeyer, R. A. *Death Anxiety Handbook: Research, Instrumentation, and Application*. Washington, D.C.: Taylor & Frances, 1994.

——. *Lessons of Loss: A Guide to Coping*. Philadelphia: Brunner Routledge, 2001.

Parkes, C. M. *Bereavement: Studies of Grief in Adult Life*. Madison, Conn.: International Universities Press, 1998.

Parkes, C. M., and R. S. Weiss. *Recovery from Bereavement*. New York: Basic Books, 1983.

Stillwell, E. A. *Forever Angels*. Omaha, Nebr.: Centering Corporation, 2000.

——. *A Forever Angel.* Omaha, Nebr.: Centering Corporation, 2001.

——. *The Death of a Child: Reflections for Grieving Parents.* Chicago: ACTA Publications, 2004.

Stroebe, M. S., W. Stroebe, and R. O. Hansson (eds.). *Handbook of Bereavement: Theory, Research and Intervention.* Cambridge, England: Cambridge University Press, 1993.

Wass, H., F. Berardo, and R. Neimeyer. *Dying: Facing the Facts.* Washington: Hemisphere, 1988.

Animal Loss—Books

Coleman, J. *Forever Friends: Resolving Grief After the Loss of a Beloved Animal.* Las Vegas, Nev.: J. C. Tara Enterprises, 1993.

Kay, W. J., et al. (eds.). *Pet Loss and Human Bereavement.* Ames, Iowa: Iowa State University Press, 1984.

Montgomery, M., and H. Montgomery. *Good-bye My Friend: Grieving the Loss of a Pet.* Minneapolis, Minn.: Montgomery Press, 1991.

Moody R., and D. Arcangel. *Life After Loss: Conquering Grief and Finding Hope.* San Francisco: HarperSanFrancisco, 2001.

Nieburg, H. A., and A. Fischer. *Pet Loss: A Thoughtful Guide for Adults and Children.* New York: HarperCollins, 1982.

Quackenbush, J., and D. Graveline. *When Your Pet Dies: How to Cope with Your Feelings.* New York: Simon & Schuster, 1985.

Ross, C. B., and J. B. Sorensen. *Pet Loss and Human Emotion.* Philadelphia, Pa.: Accelerated Development, 1998.

Sheldrake, R. *Dogs That Know When Their Owners Are Coming Home: And Other Unexplained Powers of Animals.* New York: Crown, 1999.

Sife, W. *The Loss of a Pet, The Human-Animal Bond.* New York: Macmillan, 1993.

Children's Bereavement—Books

Adams, D. W., and E. J. Deveau. *Beyond the Innocence of Childhood: Helping Children and Adolescents Cope with Death and Bereavement.* Amityville, N.Y.: Baywood Publishing, 1995.

Alderman, L. *Why Did Daddy Die?* New York: Simon & Schuster, 1989.

Arnold, C. *What We Do When Someone Dies.* New York: Franklin Watts, 1987.

Aub, K. A. *Children Are Survivors Too: A Guidebook for Young Homicide Survivors.* Boca Raton, Fla.: Grief Education Enterprises, 1991.

Blackburn, L. B. *The Class in Room 44*. Omaha, Nebr.: Centering Corp., 1991.

Bluebond-Langner, M. *The Private Worlds of Dying Children*. Princeton, N.J.: Princeton University Press, 1978.

Center for Attitudinal Healing. *There Is a Rainbow Behind Every Dark Cloud*. Millbrae, Calif.: Celestial Arts, 1978.

Coles, R. *The Spiritual Life of Children*. Boston: Houghton Mifflin, 1990.

Corr, C. A. and J. N. McNeil (eds.). *Adolescence and Death*. New York: Springer, 1986.

Dyregrov, A. *Grief in Children: A Handbook for Adults*. London: J. Kingsley, 1991.

Fitzgerald, H. *The Grieving Child: A Parent's Guide*. New York: Fireside Simon & Schuster, 1992.

Furman, E. *A Child's Parent Dies: Studies in Childhood Bereavement*. New Haven: Yale University Press, 1981.

Goldman, L. *Life and Loss: A Guide to Help Grieving Children*. Muncie, Ind.: Accelerated Development, 1993.

Gordon, A. K., and D. Klass. *They Need to Know: How to Teach Children About Death*. Englewood Cliffs, N.J.: Prentice-Hall, 1979.

Grollman, E. A. *Explaining Death to Children*. Boston, Mass.: Beacon, 1987.

——. *Talking About Death: A Dialogue Between Parent and Child*. Boston, Mass.: Beacon, 1990.

——. *Straight Talk About Death for Teenagers: How to Cope with Losing Someone You Love*. Boston, Mass.: Beacon Press, 1993.

—— (ed.). *Bereaved Children and Teens: A Support Guide for Parents and Professionals*. Boston, Mass.: Beacon, 1995.

Hartnett, J. *Children and Grief: Big Issues for Little Hearts*. Burlington, Vt.: Good Mourning, 1993.

Huntley, T. *Helping Children Grieve: When Someone They Love Dies*. Minneapolis, Minn.: Augsburg Fortress, 2002.

Jewett, C. J. *Helping Children Cope with Separation and Loss*. Boston, Mass.: Harvard Common Press, 1994.

Kolehmainen, J., and S. Handwerk. *Teen Suicide: A Book for Friends, Family, and Classmates*. Minneapolis, Minn.: Lerner Publications, 1986.

Kübler-Ross, E. *On Children and Death*. New York: Scribner, 1983.

LaTour, K. *For Those Who Live: Helping Children Cope with the Death of a Brother or Sister*. Omaha, Nebr.: Centering Corp, 1983.

Lombardo, V. S., and E. R. Lombardo. *Kids Grieve Too!* Springfield, Ill,: Charles C. Thomas Publisher, 1986.

Lonetto, R. *Children's Conceptions of Death.* N.Y.: Springer, 1980.

Schaefer, D., and C. Lyons. *How Do We Tell the Children?: A Step-by-Step Guide for Helping Children Two to Teen Cope When Someone Dies.* New York: Newmarket Press, 1993.

Schowalter, J. E. et al. (eds.). *The Child and Death.* New York: Columbia University Press, 1983.

Stillwell, E. A. *Forever Angels.* Omaha, Nebr.: Centering Corporation, 2000.

———. *A Forever Angel.* Omaha, Nebr.: Centering Corporation, 2001.

Wass, H., and C. A. Corr. *Helping Children Cope with Death: Guidelines and Resources.* Washington, D.C.: Hemisphere, 1984.

Wolfelt, A. D. *Helping Children Cope with Grief.* Muncie, Ind.: Accelerated Development, 1983.

———. *A Child's View of Grief: A Guide for Caring Adults.* Fort Collins, Colo.: Companion Press, 1991. [Video also available.]

Survival-Related Literature
Afterlife Encounters—Books

Almeder, R. F. *Death and Personal Survival: The Evidence for Life After Death.* Lanham, Md.: Rowen & Littlefield, 1992.

Auerbach, L. *ESP, Hauntings and Poltergeists: A Parapsychologist's Handbook.* New York: Warner, 1986.

Baird, A. T. *One Hundred Cases for Survival After Death.* New York: B. Ackerman, 1944.

Barrett, S. W. *Death-bed Visions: The Psychical Experiences of the Dying.* New York: Aquarian Press, 1986.

Bayless, R. *Apparitions and Survival of Death.* New Hyde Park, N.Y.: Basic Books, 1973 (out of print).

Bennett, E. *Apparitions and Haunted Houses: A Survey of Evidence.* Ann Arbor, Mich.: Gryphon Books, 1971.

Carrington, H. *The Case for Psychic Survival.* New York: Citadel Press, 1957.

Devers, E. *Goodbye Again.* Kansas City, Mo.: Andrews and McMeel, 1997.

Doore, G. (ed.). *What Survives?* Los Angeles: Jeremy P. Tarcher, 1990.

Ducasse, C. J. *Critical Examination of the Belief in a Life After Death.* Springfield, Ill.: Charles C. Thomas, 1961.

Duncan, L., and W. Roll. *Psychic Connections.* New York: Delacorte Press, 1995.

Edwards, D. L. *After Death? Past Beliefs and Real Possibilities.* London: Cassell, 1999.

Finucane, R. C. *Appearances of the Dead: A Cultural History of Ghosts.* New York: Prometheus, 1984.

Flammarion, C. *Haunted Houses.* Detroit: Gale Research, 1971.

Gauld, A. Discarnate survival, in B. B. Wolman (ed.), *Handbook of Parapsychology.* New York: Van Nostrand Reinhold, 1977.

Green, C., and C. McCreery. *Apparitions.* New York: State Mutual Book & Periodical Service, 1989 (out of print).

Grof, S., and J. Halifax. *The Human Encounter with Death.* New York: E. P. Dutton, 1978.

Guggenheim, B., and J. Guggenheim. *Hello from Heaven.* New York: Bantam Books, 1996.

Gurney, E., F. W. H. Myers, and F. Podmore. *Phantasms of the Living* (2 volumes). London: Trübner, 1886.

———. *Phantasms of the Living* (1 volume). New York: Arno Press, 1975.

Haraldsson, E., and K. Osis. *At the Hour of Death.* New York: Avon Books, 1977.

Holzer, H. *Ghosts.* New York: Black Dog and Leventhal, 1998.

Hyslop, J. H. *Contact with the Other World.* New York: Century, 1919.

Iverson, J. *In Search of the Dead: A Scientific Investigation of Evidence for Life After Death.* San Francisco: HarperSanFrancisco, 1992.

Jung, C. G. *Memories, Dreams, Reflections.* New York: Pantheon, 1965.

LaGrand, L. *After Death Communication: Final Farewells.* St. Paul, Minn.: Llewellyn Publications, 1997.

———. *Messages and Miracles: Extraordinary Experiences of the Bereaved.* St. Paul, Minn.: Llewellyn Publications, 1999.

Linn, E. *Premonitions, Visitations and Dreams of the Bereaved.* Incline Village, Nev.: The Publisher's Mark, 1991.

MacKenzie, A. *Apparitions and Ghosts.* London: Arthur Barker, 1971.

———. *Hauntings and Apparitions.* London: Heinemann, 1982.

Martin, J., and P. Romanowski. *Love Beyond Life: The Healing Power of After-Death Communications.* New York: HarperCollins, 1997.

McCready, W., and A. Greeley. *The Ultimate Values of the American Population.* Beverly Hills: Sage, 1976.

Myers, F. W. H. *Human Personality and Its Survival of Bodily Death.* New Hyde Park, N.Y.: University Books, 1961.

———. *Human Personality and Its Survival of Bodily Death.* New York: Arno Press, 1975 (originally published in 1903).

Osis, K. *Deathbed Observations by Physicians and Nurses.* New York: Parapsychology Foundation, 1961.

Osis, K., and E. Haraldsson. *At the Hour of Death: A New Look at Evidence for Life after Death* (3rd edition). Norwalk, Conn.: Hastings House, 1993.

Osty, E. *Supernormal Faculties in Man.* London: Methuen, 1923.

Parkes, C. M. *Bereavement: Studies of Grief in Adult Life.* Madison, Conn.: International Universities Press, 1987.

Parkes, C. M., and R. S. Weiss. *Recovery from Bereavement.* New York: Basic Books, 1983.

Podmore, F. *Studies in Psychical Research.* London: G. P. Putnam's Sons, 1897.

Rogo, D. *NAD: A Study of Some Unusual "Other-world" Experiences.* New Hyde Park, N.Y.: University Books, 1970.

———. Spontaneous contact with the dead: Perspectives from grief counseling, sociology and parapsychology, in G. Doore (ed.), *What Survives?* (pp.76–91). Los Angeles: Jeremy P. Tarcher, 1990.

Salter, W. H. *Ghosts and Apparitions.* London: G. Bell and Sons, 1938.

Shucter, S. R., and S. Zisook. The course of normal grief, in M. S. Stroebe, W. Stroebe, and R. O. Hansson (eds.), *Handbook of Bereavement: Theory, Research and Intervention* (pp. 23–43). New York: Cambridge University Press, 1993.

Sidgwick, H., E. Sidgwick, and A. Johnson, et al. Report on the census of hallucinations. *Proceedings of the Society for Psychical Research,* 10, 25–422, 1894.

Tyrrell, G. N. M. *Apparitions.* London: Society for Psychical Research, 1973.

Wiitala, G. C. *Heather's Return: The Amazing Story of a Child's Communications from Beyond the Grave.* Virginia Beach, Va.: A.R.E. Press, 1996.

Afterlife Encounters—Articles

Arcangel, D. "Investigating the relationship between the Myers-Briggs Type Indicator and facilitated reunion experiences." *Journal of the American Society for Psychical Research,* 91, 82–95, 1997.

———. "Afterlife Encounters Survey: The Results." *Journal of the American Society for Psychical Research,* in press.

Balfour, G. W. "The ear of Dionysius; further scripts affording evidence of personal survival." *Proceedings of the Society for Psychical Research,* 29,197–243, 1918.

Berger, A. S. "Quoth the raven: Bereavement and the paranormal." *Omega: Journal of Death & Dying,* 31(1), 1–10, 1995.

Burton, J. "Contact with the dead: A common experience?" *Fate,* 35(4), 65–73, 1982.

Cook, E. W. "The survival question: Impasse or crux?" *Journal of the American Society for Psychical Research,* 81, 125–139, 1987.

Cook, E. W., B. Greyson, and I. Stevenson. "Do any near-death experiences provide evidence for the survival of human personality after death? Relevant features and illustrative case reports." *Journal of Scientific Exploration,* vol. 12, no. 3, pp. 377–406, 1998.

Fontana, D. "Apparent post-mortem communication from Professor Arthur Ellison." *Journal of the Society for Psychical Research,* 67.2, 131–142, 2003.

Gauld, A. Discarnate survival. In B. B. Wolman (ed.), *Handbook of Parapsychology* (pp. 577–630). New York: Van Nostrand Reinhold, 1977.

Greeley, A. "Hallucinations among the widowed." *Sociology and Social Research,* 71(4), 258–265, 1987.

Greyson, B. "Near-death experiences" pp. 315–352. *Varieties of Anomalous Experience: Examining the Scientific Evidence.* Edited by E. Cardena, S. Lynn, and S. Krippner. Washington: American Psychological Association, 2000.

Gurney, E., and F. W. H. Myers. "On apparitions occurring soon after death." *Proceedings of the Society for Psychical Research,* 5, 403–485, 1888–89.

Hallson, P. "Can we make progress in the study of apparitions?" *Paranormal Review, Magazine of the Journal of the Society for Psychical Research.* January, 21, 3–6, 2002.

Haraldsson, E., and I. Stevenson. "An experiment with the Icelandic medium Hafsteinn Bjornsson." *Journal of the American Society for Psychical Research,* 68, 201, 1974.

———. "A communicator of the 'drop in' type in Iceland: Case of Gudni Magnusson." *Journal of the American Society for Psychical Research* 69, 245–261, 1975.

———. "A communicator of the 'drop in' type in Iceland: Case of Runolfur Runolfsson." *Journal of the American Society for Psychical Research,* 69, 33–59, 1975.

Hart, H. "Six theories about apparitions." *Proceedings of the Society for Psychical Research,* 50,153–239, 1976.

Hart, H., and E. B. Hart. "Visions and apparitions collectively and reciprocally perceived." *Proceedings of the Society for Psychical Research,* 41, 205–249, 1976.

Kalish, R. A., and D. K. Reynolds. "Phenomenological reality and post-death contact." *Journal for the Scientific Study of Religion,* 12, 209–221, 1973.

Lindstrom, B. "Exploring paranormal experiences of the bereaved." *Creativity in Death Education and Counseling,* Charles A. Corr, et al. (eds.) pp. 117–143. Association for Death Education and Counseling, 1983.

Osis, K. "Linkage experiments with mediums." *Journal of the American Society for Psychical Research,* 60, 91–124, 1966.

Osis, K., and E. Haraldsson. "Deathbed observations by physicians and nurses: A cross-cultural survey." *Journal of the American Society for Psychical Research, 71,* 237–259, 1977.

Radin, Dean, and J. Rebman. "Are phantasms fact or fantasy? A preliminary investigation of apparitions evoked in the laboratory." *Journal of the Society for Psychical Research,* 65–87, 1996.

Rees, W. "The hallucinations of widowhood." *British Medical Journal,* 4, 37–41, 1971.

———. "Bereavement and illness." *Journal of Thanatology,* 2(3–4), 814–819, 1972.

Rhine, J. B. "The value of reports of spontaneous psi experiences." *Journal of Parapsychology,* 12, 231–235, 1954.

———. "Incorporeal personal agency: The prospect of a scientific solution." *Journal of Parapsychology,* 24, 279–309, 1960.

Rhine, L. E. "Conviction and associated conditions in spontaneous cases." *Journal of Parapsychology,* 15,164–191, 1951.

———. "Hallucinatory psi experiences: The initiative of the percipient in hallucinations of the living, the dying, and the dead." *Journal of Parapsychology,* 21, 13–46, 1957.

Rogo, D. S. "Research on deathbed experiences: Some contemporary and historical perspectives." *Parapsychology Review,* January–February, 9, 20–27, 1978.

Roll, W. G. The changing perspective of life after death. In S. Krippner (ed.), *Advances in Parapsychological Research: Vol. 3* (pp. 147–291). Cambridge, Mass.: Perseus Books, 1982.

Schwartz, G., L. Russek, L. A. Nelson, and C. Barentsen. "Accuracy and replicability of anomalous after-death communication across highly skilled mediums." *Journal of the American Society for Psychical Research,* 65, 862: 1–25, 2001.

Sherwood, S. "Apparitions of black dogs." *Paranormal Review,* magazine of the *Journal of the Society for Psychical Research,* April, 22, 3–6, 2002.

Stevenson, I. "Survival after death: Evidence and issues," in I. Grattan-Guinness (ed.), *Psychical Research: A Guide to Its History, Principles and Practices* (pp. 109–122). Wellingborough, Northamptonshire, England: Aquarian Press, 1982.

———. "Do we need a new word to supplement 'hallucination'?" *American Journal of Psychiatry,* 140(12), 1609–1611, 1983.

Thouless, R. H. "Do we survive bodily death?" *Proceedings of the Society for Psychical Research,* 57, 1–52, 1984.

White, R. A. "Implications for the study of exceptional human experience in a new philosophy of science." *Exceptional Human Experience,* 8, 40–43, 1990.

———. "Exceptional Human Experiences: A Brief Overview" (2nd ed.). New Bern, N. C.: EHE Network, 1999. (Flyer available upon request)

Yamamoto, J., K. Okonogi, T. Iwasaki, and S. Yoshimura. "Mourning in Japan." *American Journal of Psychiatry*, 125(12), 1660–1665, 1969.

Device-Encounters—Books and Articles

Bander, P. *Voices from the Tapes.* New York: Drake Publications, 1973.

MacRae, A. "A means of producing the electronic voice phenomenon based on electro-dermal activity." *Journal of the Society for Psychical Research*, 68.1, 874, 35–50, 2004.

Ostrander, S., and L. Schroeder. *Handbook of PSI Discoveries.* New York: Berkeley (section 5 and section 6), 1974.

Raudive, K. *Breakthrough: An Amazing Experiment in Electronic Communication with the Dead.* New York: Taplinger; London: Colin Smythe, 1971. (Available through Samuel Weiser, Inc., 734 Broadway, New York, NY 10003.)

Rogo, D. S., and R. Bayless. *Phone Calls from the Dead.* Englewood Cliffs, N.J.: Prentice-Hall, 1979.

Smith, S. *Voices of the Dead?* Bergenfield, N.J.: The New American Library, 1977 (out of print).

Welch, W. A. *Talks with the Dead.* New York: Pinnacle Books, 1975.

Mediumship Literature—Books and Articles

Anderson, G., and A. Barone. *Lessons from the Light.* New York: G. P. Putnam's Sons, 1999.

———. *Walking in the Garden of Souls.* New York: G. P. Putnam's Sons, 2001.

Edward, J. *Crossing Over: The Stories Behind the Stories.* San Diego: Jodere Group, 2001.

Garrett, E. J. *Adventures in the Supernormal.* New York: Helix Press. Available through the Parapsychology Foundation, 228 East 71st Street, New York, NY 10021, USA, 2000. www.parapsychology.org.

Gauld, A. *Mediumship and Survival: A Century of Investigations.* London: Heinemann, 1882.

LeShan, L. *The Medium, the Mystic, and the Physicist: Toward a General Theory of the Paranormal.* New York: Allworth Press, 2003.

McMahon, J. D. S. *Eileen J. Garrett: A Woman Who Made a Difference.* New York: Helix Press, 1994. (Available through the Parapsychology Foundation: www.parapsychology.org.)

Schwartz, G. E., with W. L. Simon (2002). *The Afterlife Experiments: Breakthrough Scientific Evidence of Life After Death.* New York: Pocketbooks, 2002.

Schwartz, G., L. Russek, and C. Barentsen. "Accuracy and replicability of anomalous after-death communication across highly skilled mediums." *Journal of the Society for Psychical Research*, 65, 862, 1–25, 2001.

Schwartz, G., L. S. Geoffrion, J. Shamini, S. Lewis, and L. Russek. "Evidence of anomalous information retrieval between two mediums." *Journal of the Society for Psychical Research*, 67.2, 871, 115–130, 2003.

Survival—Books

Almeder, R. F. *Death and Personal Survival: The Evidence for Life After Death.* Lanham, Md.: Rowen & Littlefield, 1992.

Becker, C. B. *Paranormal Experience and Survival of Death.* Albany: State University of NewYork Press, 1993.

Berger, A. S. *Evidence of Life After Death: A Casebook for the Tough-Minded.* Springfield, Ill.: Charles C. Thomas, 1988.

——. *The Aristocracy of the Dead: New Findings in Post-Mortem Survival.* Jefferson, N.C.: McFarland, 1987.

Berger, A. S., and J. Berger. *Fear of the Unknown: Enlightened Aid-in-Dying.* Westport, Conn.: Praeger, 1995.

Cardena, E., S. J. Lynn, and S. Krippner (eds.). *Varieties of Anomalous Experience: Examining the Scientific Evidence.* Washington, D.C.: American Psychological Association, 2000.

Carrington, H. *The Case for Psychic Survival.* New York: Citadel Press, 1957.

Colaizzi, P. "Psychological research as the phenomenologist views it," in Valle and King (eds.), *Existential-phenomenological Alternatives for Psychology.* New York: Oxford University Press, 1978.

Greyson, B., and C. Flynn (eds.). *The Near-Death Experience: Problems, Prospects, Perspectives.* Springfield, Ill.: Charles C. Thomas, 1984.

Grof, S. *The Adventure of Self-Discovery.* Albany: State University of New York Press, 1988.

Hart, H. *The Enigma of Survival: The Case for and Against an After Life.* Springfield, Ill.: Charles C. Thomas, 1959.

Hastings, A. *With the Tongues of Men and Angels: A Study of Channeling.* Ft. Worth, Tex.: Holt, Rinehart, and Winston, 1991.

James, W. *Varieties of Religious Experience.* New York: Longmans, Green & Co., 1902.

Johnson, C. J., and McGee, M. G. (eds.). *How Different Religions View Death and Afterlife.* Philadelphia: Charles Press, 1998.

Jung, C. *Memories, Dreams, Reflections.* New York: Random House, 1965.

Kuhn, T. S. *The Structure of Scientific Revolutions* (2nd ed.). Chicago: University of Chicago Press, 1970.

Lorimer, D. *Survival? Body, Mind, and Death in the Light of Psychic Experience.* London: Routledge & Kegan Paul, 1984.

Maslow, A. H. *Religions, Values, and Peak-Experiences.* New York: Viking, 1964.

Morse, M., and P. Perry. *Closer to the Light: Learning from the Near-Death Experiences of Children.* New York: Macmillan, 1991.

——. *Transformed by the Light: The Powerful Effect of Near-Death Experiences on People's Lives.* New York: Villard, 1992.

Myers, F. W. H. *Human Personality and Its Survival of Bodily Death.* New Hyde Park, N.Y.: University Books, 1961.

Naparstek, B. *Your Sixth Sense.* San Francisco: HarperSanFrancisco, 1997.

Palmer, G. *Death: The Trip of a Lifetime.* San Francisco: HarperSanFrancisco, 1993.

Radin, D. *The Conscious Universe: The Scientific Truth of Psychic Phenomena.* SanFrancisco: HarperSanFrancisco, 1997.

Ring, K. *Life At Death: A Scientific Investigation of the Near-Death Experience.* New York: Quill, 1982.

——. *Heading Toward Omega: In Search of the Meaning of Near-Death Experience.* New York: W. Morrow, 1984.

Ring, K., and E. Valarino. *Lessons from the Light: What We Can Learn from the Near-Death Experience.* Portsmouth, N.H.: Moment Point Press, 2000.

Ring, K., S. Cooper, and C. Tart. *Mindsight: Near-Death and Out- of-Body Experiences in the Blind.* Palo Alto, Calif.: William James Center for Consciousness Studies at the Institute of Transpersonal Psychology, 1999.

Rinpoche, S. *The Tibetan Book of Living and Dying.* New York: HarperCollins, 1994.

Ritchie, G. *Ordered to Return: My Life After Dying.* Charlottesville, Va.: Hampton Roads, 1998.

Rogo, D. S. *The Welcoming Silence: A Study of Psychical Phenomena and Survival of Death.* Secaucus, N.J.: University Books, 1973.

Sabom, M. *Light and Death: One Doctor's Fascinating Account of Near-Death Experiences.* Grand Rapids, Mich.: Zondervan, 1998.

Sharp, K. C. *After the Light: The Spiritual Path to Purpose.* N.Y.: W. Morrow, 1995.

Smith, S. *Life Is Forever: Evidence for Survival of Death.* New York: Putnam, 1974.

Targ, R., and J. Katra. *Miracles of Mind.* Novato, Calif.: New World Library, 1998.

Wilson, I. *The After Death Experience.* New York: William Morrow & Co., 1989.

Parapsychology—Books

Bohm, D. *Wholeness and the Implicate Order.* London: Routledge, 1980.

Chauvin, R. *Parapsychology: When the Irrational Rejoins Science.* Jefferson, N.C.: McFarland, 1985.

Edge, H. L., R. L. Morris, J. H. Rush, and J. Palmer. *Foundations of Parapsychology: Exploring the Boundaries of Human Capability.* Boston: Routledge & Kegan, 1986.

Gurney, E., F. W. H. Myers, and F. Podmore. *Phantasms of the Living.* New York: Arno Press, 1975. (The classic reprinted in 1 vol.)

Heywood, R. *Beyond the Reach of Sense: An Inquiry into Extra-Sensory Perception.* New York: E. P. Dutton, 1974.

Hintze, N. A., and J. G. Pratt. *The Psychic Realm: What Can You Believe?* New York: Random House, 1975.

Irwin, H. J. *An Introduction to Parapsychology* (3rd edition). Jefferson, N.C.: McFarland, 1999.

Krippner, S. (ed.). *Advances in Parapsychological Research,* 8 volumes (vol. 1 Cambridge, Mass.: Perseus Books, 1977; vol. 2 Cambridge, Mass.: Perseus Books, 1978; vol. 3 Cambridge, Mass.: Perseus Books, 1982; vol. 4 Jefferson, N.C.: McFarland, 1984; vol. 5 Jefferson, N.C.: McFarland, 1987; vol. 6 Jefferson, N.C.: McFarland, 1990; vol. 7 Jefferson, N.C.: McFarland, 1994; vol. 8 Jefferson, N.C.: McFarland, 1997), 1977–1997.

Kurtz, P. (ed.). *A Skeptic's Handbook of Parapsychology.* New York: Prometheus Books, 1985.

Murphy, G., with L. A. Dale. *Challenge of Psychical Research.* Westport, Conn.: Greenwood Press, 1979.

Myers, F. W. H. *Human Personality and Its Survival of Bodily Death.* New York: Arno Press, 1975. (Originally published in 1903.)

Podmore, F. *Studies in Psychical Research.* London: G. P.. Putnam's Sons, 1897.

Radin, D. *The Conscious Universe: The Scientific Truth of Psychic Phenomena.* San Francisco: HarperSanFrancisco, 1997.

Rhine, L. E. *Psi: What Is It?* New York: Harper and Row, 1976.

———. *The Invisible Picture: A Study of Psychic Experiences.* Jefferson, N.C.: McFarland, 1981.

Ring, K. *Life at Death.* New York: Coward, McCann & Geoghegan, 1980.

Rogo, D. *The Poltergeist Experience.* New York: Penguin Books, 1979.

Roll, W., and V. Storey. *Unleashed: Of Poltergeists and Murder.* New York: Paraview Pocket Books, 2004.

Rossi, E. L. *The Psychobiology of Mind-Body Healing: New Concepts of Therapeutic Hypnosis* (revised ed.). New York: Norton, 1993.

Sheldrake, Rupert. *Dogs That Know When Their Owners Are Coming Home: And Other Unexplained Powers of Animals.* New York: Crown, 1999.

Stokes, D. M. *The Nature of Mind: Parapsychology and the Role of Consciousness in the Physical World.* Jefferson, N.C.: McFarland, 1997.

White, R. *Parapsychology: Sources of Information 1973-1989.* Metuchen, N.J.: Scarecrow Press, 1990.

Wolman, B. B. (ed.). *Handbook of Parapsychology.* Jefferson, N.C.: McFarland, 1986.

Education and Research Services

Academy of Religion and Psychical Research. Publishes *Journal of Religion and Psychical Research.* PO Box 614, Bloomfield, CT 06002. Telephone: 860.242.4593. Website: www.lightlink.com/arpr.

Afterlife Encounters. My website presents information, research data, and links. www.afterlife-encounters.com.

American Society for Psychical Research (ASPR). First American parapsychological research organization, began in 1885. Publishes *Journal of the American Society for Psychical Research,* which offers the latest research data and other information surrounding the concept of survival and other phenomenon; hosts meetings, lectures, and conferences. 5 West 73rd Street, New York, NY 10023. Telephone: 212.799.5050. www.aspr.com.

Association for Research and Enlightenment (ARE). Founded in 1931 by Edgar Cayce, offers programs and conferences; houses a massive library and archives; bookstore on site. 215 67th Street, Virginia Beach, VA 23451-2061. Telephone: 800.333.4499. www.are-cayce.com.

Association for Transpersonal Psychology (ATP). Founded by Abraham Maslow and Anthony Sutich in 1969. Publishes *Journal of Transpersonal Psychology.* PO Box 50187, Palo Alto, CA 94303. Telephone: 650.424.8764. www.atpweb.org.

Division of Personality Studies, University of Virginia Health System. Program under the direction of Bruce Greyson, M.D. Conducts premier studies surrounding mediumship, near-death experiences, reincarnation, and consciousness. P.O. Box 800152, Charlottesville, VA 22908-0152. Telephone: 434.924.2281. www.med.virginia.edu.

Exceptional Human Experiences. EHE is a forum for ideas, research, and personal accounts such as near-death experiences, afterlife encounters, and events that lead to transformation. Founded by Rhea White, EHE Network offers journals and other publications; original articles are available via their web site. EHE Network, 414 Rockledge Road, New Bern NC 28562. www.ehe.org.

Institute of Transpersonal Psychology (ITP). Offers classes, research opportunities, conferences, and more. 1069 E. Meadow Circle, Palo Alto, CA 94303. Telephone: 650.493.4430. www.itp.edu.

International Association for Near-Death Studies (IANDS). Hosts annual conferences on the topic and is an excellent resource for education, information, and research. Web site hosts resources for those interested in near-death experiences as well as support for experiencers. www.iands.org.

International Foundation for Survival Research. Internet site offers research plans, results, information, links, and more. www.expbeyond.org.

International Survivalist Society. Internet site offers articles, experiments, photographs, online library, and other resources. www.survivalafterdeath.org.

Koestler Chair of Parapsychology, Department of Psychology, University of Edinburgh. Offers lectures and accredited degree programs related to survival. Publishes: *European Journal of Parapsychology*. 7 George Square, Edinburgh EH8 9JZ. www.moebius.psy.ed.ac.uk.

Parapsychological Association (PA). Founded in 1957 by J. B. Rhine; professional organization; hosts annual conferences; information and resources appear on their web site www.parapsych.org.

Parapsychology Foundation (PF). Founded in 1951 by Eileen Garrett, the PF houses one of the world's largest parapsychological libraries open to the public. It publishes the *International Journal of Parapsychology*. www.parapsychology.org.

Rhine Research Center. Founded by J. B. Rhine, the center is successor to the Duke University Parapsychology Laboratory. Publishes the *Journal of Parapsychology*; offers study opportunities, research, and an expansive library that is open to the public. 2741 College Park Avenue, Building 500, Durham, NC 27705. Telephone: 919.309.4600. www.rhine.org.

Society for Psychical Research (SPR). Founded in 1882 for the scientific investigation of life beyond physical death. Its publication, *Journal of the Society for Psychical Research,* remains prominent in the field. 49 Marloes Road, Kensington, London, W8 6LA. Telephone: 020.7937.8984. www.spr.ac.uk.

Society for Scientific Exploration (SSE). Founded in 1982 by a committee of fourteen scientists and scholars, the SSE hosts programs throughout the world and publishes the *Journal of Scientific Exploration*. www.scientificexploration.org.

The Afterlife Experiments. Gary Schwartz Internet site offers opportunities to participate in mediumship experiments, the latest research data, and more. www.openmindsciences.com.

Works Consulted

Arcangel, D. "Investigating the relationship between the Myers-Briggs Type Indicator and facilitated reunion experiences." *Journal of the American Society for Psychical Research,* 91, 82–95, 1997.

——. "Afterlife Encounters Survey: The results." *Journal of the American Society for Psychical Research,* in press.

Barrett, W. F. *Death-bed Visions.* London: Methuen, 1926.

Bennett, G., and K. Bennett. "The presence of the dead: An empirical study." *Mortality,* 5, 139–157, 2000.

Bowlby, J. *Loss: Sadness and Depression vol. 3.* New York: HarperCollins, 1980.

——. *Loss: Attachment and Loss vol. 1.* New York: Harper Collins, 1982.

Carrington, H. *The Story of Psychic Science.* London: Rider, 1930.

Carverhill, P. "Qualitative research in thanatology." *Death Studies,* 26 (3), 195–207, 2002.

Childs, A. "Positive emotional effects of the near-death experience and facilitated altered states of consciousness." Unpublished doctoral dissertation, California Coast University, 1997.

Cohen, S. S. *Looking for the Other Side.* New York: Clarkson Potter, 1997.

Conant, R. D. "Widow's experiences of intrusive memory and 'sense of presence' of the deceased after sudden and untimely death of a spouse during mid-life." Unpublished doctoral dissertation, Massachusetts School of Professional Psychology, West Roxbury, Mass., 1992.

Cook, E. W. "The subliminal consciousness: F. W. H. Myers's approach to the problem of survival." *Journal of Parapsychology,* 58, 39–58, 1994.

Datson, S. L., and S. J. Marwit. "Personality constructs and perceived presence of deceased loved ones." *Death Studies,* 21 (2), 131–147, 1997.

DeSpelder, L. A., and A. L. Strickland. *The Last Dance: Encountering Death and Dying.* Palo Alto, Calif.: Mayfield Publishing Company, 1983.

Devers, E. "Experiencing an encounter with the deceased." Unpublished master's thesis, University of Florida, Gainesville, 1987.

——. "Experiencing the deceased." *Florida Nursing Review*, 2 (3), 7–13, 1988.

——. "Experiencing the Deceased: Reconciling the Extraordinary." Unpublished doctoral dissertation, University of Florida, 1994.

——. *Goodbye Again: Experiences with Departed Loved Ones*. Kansas City, Mo.: Andrews and McMeel, 1997.

Devers, E., and K. M. Robinson. "The making of a grounded theory: After death communication." *Death Studies*, 26, 241–254, 2002.

Doka, K., with J. Morgan, (eds.). *Death and Spirituality*. New York: Baywood, 1993.

Drewry, M. D. J. "Purported after-death communication and its role in the recovery of bereaved individuals: A phenomenological study." Unpublished doctoral dissertation, California Institute for Human Science, 2002.

Ellison, A. "Do we see what we expect to see?" *Paranormal Review*, magazine of the *Journal of the Society for Psychical Research*, 22, 8, 2002.

Fontana, D. "Apparent post-mortem communication from Professor Arthur Ellison." *Journal of the Society for Psychical Research*, 67.2, 131–142, 2003.

Fontana, D., and M. Keen. "Report of the Survival Research Committee." *Journal of the Society for Psychical Research* 22, 6–7, 2002.

Gamino, L. A., K. N. Sewell, and L. W. Esterling. "Scott and White Study – Phase 2: Toward an adaptive model of grief." *Death Studies*, 24 (7), 633–661, 2000.

Gilliss, C. L., I. M. Moore, and I. Marie. "Measuring parental grief after childhood cancer: Potential use of the SCL-90R." *Death Studies*, 21 (3), 277–288, 1997.

Glick, I. O., R. S. Weiss, and C. M. Parkes. *The First Year of Bereavement*. New York: John Wiley, Interscience, 1974.

Gorer, G. Death, grief and mourning in Britain. In E. J. Anthony & C. Koupernik (eds.), *The Child in His Family: The Impact of Disease and Death*. New York: John Wiley, 1973.

Greeley, A. M. Hallucinations among the widowed. *Sociology and Social Research*, 71 (4), 258–265, 1987.

——. *Religious Change in America*. Harvard University Press, 1989.

Guggenheim, B., and J. Guggenheim. *Hello From Heaven*. New York: Bantam Books, 1996.

Gurney, E., and F. W. H. Myers. "On apparitions occurring soon after death." *Proceedings of the Society for Psychical Research*, 5, 403–485, 1888–89.

Gurney, E., F. W. H. Myers, and F. Podmore. *Phantasms of the Living* (2 vols.). London: Trübner, 1886.

Hallson, P. "Can we make progress in the study of apparitions?" *Paranormal*

Review, Magazine of the Journal of the Society for Psychical Research, January, 21, 3–6, 2002.

Haraldsson, E. "Survey of claimed encounters with the dead." *Omega, the Journal of Death and Dying,* 19(2), 103–113, 1988–89.

———. Apparitions of the dead: Analysis of a new collection of 357 reports. In E. W. Cook and D. L. Delanoy: *Research in Parapsychology 1991.* Metuchen & London: Scarecrow Press, 1–6, 1994.

———. 350 case survey (unpublished), 2003.

Institute for Parapsychology. *Parapsychology and The Rhine Research Center.* Durham, N.C.: Parapsychology Press, 2001.

Irwin, H. J. "Proneness to self-deception and the two-factor model of paranormal belief." *Journal of the Society for Psychical Research,* 66.2, 867, 80–87, 2002.

James, W. *The Varieties of Religious Experience.* New York: New American Library, 1958.

Jung, C. G. *Memories, Dreams, Reflections.* New York: Vintage Books, 1965.

Kalish, R. A., and D. K. Reynolds. "Phenomenological reality and post-death contact." *Journal for the Scientific Study of Religion,* 12, 209–21, 1973.

———. *Death and Ethnicity: A Psychocultural Study.* Farmingdale, N. Y.: Baywood Publishing Company, 1981.

Kastenbaum, R. *Psychology of Death.* New York: Springer, 1992.

Kelly, E. W. "Near-death experiences with reports of meeting deceased people." *Death Studies,* 25 (3), 229–249, 2001.

Kingsford, S. M. *Psychical Research for the Plain Man.* Kila, Montana: Kessinger, 1920.

Kircher, P. *Love Is the Link: A Hospice Doctor Shares Her Experience of Near-Death and Dying.* Burdett, N.Y.: Larson Publications, 1995.

Klass, D. "Solace and immortality: Bereaved parents continuing bond with their children." *Death Studies,* 17, 343–368, 1993.

Krippner, S. (ed.). *Advances in Parapsychological Research, Vol 3.* Cambridge, Mass.: Perseus Books, 1982.

Kübler-Ross, E. *On Death and Dying.* New York: Macmillan, 1969.

———. *Death: The Final Stage of Growth.* Englewood Cliffs, N.J.: Prentice-Hall, 1975.

Kurtz, P. (ed.). *A Skeptic's Handbook of Parapsychology.* New York: Prometheus Books, 1985.

LaGrand, L. E. *After Death Communication: Final Farewells.* St. Paul, Minn.: Llewellyn Publications, 1997.

——. *Messages and Miracles*. St. Paul, Minn.: Llewellyn Publications, 1999.

Laski, M. *Ecstasy: A Study of Some Secular and Religious Experiences*. New York, Greenwood Press, 1968.

——. *Ecstasy in Secular and Religious Experiences*. Los Angeles: J. P. Tarcher, 1990.

Lee, D. "An infrared look at personal insulation," in K. Weaver's "Our Energy Predicament." *National Geographic: Special Report*. February, 6–15, 1981.

Lindstrom, T. C. "Experiencing the presence of the dead: Discrepancies in the sensing experience and their psychological concomitants." *Omega*, 31, 11–21, 1995.

Lodge, S. O. J. *Raymond or Life and Death*. New York: G. H. Doran, 1916.

Martinson, I., B. Davies, and S. McClowry. "Parental depression following the death of a child." *Death Studies*, 15, 259–267, 1991.

McClowry, S., E. Davies, K. May, E. Kulenkamp, and I. Martinson. "The empty space phenomenon: The process of grief in the bereaved family." *Death Studies*, 11, 361–74, 1987.

Moody, R., and D. Arcangel. *Life After Loss: Conquering Grief and Finding Hope*. San Francisco: HarperSanFrancisco, 2001.

Myers, F. W. H. *Human Personality and Its Survival of Bodily Death*. (2 vols.). London: Longmans, Green, 1903.

Neimeyer, R. A. *Death Anxiety Handbook: Research, Instrumentation, and Application*. Washington, D.C.: Taylor & Frances, 1994.

——. *Lessons of Loss: A Guide to Coping*. Philadelphia: Brunner Routledge, 2001.

Olson, P. R., J. A. Suddeth, P. J. Peterson, and C. Egelhoff. "Hallucinations of widowhood." *Journal of the American Geriatric Society*, 33, 543–547, 1985.

Osis, K. *Deathbed Observations by Physicians and Nurses*. New York: Parapsychology Foundation, 1961.

——. "In search of life after death: Science, experience or both?" *Academy of Religion and Psychical Research Annual Conference Proceedings*, 24, 1995.

Osis, K., and E. Haraldsson. *At the Hour of Death*. New York: Hastings House, 1993.

Parkes, C. *Bereavement: Studies of Grief in Adult Life*. New York: International Universities Press, 1972.

Podmore, F. *Studies in Psychical Research*. London: G.P. Putnam's Sons, 1897.

Radin, D., and J. Rebman. "Are phantasms fact or fantasy? A preliminary investigation of apparitions evoked in the laboratory." *Journal of the Society for Psychical Research*, 65–87, 1996.

Rando, T. A. *Grief, Dying, and Death: Clinical Interventions for Caregivers*. Champaign, Ill.: Research Press Company, 1984.

———. *Treatment of Complicated Mourning.* Champaign, Ill.: Research Press Company, 1993.

Raudive, K. *Breakthrough: An Amazing Experiment in Electronic Communication with the Dead.* New York: Taplinger, 1977.

Rees, W. D. "The hallucinations of widowhood." *British Medical Journal,* 4, 37–41, 1971.

——— "The bereaved and their hallucination," in Bernard Schoenberg et al. (eds.), *Bereavement: Its Psychosocial Aspects.* New York: Columbia University Press, 1975.

Rhine, J. B. *New World of the Mind.* New York: William Sloanne Associates, 1953.

Rogo, D., and R. Bayless. *Phone Calls from the Dead.* Englewood Cliffs, N.J.: Prentice-Hall, 1979.

Roll, W. G. "Changing perspective on life after death," in S. Krippner (ed.), *Advances in Parapsychological Research, Vol. 3.* Cambridge, Mass.: Perseus Books, 1982.

Rosenblatt, P. C. *Bitter, Bitter Tears: Nineteenth Century Diarists and Twentieth Century Grief Theories.* Minneapolis: University of Minnesota Press, 1983.

Rosenblatt, P.C., R. P. Walsh, and D. A. Jackson. *Grief and Mourning in Cross-Cultural Perspective.* New Haven, Conn.: Human Relations Area Files Press, 1976.

Sanders, C. M. *Grief: The Mourning After, Dealing with Adult Bereavement.* New York: Wiley, 1989.

Schwartz, G. E., with W. L. Simon. *The Afterlife Experiments: Breakthrough Scientific Evidence of Life After Death.* New York, Pocket Books, 2002.

Sheldrake, R. *A New Science of Life: The Hypothesis of Formative Causation.* London: Blond and Briggs, 1981.

———. *The Presence of the Past: Morphic Resonance and the Habits of Nature.* New York: Times Books, 1988.

———. *Seven Experiments That Could Change the World: A Do-it-Yourself Guide to Revolutionary Science.* Rochester, Vt.: Park Street Press, 1994.

———. *Dogs That Know When Their Owners Are Coming Home: And Other Unexplained Powers of Animals.* New York: Crown, 1999.

———. *The Sense of Being Stared At.* New York: Crown, 2003.

———. "The sense of being stared at: Experiments in schools." *Journal of the Society of Psychical Research,* 62: 311–23, 1998.

Sheldrake, R., and P. Smart. "Experimental tests for telephone telepathy." *Journal of the Society for Psychical Research,* 67,3: 184–199, 2003.

Sherwood, S. "Apparitions of black dogs." *Paranormal Review,* magazine of the *Journal of the Society for Psychical Research,* April, 22, 3–6, 2002.

Shuchter, S. R., and S. Zisook. "The course of normal grief," in Stroebe, Margaret S., Wolfgang Stroebe, and Robert O. Hansson (eds.) *Handbook of Bereavement: Theory, Research, and Intervention.* New York: Cambridge University Press, 1993.

Sidgwick, H. "Phantasms of the living." *Proceedings of the Society for Psychical Research,* 33, 23–429, 1923.

Sidgwick, H., and Committee. Report on the census of hallucinations. *Proceedings of the Society for Psychical Research,* 10, 25–422, 1894.

Silverman, P. R., and J. W. Worden. "Children's reactions to the death of a parent," in Stroebe, M. S., W. Stroebe, and R. O. Hansson (eds.). *Handbook of Bereavement: Theory, Research, and Intervention.* New York: Cambridge University Press, 1993.

Smith, S. *ESP.* New York: Pyramid, 1972.

Stroebe, M. S., W. Stroebe, and R. O. Hansson (eds.). *Handbook of Bereavement: Theory, Research, and Intervention.* New York: Cambridge University Press, 1999.

Taylor, S. E., and J. D. Brown. "Illusion and well-being: A social psychological perspective on mental health." *Psychological Bulletin,* 103 (2), 193–210, 1988.

Tyrrell, G. N. M. *Apparitions.* New Hyde Park, N.Y.: University Books, 1961.

Wiitala, G. C. *Heather's Return: The Amazing Story of a Child's Communications from Beyond the Grave.* Virginia Beach, Va.: A.R.E. Press, 1996.

Wolfelt, A. D. *Death and Grief: A Guide for Clergy.* Muncie, Ind.: Accelerated Development, 1988.

Worden, W. J. *Grief Counseling & Grief Therapy: A Handbook for the Mental Health Practitioner.* New York: Springer, 1991.

Wright, S. *When Spirits Come Calling: The Open-Minded Skeptic's Guide to After-Death Contacts.* Nevada City, Calif.: Blue Dolphin, 2002.

Zisook, S., R. DeVaul, and M. Click. "Measuring symptoms of grief and bereavement." *American Journal of Psychiatry,* 139, 1590–1593, 1982.

Zisook, S., and S. R. Shuchter. "The first four years of widowhood." *Psychiatric Annals,* 15, 288–294, 1986.

Index

adversaries, 165
afterlife encounters (AEs)
   belief in, 65
   expectations of, 99, 101
   features/forms of, 17
   longevity of, 99
   occurrences of, 115–116
   purpose of
      growth and, 20, 50, 124–148
      individual nature of, 134–135
      need and, 30, 135–140
      spiritually correct nature of, 140–148
   states of, 115
   therapeutic value of, 113
   see also discarnates; transitional periods
afterlife-encounters.com (website), 42, 103
Afterlife Encounters Survey (AES)
   phase 1 of, 17, 50–51, 102
   phase 2 of, 103
alcohol abuse, 99
Alexander the Great, 148
Allred, Kathy, 22
Americans, 65, 105
Anderson, George, 141, 176–198
anecdotes, 75, 98
animals, domesticated, 30–31, 44–47, 189, 191
answering machines, 17, 20, 32, 37–39, 169
apparitions, 20–32
aromas, 20, 31–32
audiovisual equipment, 169

Barrett, Sir William, 106
Beatles, 168
believers/nonbelievers, 104, 106–108
bereaved
   expectations of, 99, 101, 198, 200
   hallucinations of, 102
   incidents of AEs and, 51, 110–114
   mediums and
      benefits from, 200–201
      cautions of, 198–200
   parents, 73, 91, 156, 157
   playing on, 172, 174–175
   Special Protection Group, 198

Bigelow Holding Company, 105
biofeedback instrumentation, 187, 188
bodily death
   survival after, 9, 66, 173
   see also postmortem existence, proof of
Bok, Edward, 106
Botti, Diane, 135–139
brain mechanisms, 167
Break Through (Raudive), 167
Buddha, 148
butterflies, 48

cameras, 21, 160, 174, 187, 188
Carter, Jimmy, 107
Carter, Roslyn, 107
cave paintings, 65
Cayce, Edgar, 106
charlatans, 104, 173, 175, 186
children
   appearance of, physical, 156–161
   as discarnates, 26, 52, 54, 156, 169–172
   images of, 157, 161
   loss of, 56–63, 57–58, 95–97, 139–140
   as mediums, 171–172
Churchill, Winston, 106, 148
clocks, 21
coincidence, 46, 123, 175, 193
cold, sensation of, 20, 162
Coleridge, Samuel Taylor, 115
College Conservatory of Music (CCM), 61, 62
Columbia (space shuttle) memorial service, 108
comfort, 51–55, 64
communication
   conduits for, 20–21, 32, 37
   conscious awareness, below, 7
   discarnate, 167–168
   evidence of, 168
   lack of, 22–25
   silent, 150
   spiritual, 123–124
   telepathy and, 24, 166–167
Compassionate Friends Conference, 194
computers, 17, 21, 32, 37, 40–42
consciousness

energy and, 98
exploration of, funding for, 167
states of, 115
survival of, after bodily death, 47, 87
controversy, 165–170
couriers, 82
Crookes, Sir William, 106

Daily News (newspaper), 106
Davidson, George, 178
death anxiety, 54
deception, 99, 100, 175, 193
DelSoldato, Patti, 73–74, 151–153
    Civilian Award of Merit, 152–153
Diehl, Dr. Alan, 196
DiMaggio, Joe, 150
Dioca, Angela, 37–39, 153–155
Dioca, Joe, 111–112
Dioca-Bevis, Carol, 153–155
direct encounters
    auditory, 20, 25, 178
    olfactory, 20, 31–32
    sight/touch combinations, 26–27
    tactile, 20, 26–27, 30, 131, 162
    visual, 20–27, 124–125
    visual/auditory combinations, 25–26
    see also presence, sense of
discarnates
    appearance of
        environmental, 161–162
        physical, 155–161
        in recognizable forms, 162, 164
        tangible, 162–163
        to third party, 73–74
    authority figures as, 52–53
    categories of, 17
        historical/famous figures, 148, 149–150
        personal figures, 148–149
        spiritual figures, 151–154
        unknown figures, 153–155
    emotions of, 155, 157
    energy of, 155
    information known by, exclusive, 9
    interaction of, 93
    judgment/negativity of, 53
    purpose of, 115
    silence of, 150
    spirituality of, 155
    see also children
    discerning, art of, 175–176
discomfort, 52–55
disembodied existence, evidence of, 82, 108

disenfranchise, 48, 104, 275–276
dogmatic skeptics, 98–99
    claims of, 99–104
dogs, black, 107
dreams
    consciousness and, 131
    messages in, 50
    spirit visits in, 45
Dubé, Deanna, 128–134
Dudley, Valerie, 44–47

Edison, Thomas, 107, 167
elapsed-time theory, 101–103
Electronic Voice Phenomena, 167
Elisabeth Kübler-Ross Centers, 16, 128, 149, 163, 176
e-mail encounters, 42–44
emotions
    of bereaved, 198
    climates of, 115
    of discarnate loved ones, 155, 157
    externalizing, 125–128, 200
    of Feelers, 109
    in messages, 168
    state of, 99, 100, 115, 139
    ties of posthumous contacts and, 93, 165
    transitional period and, 123–124
energy, 98, 155, 165
England, 105
enlightenment, 16, 104, 125, 143, 148
ESP Research Associates Foundation, 23, 24
ethereal images, 19, 20, 63, 153–155
Europe, 167
exaggeration, 16, 99
Extrovert-type personalities, 108, 109

Fancher, Debbie, 82, 83–89
Fancher, Karl, 44, 103
feathers, 20, 62
Feeling-type personalities, 108–109
film, 11, 159, 160
Finland, 65
Five Stages of Loss Theory (Kübler-Ross), 106
Ford, Henry, 106
fortune-telling, 48
France, 105
Franklin, Benjamin, 106
fraud, 99, 100, 175, 193
Freud, Sigmund, 104

Gateway Center (New York), 16
Germany, 105

ghosts, 17–20, 106
God, 148
Great Beyond, 5, 103, 167
Green-Studer, Barbara, 161–162
grief
    affect of AEs on, 55–64
    comfort from, 51–52
    exacerbation of, 200
    support, 125
    see also bereaved
Grimaldi, Joseph, 106

hallucinations, 23, 99–100, 102, 112
Hamlet (Shakespeare play), 63
Haraldsson, Erlendur, 103
Head Waters, Virginia, 163–164
Heather's Return (Wiitala), 89, 91
hieroglyphics, 65
High School for the Performing and
    Visual Arts (Houston), 122
Holmes, Oliver Wendell, 106
Houston (Texas), 16, 122, 184, 191, 193,
    194
Howe, Emily, 131–134
Huber, Terri, 194, 195
Hugo, Victor, 106

illusion, 73, 99, 101, 174, 193
images
    bodily, 187
    camera reproduction of, 187–188
    of children, 157, 161
    describing, 89
    ethereal, 19, 20, 63, 153–155
    hallucinations and, 99–100
    mirror, 89
    prerecorded, 18
    repetitive, 99
    thermal, 187
immortality, 65
Incarnate Word, 48
indirect encounters, 20–21, 32–48,
    142–148
ineffability, 151
Influential Americans group, 106
Institute for Psychotherapy, 171
Instrumental Communication, 167
Instrumental Trans-communication, 167
Introvert-type personalities, 108, 109
Intuitive-type personalities, 108
Italy, 65

Jesus, 148
John Paul, Pope, 106

Johnson, Debbie, 39–40
journals/diaries, 37, 48, 100–101, 123,
    124, 159
Judging-type personality, 109
Jung, Carl, 106

Kjäll, Thomas, 40–42
Klass, Dennis, 16
Kübler-Ross, Elisabeth, 106–107

Ladies Home Journal (magazine), 106
Landers, Marsha, 160
Lewis, Marti, 47–48
Lincoln, Abraham, 106
Lodge, Sir Oliver, 106

Mac, Jackie, 196–197
Mann, Thomas, 106
Mantle, Mickey, 148
Marie, Teresa, 134–135
Markham, Andrew, 129–134
May, Jane, 32–34, 95, 101
May, Jim, 58–63
May, J. R., 122
mediums
    bereaved and
        cautions to, 198–200
        playing on, 172, 174–175
    categories of, 175, 176
    expectations and, 198
    fraudulent nature of, 175
    generalizations made by, 172–174
    George Anderson, 176–184
    skepticism and, 171–173
mediumship practitioners, 175–176,
    198–200
memory, false, 99
Mendez, Alexandra Sucre, 139–140
mental health, 16, 40, 99, 115, 198
messages
    couriers of, 82
    delivery of, 133–134, 189–190
    in dreams, 50
    from indirect encounters, 20–21, 142
    from spirit voices, 168
    telepathic, 24–25
    third party, 134–135
mistaken identity, 99, 100
monitoring devices, 21, 32, 37, 39–40,
    187–188
Monroe, Marilyn, 148, 149–150
morphic resonance, 166
Mother Teresa, 148
music boxes, 21, 32–35, 57, 95, 101

Myers, F. W. H., 171
Myers-Briggs Type Indicator (MBTI),
    108–109

National Aerospace and Science
    Administration (NASA), 108
National Institute for Discovery
    Science (NIDS), 93, 135
Netherlands, 65
New York City, 171, 196
Norway, 65
Noss, Valerie, 48–50

occult, 48
Osment, Haley Joel, 131
Owen, Dana, 22–23

pagers, 21
paranormal events, 16, 60, 92, 97, 101, 109
parapsychologists, 95, 171, 187
pennies, 20, 134–135
perceivers
    candidates for, most likely, 113–114
    defined, 16
    emotional condition of, 100
    profiles of
        personality, 108–109
        social, 105–108
        spirituality, 110–114
    skeptics of, 99
Perez, Donna, 21
personality tests, 108–109
pets, 30–31, 44–47, 189, 191
photographs, 159–160
    see also cameras
Poole, Carol, 140–142
postmortem existence, proof of, 66
    anonymity of apparition, later identi-
        fied, 82–93
    autonomously manipulated objects, 7,
        95–97
    collective encounter, 74–82
    current event unknown by perceiver,
        later found to be true, 93–95
    mediums, 200
    purpose exhibited, 97–99
    research/anecdotes, 65–66, 98
    unknown information revealed, 27,
        66–74
postmortem survival, criteria for, 65–66
pre-death encounters, 110, 116–120, 121
presence, sense of
    cold, feeling of, 20, 162
    comfort from, 50, 98, 139

defined, 20
    grief support and, 125
    seventh sense and, 27–30
Princeton Imaging, 187
proxy encounters, 165, 191
pseudomediums, 175
psychics, 175
psychokinesis (PK, mind over matter),
    47, 95

Radin, Dean, 187
rainbows, 10–11, 20, 61, 142
Raminger, Kent, 108
Raudive, Konstantin, 167
Rebman, Jannine, 187
recording devices, 21, 39, 168–170, 187
Red Skelton's Favorite Ghost Stories
    (Skelton), 106
religion, 65
research
    on body temperature and supernor-
        mal perception, 162
    on discarnate communications,
        recordings of, 167–168
    documentation of events for, 21
    on elapsed-time theory, 102–103
    financing of, 107–108
    with George Anderson, 186–194
    on grief, postmortem sightings and,
        110–114
    on morphic resonance, 166
    Rorschach ink blot test and, 168
    skeptics and, 98, 104
    support of findings, 108
    survival evidence, 15–16, 47, 98, 104
    on telepathy, 167
    transpersonal experiments, 166
researchers
    expenses/funding of, 167
    Gurney, Myers, Podmore, 102, 165
    Haraldsson, 103
    Roll, 168
    Schwartz, 104
    scientists, 93, 104
    Sherman, 23
reverie, 115
Rhine, J. B., 65
rites of passage, 121–122
Roll, William, 168
Roonan, Gary, 123–124
Roper Center for Public Opinion
    Research, 105, 106
Rose, Phyllis, 169–170, 200–201

Sands, Jackie, 131–134
Schwartz, Gary, 104
science, 65, 98, 99
self-expectations, 198, 200
sensations, physical, 20, 26–27, 30, 131, 162
The Sense of Being Stared At (Shedrake), 166
sensitives (mediums), 175, 184, 185
Sensor-type personalities, 108, 109
sensory cues, 175, 193
seventh sense phenomenon, 28
Shakespeare, William, 1
Shared Blessings (Poole), 140
Sharp, Neta, 194–196
Shaw, George Bernard, 165
Sheldrake, Rupert, 27–28, 98, 166
Sherman, Harold, 23–25
Sherman, Martha, 23–25
Safer, Mary, 25–26
signs, 11, 96, 124
Silver Cord (American Native legend), 166
Simon, John, 93–95
The Sixth Sense (movie), 131
Skelton, Red, 105, 106
skepticism
    definition of, 98
    mediums and, 171–173
    on research findings, 98, 104
    see also dogmatic skeptics
Smith, Sheila, 184
Socrates, 106
Spain, 65
Special Protection Group, 198
spiritual
    appropriateness, 142
    awareness, 57, 63, 89, 105, 124
    communications, 123–124
    continuance, 65
    figures, 17, 148, 151, 153
    healing, 139
    health, 155, 157
    ineffability, 151
    movement, 16
    nature of AEs, 140–148
    signs, 124
    telepathy, 166–167
    transcendence, 58, 63
spirituality
    of discarnate loved ones, 155
    of perceivers, 110–114
    seeking of, 63, 89, 103, 124

Spirit Voice Recording, 167
spousal AEs, 112
Stanford, Leland, 107
Stanford Imaging, 187
Stanford University, 107
Stevenson, Robert Louis, 106
Stone, George, 27, 102–103
support groups, 100
symbols, 11

Tenanting, Maria Elena, 54
Taylor, George, 74–76
Taylor, Lori, 35–37
telephones, 11–15, 17, 21, 39, 169
    telepathy, 166
televisions, 21
Templeton, Payload, 164
terminally ill, 110, 117, 119–121, 191, 198
Texas Assessment of Academic Skills (TAAS), 157–158
Thinker-type personalities, 108–109
Thomas, Jo Ann, 125–128
Thoughts Through Space (Harold, Wilkins), 24
transcending loss, 16
transitional periods
    life-continuing, 121–124
    physical death and, 116–121
transmitting devices, 169
Twain, Mark, 106

United Kingdom, 65
United States, 105, 167, 175
United States Navy, 108
University of Chicago Medical Center, 106
University of Cincinnati's College Conservatory of Music (CCM), 61, 62
University of Houston, 165
University of Iceland, 103
University of Nevada, Las Vegas (UNLV), 135, 187
University of Virginia, 44
Unusual Events Survey, 105

validation
    disenfranchisement and, 48, 275–276
    dogmatic skeptics and, 98
    of George Anderson's statements, 191
    by healthcare practitioners, 113
    by source examination, 34
    by unfamiliar discarnates, 87
    by witnesses, 34, 82

Vance, Charles, 74–82
Vanckhoven, Jenny, 157–160
voice mail, 169
voice recordings, 167–170

Walker, Danton, 106
walkie-talkies, 21
Way, Michael, 30–31
We Are Not Forgotten (Anderson), 176
*We Don't Die: George Anderson's
    Conversations with the Other Side*
    (Martin), 141, 176
West, Helen, 185
White Album (Beatles' album), 168
Wiitala, Geri, 89–92
Wilk, Adam, 142–148
Wilkens, Sir Hubert, 24
wishful thinking, 9, 101

witnesses
    of audible sounds, 20
    cold sensations felt by, 162
    conversation initiated by, 150
    of disembodied existence, 82
    emotions of, 115
    inaccurate reporting of, 99, 100
    of indirect encounters, 32
    influence of AEs on, 17
    validation of AEs by, 34
Wood, Mary, 56–58, 124–125
World's Fair (Chicago), 3, 7, 171
World Trade Center, attack survivors
    of, 196

Zimmerman, Eric Michael, 135
Zimmerman, Marilyn and Fred, 135

About the Author

 Dianne Arcangel, M.S., is the former director of the Elisabeth Kübler-Ross Center of Houston and chaplain for The Hospice At The Texas Medical Center. She was on the board of directors for the Rhine Research Center and the National Institute for Discovery Science, where she also led workshops and conducted research. Dianne currently writes, lectures, and investigates afterlife encounters independently and through the University of Virginia. She is available via her websites www.afterlife-encounters.com and www.Arcangel.net.

Hampton Roads Publishing Company

. . . for the evolving human spirit

HAMPTON ROADS PUBLISHING COMPANY publishes books on a variety of subjects, including metaphysics, spirituality, health, visionary fiction, and other related topics.

We also create on-line courses and sponsor an *Applied Learning Series* of author workshops. For a current list of what is available, go to www.hrpub.com, or request the ALS workshop catalog at our toll-free number.

For a copy of our latest trade catalog, call toll-free, 800-766-8009, or send your name and address to:

HAMPTON ROADS PUBLISHING COMPANY, INC.
1125 STONEY RIDGE ROAD • CHARLOTTESVILLE, VA 22902
e-mail: hrpc@hrpub.com • www.hrpub.com